THE DECADE OF DISILLUSION

The Decade of Disillusion:

British Politics in the Sixties

Edited by

DAVID McKIE
Political staff, The Guardian

and

CHRIS COOK
Director, Historical Records Project, London School of Economics

Macmillan
St. Martin's Press

First published 1972 by
THE MACMILLAN PRESS LTD
London and Basingstoke
Associated companies in New York Toronto
Dublin Melbourne Johannesburg and Madras

Library of Congress catalog card no. 72–83416

SBN 333 13064 2

Printed in Great Britain by
THE BARLEYMAN PRESS
Bristol

Contents

Introduction

DAVID McKIE

The persistence of full employment for more than a decade of peace has now largely cured the depression psychosis which dominated industrial attitudes, with such insidious results, in the inter-war period. The business community accepts the fact that prosperity is here to stay, not only because full employment will be maintained, but also because we have entered a period of rapid growth in personal incomes and consumption. . . .

There is no intelligent sense in which one can speak of a likely excess of potential output over potential demand in Britain in the foreseeable future. . . .

Such primary poverty as remains will disappear within a decade, given our present rate of economic growth; and the contemporary mixed economy is characterised by high levels both of employment and productivity and by a reasonable degree of stability. . . .

Anthony Crosland, *The Future of Socialism* (London, 1956)

Eighteen per cent – not far short of one in five – of those who were entitled to vote in the British General Election of 1970 didn't do so. It was the sixth successive election in which the turnout at the polls had fallen: even allowing for the thousands away on holiday, it hardly suggested that Britain had faced the prospect of making its choice between the Parties with any passionate enthusiasm.

It could, of course, have been a healthy sign. If people are wildly discontented, one might argue, they will surely flock to the polls to make sure the Government is turned out. Perhaps their abstention simply indicates that they are not greatly disturbed by the way things are going.

Maybe. But that was hardly how it seemed to people who went round knocking on doors in the British elections of the sixties. What one found, increasingly, was the weary complaint that there was 'nothing to choose between them'; that they were 'both as bad as each other'; that it 'doesn't make a blind bit of difference who gets in'.

It is, of course, no new thing for people to think about their rival leaders in this way. The same assessment was no doubt made of the relative merits of Moses and Aaron. And in some ways the verdict had never, in strictly factual terms, been more justified. For the sixties were years of consensus, when the spirit of Butskell remained strong in the land (even if, before long, one half of the horse was dead and the other unlikely to win any more races); when Conservatives presided over the 'giving away' of Africa, and were content to let responsibility for education rest in the hands of that least militantly true-blue of figures, Sir Edward Boyle. The contest was less, now, between competing philosophies; much more about which set of managers was likely to get better results.

The fulcrum of the politics of the sixties, to which so many of the essays in this book return, was the 1964 General Election, and most of all the campaign which won it for Harold Wilson. What mattered in that campaign was less the clash of competing ideologies (though these of course could never be completely buried) than the conflicting claims as to whether Home's side or Wilson's could be more confidently backed to deliver the goods.

Labour's victory, too, marks the point at which the popular political fashions of the early sixties (so many of them built around the concept of managerial efficiency), and most of all the commitment to planning, became at last enshrined at the heart of official thinking. This is not to say that the Conservatives had remained impervious to them: as John Barnes and Victor Keegan show, the great period in which Government became involved in planning and began to interfere at every level of industry comfortably predates the arrival of Harold Wilson at Number 10. But certainly there was now a sense that the critics had won: the doors of Whitehall opened, and such erstwhile hammers of the Treasury as Samuel Brittan and Michael Shanks found themselves courteously invited in. With pleasing symmetry, though with a great deal of truly unpleasant anguish and pain, the late sixties were to see many of the fine political enthusiasms of the early years dwindle and die away.

The mood of those exhilarating days of 1963-4, when Wilson was making his great speeches up and down the country (there were even comparisons with Kennedy) was above all one of: 'if only'. *If only* we could get the old guard out, those graceful, obsolete amateurs in a new professional world, so neatly symbolised by the improbable appearance as Prime Minister of Sir Alec Douglas-Home; *if only* we could cut out the snobbery, treat people on their merits rather than their antecedents, cast off the old school mufflers of tradition and behave as our international competitors were accustomed to do; *if only* the genius of our scientists and technologists could be put to efficient productive use; *if only* all those hopelessly hidebound assumptions could be hunted out of the Treasury and replaced by something more twentieth-century, more closely related to common sense – then, said Harold Wilson, and found an echo in many thousand hearts, we might so easily attain those gifts which many men desire; of which the greatest and the best, the key indeed to almost all others, both at home and overseas, is growth.

This optimism about our national potential, this demand for pragmatic reform, was not the mood of Labour supporters alone: it was the mood of a great many of those uncommitted, unideological, largely unpolitical voters on whom Wilson had long ago set his accurate eye. Labour won many such voters in 1964; and in 1966, it was able – despite all the Conservative warnings of looming economic disaster – to build a far greater majority, mainly on two counts: first, a general confidence in Wilson as an effective political leader; and second, a feeling that Labour, saddled from the start with the legacy of Conservative mismanagement, had not yet had a fair chance to show what it could do. One found this goodwill towards Labour during the 1966 Election campaign even among devoted Conservatives. As David Butler and Donald Stokes say in their book, *Political Change in Britain* (London, 1969):

Electors ... while themselves staying loyal to a long-standing party allegiance, may nevertheless feel the pull of issues and leaders that have caused others of less fixed allegiance to change sides. In this sense, those who change act as surrogates for those who, although they do not change, recognise in themselves the reactions which have moved the less committed.

What followed, of course, were years of economic crisis far worse than all the widely condemned misfortunes that had gone before, with an administration which had been intent on purposive leadership, on 'the smack of firm government', becoming increasingly the prisoner of events way beyond its control. Far from sweeping us forward on a new course of growth, Labour found itself struggling desperately to avert an accelerating downward slide. 'Stop-go', that label which Labour had so effectively hung around the neck of Selwyn Lloyd, was, as promised, swept away – but not by slaughtering 'stop'; it was the 'go' phase which was obliterated. The great professional economist fared no better than the genteel amateur who not only calculated with matchsticks but was unworldly enough to publicise the fact. Sir Alec's apparently mindless claim that the economy had 'seldom been stronger' was matched by the no less unwary boast of George Brown that Labour had been trying to manage the economy 'in a way that no economy has ever been managed before'.

The disillusion with Labour – and from there, with party politics in general – which now began to set in was bitterest of all on the Left. Mounting unemployment; curbs on trade unions, and wage restraint – not even stopping short of the threat of prison; support for the American adventure in Vietnam; limits on immigration, culminating in the panic moves, chronicled here by Roy Hattersley, to slam the door on the Kenya Asians; the maintenance of an independent deterrent; prescription charges, charges for school milk, and dearer school meals; cutbacks in the rate of building new homes – all these and other similar practices, natural, if thoroughly disgusting, when the Tories were in power, but unthinkable from any other source, were now to be seen issuing forth in the name of a Labour administration. The Government was able to point to priorities which it had maintained through thick and thin; not every inhabitant of the sacred cowshed had fallen under the cleaver. But too much had been sacrificed for many to stomach. The monument to it all could be seen in the empty committee room, the lapsed membership, the tireless activist of former years now nodding gently before the television screen; also in the success of Nationalist parties and Far Left groups, reported here by Chris Cook and Hugo Young.

But disillusion hit hard in the centre too. The Conservatives had been dismissed because they were not thought capable of delivering the goods; but the alternative government installed for precisely that purpose had proved no more adept. Could anyone be trusted? Otherwise quite sensible people found themselves distinctly tempted by the calls for a coalition or government by businessmen which became fashionable as the pound, despite all the Government's attempts to protect it, sank slowly in the West.

And so all the rational assumptions which punctuate Crosland's book, and were shared by many others in the late fifties, came messily unstuck. We had not cured unemployment; we had not ensured that steady rate of investment which is essential to growth; we had not eradicated poverty – indeed, as Anne Lapping's chapter shows, there were grounds for thinking that under Labour poverty actually grew worse. The party politicians on both sides had failed to come up to promises or expectations – either through mismanagement and misjudgement, or because, as Peter Sinclair argues, they were promising goods which were never there to deliver, making assumptions about the potentialities of the British economy which bore no real resemblance to the facts.

The resulting sour disillusion worried politicians too. In a speech to the 1971 Labour Conference at Brighton, made while this book was being prepared, the Party's Deputy Leader, Roy Jenkins, warned:

> We do not want the period in which we live to be remembered as the age of the politics of disillusion. And there is some danger of that. In the last ten years or so, perhaps to a greater extent than ever before, under the Tories and under us, Governments have been humiliated in by-elections.
>
> The electorate have expected more than was delivered. They have withdrawn their support almost as soon as they gave it. I believe that one of our central objectives should be to ensure that the next Labour Government breaks the pattern of General Election victories followed by the disillusionment and sulky resentment which is now in danger of settling over British politics.

The revulsion with the fashions of the early sixties which had set in by 18 June 1970 was exploited by Edward Heath as those fashions themselves had been by Harold Wilson. There was to be an end to the overnight rescue operation, the beer and sandwiches compromise at midnight at Number 10, the dashing new initiative which launched a thousand headlines but precious little else. Some of the planning apparatus remained: the Prices and Incomes Board might disappear, but no one seemed set to pronounce the sentence of death on the National Economic Development Council. Ministers were still to be seen in earnest conclave with leaders of the C.B.I. and T.U.C. as they had been in Labour's day. What was more, the new Conservative Government found itself – as in the crises at U.C.S. and Rolls-Royce – ordered about by events, abandoning deeply-held principles, under the same impulses – necessity and fear – which had moved its predecessors.

Even so, the optimistic assumption that most problems could be resolved if only men of goodwill could be brought together around a table was badly mangled by the end of the sixties. Its unreliability was demonstrated most clearly and most terrifyingly in Ireland.

Ireland, as Harold Jackson's chapter shows, had turned out to be the kind of deeply intractable problem which we had come to expect on other people's doorsteps, but not on our own. (But then, few in Britain, politicians included, had thought of it as being on our doorstep until the violence began.) By the end of 1971, more British soldiers had been killed there than in Aden; and the end of the slaughter still looked far away. As for that familiar sixties tactic, the appeal to the moderate centre – that had been tried; and the resulting electoral débâcle, leading to the downfall of Prime Minister O'Neill, suggested that it was not very likely to be fetched out of the armoury again.

So the great hope, at the end of the decade as at the beginning, was Europe. Europe, the great new opportunity – or alternatively, the great old alibi. If we could not attain our cherished economic ambitions on our own, then perhaps, within a wider community, all things might still be possible. It was always *perhaps*: all estimates were unbelievable; depending on your position, you called it an Act of Faith or a leap in the dark.

Both in the short term and in the long, Europe now seems likely to determine the way in which people look at party politics in Britain. If all goes well, it may in time supply the magic ingredient which has so long been absent from political management in this country: success. If things go badly, if people feel that they have come to suffer rather than to gain from a political initiative taken against the apparent will of the majority of the nation – then disillusion will persist, and deepen. The seventies start with a great deal less optimism, a great deal more scepticism and suspicion, than did the sixties. Perhaps, for that reason, they are unlikely to end in so much disappointment.

Part One

THE RECORD

The Record

JOHN BARNES

When, on 19 June 1970, a Conservative Prime Minister returned to Downing Street, the wheel seemed to have turned full circle. Nearly a decade before the Conservative Party had stood at the high tide of its post-war fortunes. Political scientists of note were speculating on the democratic prospects of one-Party government. The Labour Party was divided on nationalisation and on defence: in the autumn of 1960, Conference rejected the defence policy of the Party's leader and Parliamentary Party. Their support fell to only 37 per cent of the electorate. Few would then have forecast a dramatic reversal of fortunes, but by mid-decade Macmillan had shuffled from the political stage, seemingly discredited, and a new Labour leader had stamped his personality on the decade. The Labour Party was within sight of the pastures of permanent power. Even after traumatic electoral reverses, that still seemed possible a week before polling day. But the English people, almost unknown to themselves, had resolved to put an end to Wilson's quasi-Presidential role. In his place they set one of Macmillan's principal lieutenants, Edward Heath. The apparent return of 'yesterday's men', however, paradoxically masked a dramatic shift of emphasis. Heath's Conservatism, in certain important respects, marks out a challenge to the past decade, and perhaps not just to that decade.

A decade of consensus has come to an end. It is with that consensus that this essay deals and with the failure of either party to consolidate the predominant position in politics which the commentators were ready to concede it.

The Conservatives' third successive electoral victory – the fourth in which they improved their position – triggered off in the Labour Party fresh doctrinal disputes. The 1959 result had been the final recognition that the age of affluence had arrived, altering the entire social and economic base of politics. Hugh Gaitskell admitted publicly the large number of trade unionists who must have voted Conservative. Macmillan proclaimed the class war obsolete. 'Labour Party supporters see the Conservatives as exercising a much greater attraction for ambitious people, middle-class people, young people, office workers and scientists', Mark Abrams found. 'The image of the Labour Party, held by both its supporters and its non-supporters, is one which is increasingly obsolete in terms of contemporary Britain.'

In November 1959, at the special post-election conference, Gaitskell provoked anger with a blunt hint that Clause Four of the Party's con-stitution (the public ownership clause) should be amended. Normally loyal trade unionists backed the traditional Left in a storm of protest which left no one in any doubt that Gaitskell would have to compromise. Clause Four was not dropped – although the cynical noted that it was relegated to the inside of the Party membership card: instead the National Executive amplified (and qualified) it in a unanimously approved statement of the Party's aims. The key clause, suggested by Harold Wilson, made it clear that their social and economic objectives could 'only be achieved through an expansion of public ownership substantial enough to give the commu-nity power over the commanding heights of the economy'. The 'com-manding heights' were never defined, but both left and right were appeased by this retreat into meaningless metaphor.

Perhaps the most important consequence of Gaitskell's 'provocation' on Clause Four was the determination of many trade unionists to get back at him. They had not far to look for an issue. C.N.D. was already the focus for much of the frustrated idealism of youth and marked the first outburst of the new restlessness in politics which characterised the sixties. But it had not yet despaired of capturing a more orthodox political vehicle. Within the Labour Party it had a great deal of support. In quick succession a number of the larger unions, the A.E.U., U.S.D.A.W. and the N.U.R., voted to join Frank Cousins' T.G.W.U. in opposition to official Labour defence policy. Gaitskell, until then a supporter of the British deterrent, found his position within the party undermined, and the death of Aneurin Bevan in July 1960 robbed him of his buckler against the Left.

Wilson urged Gaitskell to compromise, to concentrate on those aspects of the defence issue which united the party, the abandonment of the independent deterrent, the making of a viable conventional contribution to NATO, and disengagement in Central Europe. A joint Labour/T.U.C. committee had already agreed a statement reaffirming support for NATO but urging that Britain's defence effort should be concentrated on con-ventional forces. The unilateralists had not been satisfied, and Gaitskell refused to adopt Wilson's approach. He was worried less that a passion for nuclear disarmament would engulf the Labour Party than that it would carry with it the threat of neutralism. That issue must be smoked out into the open and fought.

On the eve of the Scarborough Conference the Labour Party was in poor heart. It was evident that the somewhat amorphous motion proposed by Frank Cousins would be passed by the block votes of the trade unions, but Gaitskell was determined not to surrender. It was Gaitskell's defiant claim, at the close of an impassioned attack on neutralists and fellow travellers, that he and his friends would 'fight and fight and fight again' to save the party they loved, which roused the enthusiasm of the Conference and won the support of many delegates which had seemed forfeit.

Within a month Wilson contested the leadership on a platform of party unity. He was heavily defeated by 166 votes to 81. In the elections for the Shadow Cabinet, he almost paid the price, plummeting from first to ninth place. The Parliamentary Labour Party and the Conference was now at loggerheads, and there seemed no immediate prospect that the dispute would be resolved.

Macmillan's popularity now stood at its peak. The disunity of the Labour Party tempted Conservatives with thoughts of a fourth successive election victory, and the only doubt was that of the young men swept in on the tide of 1959 – was Macmillan making sufficient use of his majority? Made bold by Labour's weakness and the size of their own majority, a number of Tory backbenchers began to constitute an internal opposition of their own.

This restlessness was more than a reflection of the Government's dominant position. It reflected the profound sea-change that was coming over articulate opinion. In 1960, a P.E.P. publication *Growth in the British Economy* drew attention to the French experience of indicative planning, and there was growing industrial discontent, strengthened by the credit restrictions of April 1960, at the rhythm of 'Stop-Go' which seemed to have become a perpetual brake on investment and economic growth. It was not until the publication of Michael Shanks's *The Stagnant Society* in 1961 that the flood of 'What's Wrong' books really got under way, but the mood of buoyant self-satisfaction which had characterised the late fifties had already given place to introspection and self-doubt. It was a mood which spread from the intelligentsia to the rest of the electorate.

Macmillan had been quick to sense the mood but he found it less than easy to find an answer, harder still to convince the electorate that his party had one. There was in the Conservative Party, as Lord Poole has rightly discerned, a potential clash between those who actually liked the new Britain and those who barely tolerated it. If ever the Government lost its momentum this tension between progressive and traditionalist elements in the party might erupt into conflict, and it was natural therefore for Macmillan to be 'conscious of the need to keep the Conservative Party united by constantly renewing its idealism and corporate sense of purpose'. It would be a mistake to overestimate the effect of domestic politics on the decision to go into Europe, but many of those in the party's thinking apparatus thought it just the challenge the party now needed.

On 27 July 1960 Macmillan reshuffled his Government. The prime significance of the new appointments was obscured by the appointment of the Earl of Home to the Foreign Office. 'Insufficiently distinguished', *The Times* loftily observed. The Conservative Party received the news with stupefaction and the Labour Party was enraged. However, one unsuspected attribute in a former Commonwealth Secretary was an enthusiasm for Europe. Europe, in fact, was the purpose of the reshuffle. Keen Europeans were moved into key ministries. Duncan Sandys went to the Commonwealth Relations Office and Christopher Soames to Agriculture.

But the most important appointment of all was that of the former Chief Whip and Minister of Labour, Edward Heath, as Lord Privy Seal, to take special responsibility for European affairs and to act as principal spokesman for the Foreign Office in the House of Commons.

The cue for the reshuffle had been Amory's resignation from the Treasury, for personal reasons. Just before he went he gave the Prime Minister a clear hint of trouble. Macmillan had resisted Amory's plans for a severe budget, but agreed to the credit restrictions of 28 April. The main effect was to cause industry to reappraise the stop-go cycle and to look with a less jaundiced eye on planning. The Treasury too were embarked on reappraisal even before Selwyn Lloyd was appointed as the new Chancellor. His management of the economy, in what was admittedly a difficult period, was hardly inspired, but he inaugurated changes which (in the words of Samuel Brittan) 'transformed the long-term environment in which day-to-day management took place'.[1]

The move towards planning and the move towards Europe, often linked by the press, were in fact separate strands of policy, the latter preceding the former by some months. Modernisation was the theme which Macmillan intended to link to Europe and it was at this time that a whole series of inquiries were set up whose reports two or three years later were intended to provide the basis for a Conservative domestic programme – Beeching on railways, Hall on transport needs, Rochdale on ports, Buchanan on traffic in towns, Jenkins on company law, Molony on consumer protection, Newsom on secondary education, Robbins on higher education, Trend on civil research and Pilkington on broadcasting.[2]

Macmillan also essayed a retreat from the open emphasis on material affluence which had characterised the successful 1959 campaign. In part this was a fear of raising expectations, but much more the feeling that 'you've never had it so good' was out of keeping with the ideas of the post-war generation. This new feeling was difficult to define. It was 'anti-establishment' but not anarchic; it embraced no existing political philosophy; nor could it be explained in class or in economic terms.

Africa, then as now, was a part of the world which caught the attention of idealists, and Macmillan took a conciliatory path. Macleod was appointed to the Colonial Office after the 1959 General Election and at once embarked on a course of swift and sensible concession. Macmillan's spectacular contribution was the decision to tour Africa. His 'wind of change' speech at Cape Town, followed by the release of Dr Banda and the constitutions granted to Kenya and Nyasaland, marked his own Government's adaptation to the changing pace of Africa.

The enthusiasm of Macmillan and Macleod was not shared throughout the party. The high point of the Conservative rebellion came in June 1961 when Welensky's delegates in London successfully sought modifications to the Macleod plan for Northern Rhodesia. Yet not all the fury of the Tory Right, nor the foundation of the Monday Club to recall the Party to its principles, could divert the Government from the course they believed essential. In March, South Africa had withdrawn from the Commonwealth, and Macmillan, himself bitterly disappointed, beat off criticism from the right by pointing to their 'last great chance in Africa', the Central African Federation. Macleod, damned by Lord Salisbury as 'too clever by half', was seriously damaged in his political career by the continual opposition to his policies, and in October 1961 Macmillan moved him on to lead the Commons and act as Party Chairman, replacing him with Maudling.

It was convenient to concentrate Maudling's attention on Africa. Together with R. A. Butler and Hailsham he had been one of the most sceptical Cabinet voices about Common Market entry. Macmillan had provoked no abrupt confrontation, but used the latter half of 1960 to sound out Europe on the probable terms of any arrangement and to convince the Six that Britain's intentions were serious. There was a powerful surge of influential press and business support for entry, which allowed Macmillan to pursue a favourite tactic, edging the Cabinet towards a favourable decision while allowing the pressure of both events and opinion to work his will. By Christmas it was clear that there would be political advantages in full membership, and no chance at all of taking part in the Six's political discussions without entry. Macmillan penned a powerful Cabinet Paper putting the case in largely political terms. At the end of April Maudling could still flatly deny that the Cabinet had taken a decision, but Heath had already let the Americans know what was in the wind. At Washington in April Macmillan received President Kennedy's blessing and on 17 May Heath gave the Commons a clear indication that the Government would favour an application for full membership.

On 31 July the decision to go ahead was announced to the Commons in terms designed to damp down enthusiasm. Gaitskell moved a reasoned amendment which showed a lesser enthusiasm for, but which did not oppose the step. In effect, the negotiations did not begin until 10 October. By then the British position had, perhaps ill-advisedly, toughened under Commonwealth pressure, but the Conservative Conference had been led to approve negotiations by an overwhelming majority. Little happened for six months. The Europeans were trying to agree a common agricultural policy which they finally achieved in January 1962. The negotiations began in earnest in the spring, but by then Gaitskell was moving into open opposition to British entry.

In May 1961 the A.E.U. and U.S.D.A.W. reversed the position on unilateralism that they had taken up the previous year. Gaitskell had overwhelming support from the Parliamentary Committee, and defence debates in the Commons revealed that more than two-thirds of the Parliamentary Party backed him. He commanded a majority on the N.E.C., who asserted they were 'custodian' of the Conference decision and did nothing about it. In addition he had consistent support from a majority of the General Council of the T.U.C.

The reversal of the Scarborough decision at Blackpool[3] was a great triumph for Gaitskell. His majority approached three million, largely because the Communist dominated E.T.U. was compelled to disaffiliate after revelations in Court of the illegal electoral practices of its leadership. Increasingly Gaitskell was thought of not merely as an alternative but, as the Conservative Government ploughed the sand, the natural replacement for Harold Macmillan as Prime Minister.

The Conservative Government had been compelled in July 1961 to resort to tough measures. The balance of payments deficit in 1960 had been £450 m., but the reserves rose by £177 m. The reason for this apparent paradox was a steady influx of short-term funds into London, swollen by fears for the dollar. But in March 1961 the German mark had been revalued, and it was widely thought that this would be the prelude to a general realignment of currencies in which the pound would be devalued. The result was a massive run on sterling. Whether it was a repeat of 1957 or a trial run for 1966, the results were disastrous. Chancellor Lloyd clobbered the economy just as it was turning down. The result was two years' near-stagnation.

Undoubtedly Lloyd's policy jolted the public into awareness of the nation's problems, and in the long term it probably contributed a great deal to the acceptance by the public and press of an incomes policy; it even damped down the wage-price spiral; but the cost in political terms was high, and the Conservative Party were soon grumbling that the Government had not got its case across. In November, with the electricity pay settlement, to which Lloyd was violently opposed, and which Macmillan publicly condemned, the policy suffered a major defeat. Thereafter the political arrows were harder to bear.

The pay pause was to end officially in April 1962. The Cabinet found it hard to agree on what should follow it. In February they issued a White Paper setting out a guiding light: that incomes should rise by not more than an average of 2 per cent per person per year. To Macmillan that was not a policy but a pious platitude. He wanted an institution to help decide the priorities in incomes policy and to bring national economic considerations to bear on wage negotiations. No workable arrangement emerged from the arguments within the Treasury. In the end Macmillan lost patience and called a group of officials to Admiralty House to hammer out the broad lines of what was to become the National Incomes Commission. As far as Selwyn Lloyd was concerned it was almost the last straw. Lloyd's own initiative, N.E.D.C., was now off the ground. It met for the first time in March and by May had agreed on a 4 per cent growth target for the British economy. It now began to focus on the problems which would have to be solved if the economy were to grow so fast.

The Government at this stage was in deep political trouble. A series of disastrous by-election results culminated in defeat at Orpington, where on 14 March a rock-safe suburban seat with a Conservative majority of 14,760 became a Liberal stronghold with a majority of 7855, a swing against the Conservatives of not less than 21·9 per cent.[4] Many people blamed the Chancellor. He no longer seemed to be quite in control of the Treasury, concentrating a little too much perhaps on the details of the incomes policy, and his problems were compounded by quite the worst official forecast that the Treasury ever made. Within a week of the Budget Lloyd realised that the Treasury was wrong. Their forecast of the growth in demand was too high and they were pinning too much hope on the investment boom which they believed would follow the successful conclusion of the Common Market negotiations (timed for July).

It was not until May that a period of real negotiation began, and although this continued into August it was too late to obtain a settlement before the onset of the French presidential elections. In an effort to speed the process, Macmillan went to see de Gaulle at the Chateau de Champs at the beginning of June. He returned convinced that on the European front all would be well, and began to think about remodelling his Cabinet in readiness for an election. He would bring on young and energetic ministers to speed the work of modernisation and give a fresh image to his Cabinet. Such a reshuffle would also give him the opportunity to drop Selwyn Lloyd. Already the policy of the guiding light was in ruins. The Transport and General Workers had struck against the dock employers, and after a brief resistance the employers had given way. The Government were blamed for advising surrender. They had in fact suggested some concession, but the figure they had in mind was more than doubled.

The continuing electoral setbacks which faced the Party led to attacks on the Party chairman. *The Spectator* in an ill-judged moment wrote, 'Mr Macmillan is not going to throw out Mr Macleod to that kind of clamour, any more than he is going to throw half his Cabinet out to quieten it either'. In fact that was just what he was planning to do.

Butler was consulted about the changes on 6 July. Three days later Central Office warned that the North East Leicester by-election on the 12th would be a fresh setback to the Party. A newspaper leak accelerated the changes. Selwyn Lloyd was one of the first casualties. Badly shaken, he made it clear that he would not be leaving the Commons. Next day, an embarrassed Macmillan tried to break the news gently to the others who were to go. An irate Lord Chancellor grunted that he would have given more notice to his cook. Good cooks, somebody quipped, are harder to find than good Lord Chancellors.

The 'new men' were to be just that, with Maudling Chancellor at 45 and seven newcomers to the Cabinet. To all appearances it was a Butler Cabinet and for Butler himself there were the titles and prestige of First Secretary of State and Deputy Prime Minister. But Macmillan had no intention of letting him have his place. Instead, he must concentrate on Central Africa, a job calculated to display all his qualities; but, as nearly everyone knew, few reputations had been made over Africa.

The news was announced at 7 p.m. on Friday 13 July. There was an ominous letter in *The Times* next morning: 'For the second time the Prime Minister has got rid of a Chancellor of the Exchequer who tried to get expenditure under control. Once is more than enough.' It was signed: Nigel Birch. Birch, it was said, had also helped Lloyd with his letter of resignation which made it clear both that Macmillan had sought his resignation and that the Chancellor was concerned about the growth of public expenditure. There were cheers for Lloyd when he took his seat on the back benches. Macmillan was received in silence. When the Finance Committee met there were more rumblings, and one backbench M.P., Gerald Nabarro growled that Westminster had 'been made to look like an abattoir'.

The press were not averse to fomenting the crisis. *The Times* said of Macmillan: 'Speculation should not exclude the Prime Minister himself. He has been ruthless. His followers will admire this if it proves to have done the trick. The Tory party also has its loyalties and sentiments . . . if Mr Macmillan cannot bring about a change with so largely reconstructed a team, the question will not long be burked whether he could with any other.' But the Labour Party moved to his rescue. On 26 July their motion of no confidence was debated, and the Tory ranks closed behind the Prime Minister. Hugh Gaitskell had, perhaps, been too clever by half.[5] Macmillan's popularity in the country had, however, slumped badly. Only Neville Chamberlain in 1940 had ever been less popular as a Prime Minister.

The most pressing problem, and, Macmillan thought, his political salvation, lay in the negotiations with the Six. By August the outline of a firm deal on the Commonwealth could be seen, and with this he faced the Commonwealth Prime Ministers when they came to London in September. There was sharp criticism, but agreement in the end that Britain should do what she thought best. They offered no alternative, Macmillan's hand was not weakened, and the major effect of Commonwealth fears was to make Gaitskell an opponent of entry on any terms Britain was likely to get. The Labour Conference followed his lead, and the Conservative rebels found themselves isolated in a party clash. Gaitskell had given as one of his reasons for opposition Britain's long history, and it was Butler who best summarised the mood of the Conservative Party: 'For them a thousand years of history books. For us the future'.

Macmillan's policy was overwhelmingly endorsed, but the euphoria was short-lived. The polls showed a sharp swing away from the Conservatives and public opinion hardened against entry. A series of five by-elections in November went badly, and, what was worse, the negotiations at Brussels seemed to lose momentum once de Gaulle had won his Presidential election in France. At home there was fresh trouble over security, recalling to public memory the cases of Gordon Lonsdale and

George Blake. In September 1962 an Admiralty official, Vassall, had been arrested, and the press had a field day at the expense of the First Lord, Lord Carrington, and his deputy, Thomas Galbraith. Much was made of the friendly letters which the latter had written to Vassall, and with deep reluctance Macmillan let him resign.

The continual press demands for an independent inquiry were in no way halted by Galbraith's resignation. 'Now that his former junior has resigned Lord Carrington should quit too. And the sooner the better', screamed the *Daily Herald*. Macmillan changed his mind. 'What is now challenged is a Minister's personal integrity and character', he told the House, and that must justify a change in procedure. He spoke too of his awareness 'that there was building up, both in the press and in the House and the various places where men meet and talk and gossip on public affairs, a dark cloud of suspicion and innuendo.' The press seemed to have taken refuge in some kind of collective hysteria. The B.B.C. chose this moment to launch *That Was The Week That Was*, destined to become overnight the most successful T.V. series thus far. It brought the destructive force of the satire craze to a mass audience. The personal abuse, the savage attacks on authority of all kinds became an obsessive ritual and a suitable pointer to what was to come. It had as yet little to do with Harold Macmillan, but on 14 December a shot echoing round Wimpole Mews had reverberations that rocked the entire Government to its foundations.

It is doubtful whether Macmillan even noticed the story. Next day he was at Rambouillet to see de Gaulle. The atmosphere was cold. The French President had his election behind him. He no longer expected to see Britain in the Market. There were no misunderstandings. Even Macmillan's announcement that he was about to go to Nassau to negotiate the supply of Polaris to Britain provoked no outburst. The General took it in his stride, although he may well have found in the news confirmation of a decision already reached. Macmillan was left to hope that his negotiators might yet pull the chestnuts from the fire, that the General would not dare use the veto.

Nassau, by contrast, was an enormous and badly needed success. One of Macmillan's most insistent arguments at the Nassau talks was that he must have an alternative to Skybolt if he was to survive the pressures from his backbenchers who had erupted in angry protests over its possible loss. The subsequent agreement was, in most American eyes, a negotiating triumph for him. Polaris was substituted for Skybolt and committed to the NATO alliance, but it could be withdrawn for individual use by the British Government if 'supreme national interests' were at stake. Paradoxically this triumph was viewed with cold suspicion by Conservative defence specialists and it took a lengthy interview on 1 January to persuade them that they were wrong.

Then came a sudden and savage change in the political climate. On 16 January de Gaulle vetoed British admission to Europe in the most brutal terms. Four days later Hugh Gaitskell, who had led the Labour Party against Britain's entry, died suddenly in hospital.

Flying home from the United States, Harold Wilson's sense of occasion had never stood him in better stead. In reply to inquiries about his chance of getting the leadership, he replied: 'I don't think we can begin to think about that when the Leader has died only a few hours ago.' He had no chance of knowing it, but that morning the press had almost deified the dead leader: Wilson's reaction, almost as much as his tribute to Gaitskell – 'to a unique degree the architect of Labour's expected victory' – seemed precisely right. Brown, Gaitskell's loyal lieutenant, was less adept.

A 'Stop Wilson' movement was soon well under way, but there was no agreement on who to run. Denis Healey and another member of the Shadow Cabinet had urged Callaghan that it was his duty to stand. Wilson concentrated on a series of effective parliamentary performances that reminded everyone of his value to the party, and quietly saw that everyone knew that Brown would in no circumstances make him his deputy.

In the event, Callaghan did surprisingly well, scoring 41 votes to Brown's 88: Wilson was way out ahead with 115. Brown's instinctive reaction was counter-attack; but when the second ballot had come to its inevitable conclusion, he congratulated Wilson, insisting only, in face of the latter's invitation to continue, that he must think out his position. There were the inevitable alarms and excursions; Brown would continue, but he wanted the shadow Foreign Secretaryship; the news leaked and, even had Wilson wanted to give him the job, he could not have done so. There could be no surrender to an apparent ultimatum. Brown agreed, and within a week of the election, all Wilson's former critics had rallied behind him. The Left too returned to the fold, received perhaps a trifle more coldly than they had expected, and from then until the election there was scarcely a burst of criticism to be heard.

In the three months following his election, Wilson made thirty-two major weekend speeches and innumerable broadcasts – he even talked about religion. By late spring, he had become the most talked-about politician in Britain. He had a natural gift for publicity and a readiness to co-operate with newsmen and the T.V. cameras which they were quick to exploit. He was accused of building up a personality cult, but he has this defence: he thought he had less than seven months to establish himself before Macmillan plunged the country into a General Election. What nobody foresaw was the fantastic sequence of events that swept Wilson out of the headlines and made London the cynosure of the world for salacious goings-on in high places.

Two years before a young model, Christine Keeler, had had brief affairs with the newly promoted Secretary of State for War, John Profumo, and the Russian Naval Attaché. Rumours of this first became widespread early in 1963 when Christine Keeler became involved in a shooting affray. Rather than appear in court, she fled to Spain. Macmillan had been warned of the rumours in February, but Profumo denied the whole story. It looked like a repeat of the Galbraith case with an innocent man the victim of rumour. Macmillan was satisfied by the inquiries that had been made and chose not to see Profumo. It was a costly mistake. To make matters worse, the Tribunal enquiring into the Vassall case had that day jailed two reporters for failing to disclose their sources. The press was almost wholly alienated from the Government, and the *Daily Express* juxtaposed the story of the 'missing witness' with rumours of Profumo's resignation. Leading Labour M.P.s mentioned the rumours in Parliament, and one, Mrs Barbara Castle, linked Profumo's name with Christine Keeler's disappearance. This dangerous blend of fiction and fact offered Profumo a let-out. He denied the whole story, and subsequently obtained damages from foreign newspapers who had printed the story.

Christine Keeler's protector, the society osteopath Dr Ward, however, knew the truth, and, in a desperate attempt to buy off police enquiries into his activities, he let first Wilson and then the Home Secretary know that Profumo's story was not exactly true. Wilson saw the Prime Minister and for the first time doubt was sown in Macmillan's mind. The routine report of their talk also alerted the security authorities, who had material on the affair which had never been passed upward. Macmillan asked the Lord Chancellor to hold an inquiry; Profumo decided to anticipate the inevitable by confessing to his lie. His resignation was promptly accepted, but it was Macmillan who had to ride out the subsequent political storm.

The press were in full cry, and only Macmillan seems to have kept a sense of proportion. His first action on returning to London was to ask Hailsham to go to Moscow to negotiate the Test Ban Treaty; only then did he consult his advisers about the political impact of Profumo. It was quite clear that there would be a revolt, equally clear that a majority of Conservative M.P.s would not be prepared to see him fall on this issue. The Labour Party decided to make it an issue of confidence. Not without difficulty Macmillan rallied his Cabinet: there were press rumours of a revolt led by Powell, but it soon became clear that these had been planted by a group of Tory backbenchers who were determined to bring down Macmillan. The rumours grew steadily wilder and were not to be killed until the Denning Report appeared in September, a best-seller which did not live up to most scandalous expectations. Hailsham thundered emotionally on television against those who were trying to bring down a 'great party . . . because of a scandal by a woman of easy virtue and a proven liar'. Somewhat hypocritically the Labour Party made their main target the security aspects of the affair, but it was quickly clear that there had been no risk. When Macmillan faced the House on 17 June, he told a doleful tale. At the end his honour was unquestioned, but there remained a taint of incompetence. Wilson's speech had been restrained: if there was to be butchery, it would have to come from the Conservative backbenches.

Nigel Birch planted the dagger, quoting from Browning on 'The Lost Leader':

> . . . let him never come back to us!
> There would be doubt, hesitation and pain.
> Forced praise on our part – the glimmer of twilight,
> Never glad confident morning again!

It was a devastating blow, but not lethal. Twenty-seven backbenchers abstained. The Government's majority fell to sixty-nine. Hardly anyone thought after the vote that Macmillan could survive, but, while they were willing to wound, they seemed afraid to strike. Speculation centred on the successor, with the superficially most obvious candidate, R. A. Butler, left 'astonished . . . by the absolute rage of fire which worked through the Conservative Party in favour of a younger man'.[6] Maudling seemed to be the favourite and the chairman of the 1922 Committee advised Butler 'to take part in any government formed by a new man whoever it was'.[7] Macmillan had considered 'chucking it all in',[8] then, infuriated by the howl of the mob, and appalled at the chaos, he banged his desk. 'I'll not have this', he said.[9] Panic at Westminster was, he knew, already producing a powerful correction in the revulsion of the constituencies at what was going on. Slowly Macmillan's personal stock began to rise. Beset by further scandals over Philby, Rachmanism and the trial of Stephen Ward, the Conservative Party's standing took longer to recover, but by August Labour's huge lead had begun to melt away. Although there was a 13 per cent swing against the Government, Profumo's seat was held.

Macmillan had dug in. On 28 June he announced that he hoped 'to lead the party into the election . . . of course I must have the support of the party and I think I have it'. The audacity was breath-taking, and it was reinforced by perfectly timed talks with President Kennedy that weekend about the mixed manned fleet for NATO. The postponement of that idea was seen as a victory for Macmillan, and the conclusion of the Test Ban Treaty in July was his triumph.

The most perceptive comment on the successor by far had been Francis Boyd's in the *Guardian*: 'Many Conservatives would certainly regard Lord Home as an ideal leader at present. I conclude that if Conservative members of both Houses and candidates were asked to place the four most likely Ministers in order of preference . . . the result would be: 1. Lord Home; 2. Mr Maudling; 3. Lord Hailsham; and 4. Mr Butler . . .'[10] Six weeks later, when the House of Lords amended the Peerage Bill so as to allow peers to disclaim their titles in time for the next election, the way was clear for Macmillan to suggest Hailsham as his successor. He did not think either Butler or Maudling was of Prime Ministerial timber or that they could win an election. If the party did not want himself, perhaps they deserved the ebullient Hailsham who had the fire to win. But he had by no means decided to go, as Butler found when he saw him on 11 September, and when Home advised him to retire one September evening, his reply was that he intended to stay. He was by no means confident of his ability to do so. He was suffering from a prostate and feared a sudden incapacity. As late as 30 September he indicated to Hailsham that he was thinking of retiring before Christmas and that he felt Hailsham would be his most acceptable successor. He was under heavy family pressure to stay, and on Sunday 6 October decided that he would go on. The press were told and the following day they were unanimous: 'Macmillan to stay'. Macmillan was again less certain and told Butler he would prefer not to announce a final decision at the Conservative Party Conference in Blackpool. That evening senior Conservatives thrashed the matter out, but reached no decision; and at the Cabinet the following day, 8 October, it became clear that the Prime Minister would announce his decision to continue at the Conference.

Towards the end of the meeting Macmillan withdrew, evidently ill, and there was a long informal discussion in which most Ministers opted for the certainty of his continued leadership. If there had to be a change, the Lord Chancellor said, he would seek Ministers' opinions, and Home, declaring that he was not a candidate, said that he would be available to help in any way required. Enoch Powell was to remember these words and they influenced his later decision not to support Home. That evening while the Conference was assembling at Blackpool, Macmillan was taken to hospital for an emergency operation. Butler took charge of the Government, and he made it plain that he intended to address the final rally. In hospital Macmillan sent for Home on the afternoon of Wednesday 9 October and confirmed that he was going to resign. He suggested that Home might succeed him, but the noble Earl dismissed the suggestion. Left to a choice between Butler and Hailsham, he plumped for the latter, and both his son and son-in-law were soon to be found in Blackpool canvassing vigorously on his behalf. Hailsham had at least three other supporters in the Cabinet and that evening he was publicly offered a seat.

Home told the Conference that Macmillan would be resigning on the afternoon of Thursday 10 October and the Conference took on the atmosphere of an American convention. At the Conservative Political Centre rally that evening Hailsham stumbled through his prepared address and then, in deeply emotional tones, publicly renounced his peerage amid scenes which reminded more than one observer of the Nuremberg rallies. The platform seemed glum, but the Young Conservatives later that evening were *en fête* for Hailsham. The cold light of morning brought growing doubts, not least of Hailsham's judgement, and when the Young Conservatives attempted a standing ovation for their new hero, at the Central Council meeting on Saturday, the representatives refused to respond. Macmillan had already returned to the idea of Home, to whom the Conference had given a standing ovation for his speech on foreign affairs. Knowing this, Nigel Birch publicly set the Home bandwagon rolling, and a stream of visitors, headed by the Lord Chancellor, Selwyn Lloyd and Duncan Sandys, begged him to stand. The appeal was on grounds of party unity, but the most Home would consent to do was to see his doctor. That night on television, he defied every effort by Robin Day to get him to declare he was a contender. The effect was to convince many that he was the right choice. When he presided over Butler's closing address on the afternoon of Saturday 12 October, he was received more enthusiastically than the stand-in Prime Minister.

Back in London the following week, the Cabinet approved Macmillan's plans to sound the Party. The Cabinet were again individually polled and each member of Parliament sounded. The result was a majority but not an absolute majority, for Home in both cases, and the support for him strengthened very considerably when second preferences and 'blackballs' were taken into account. Macmillan received the results on Thursday 17 October, and to make sure there was no doubt had each of the *rapporteurs* read his conclusion over to the others. The Chief Whip gave the news to Butler, who said that he accepted the position. But that night there was a last ditch Cabinet revolt headed by Maudling, Macleod and Powell. The Prime Minister was informed that eight of the Cabinet were against the choice, but he would brook no delay. On 18 October Home was called to the Palace and invited to form a government.

Hailsham was already hard at work on another 'stop Home' gambit: he met with Butler, Maudling and Macleod while Home was at the Palace and offered to serve under the former. He also urged that the contenders should have a quadrilateral meeting with Home. This Home was determined to avoid, and his first three interviews that afternoon were with the triumvirate seen individually. Butler reserved his position, but said it was now up to Home to see if he could obtain the necessary unity. By the time the four contenders finally met that evening, he had gone a long way towards doing so, and Hailsham was reconsidering his own refusal to serve under Home. As Maudling observed, 'things were closing in'. Only Macleod and Powell had so far refused to serve.

It was not until the morning of 19 October that Butler finally consented to serve. Immediately afterwards Maudling at the fourth time of asking agreed to continue as Chancellor. A smiling, triumphant Home was able to leave for the Palace to become the first peer to be Prime Minister since 1902. The refusal of Macleod and Powell to serve in his Cabinet inevitably lent substance to Wilson's charge that he had been chosen 'through the machinery of an aristocratic cabal. In this ruthlessly competitive, scientific, technical, industrial age, a week of intrigues has produced a result based on family and hereditary connexions ... After half a century of democratic advance, of social revolution, ... the whole process has ground to a halt with a 14th Earl.'

Home had a speedy revenge when interviewed on television on 21 October. He coined a still-remembered phrase: 'I suppose Mr Wilson, when you come to think of it, is the 14th Mr Wilson.' While the nation roared, Home rubbed in his point: 'Are we to say that all men are equal except peers?' Wilson hastily backtracked. But the peerage caused genuine difficulties. Home let it be known that he did not want the Commons to meet before he met them, and that they would therefore be prorogued. Wilson branded this as an act of impertinence. On the contrary, replied the newly appointed Leader of the House, Selwyn Lloyd, it was an act of respect to the House.

In Kinross, where a by-election seat had been found for him to contest, Sir Alec waged an energetic campaign. He was determined to show that he meant business on modernisation. He looked and sounded rather old-fashioned. The Government must be made to appear progressive and up-to-date.

Sir Alec won by more than nine thousand votes. With Liberal intervention, it was an exceptionally good result and did much to compensate for the disastrous loss of Luton the previous evening where the Conservative vote fell by 15·6 per cent. 'Luton,' Sir Alec boldly proclaimed, 'was the last page of the old chapter, and Kinross . . . the first page of the new.'

Home had promised the electorate 'plain, straight talking' and his first major speech as Prime Minister at the Guildhall made his point. He called for an extra one per cent of effort from everyone and was greeted with enthusiastic applause. He was less successful in the Commons, where he stumbled unhappily through the pitfalls of Parliamentary procedure and seemed at the end to concede that Wilson would be the next Prime Minister. 'I have always faced facts – however horrible they are – even if they have not,' was his uneasy get-out. This performance may have decided the strategy he would follow. In the course of the year before the General Election he made only three more speeches in the Commons, and instead went out to meet the people. Harold Wilson thought this a mistake and he was probably right. 'He should have allowed me to go on and on making speeches, probably boring people in the process, while he gave the impression of getting on briskly and crisply with the actual job of governing the country. But as it was he made himself into a national candidate much too early . . . it was almost as if he was the Leader of the Opposition trying to get into power, not the man already supposed to be doing the job.'[11]

Certainly the Government got off to a good start, and it was by no means entirely due to Wilson's reluctance to invoke tough opposition during Home's honeymoon period. The hastily prepared Queen's Speech in November committed the Government to twenty-four specific bills, mostly in the service of modernisation; the Robbins report was accepted; and in December, the Government for the first time published its five-year forecast of public expenditure. Many Labour backbenchers complained in a bewildered way that their garments were slowly being stolen, one by one.

By the time the House broke up for the Christmas recess, Home had good reason to feel pleased. The political pendulum had not yet swung back, but the possibility no longer seemed absurd. Of the four by-elections held after his own at Kinross, three had shown swings of 9 or 10 per cent, the fourth, at Sudbury and Woodbridge, showed only a 3·7 per cent swing against the Conservatives; and for the first time there were hopes that the swing to Labour might be contained or even reversed.

In January, however, the convalescent Conservative Party found the bandages untimely ripped from its wounds by the publication of Randolph Churchill's *The Fight for the Tory Leadership*. 'Harold Macmillan's trailer for the screen play of his own memoirs', as Macleod dubbed it, provoked debate and a number of revealing leaks. But the frankest comment of all came from Macleod himself in a long review – in effect challenging Home's title to the leadership – which blamed Home's succession on an Etonian 'magic circle'. Anonymous articles appeared in *The Times* (widely believed to have been written by Enoch Powell) calling for Conservatives to slough off their illusions, including their faith in the Commonwealth. Newspaper headlines like 'When Tory Bites Tory' and 'Tories in Turmoil' were hardly a happy prelude to revival, and into this atmosphere was injected all the bitterness of the row over Resale Price Maintenance.

Heath was determined to leave his mark as Secretary of State for Industry, Trade and Regional Development. Specifically appointed to modernise Britain, he concentrated first on the regions, where he had to implement the programme for the North East and Central Scotland, and where he developed the 'growth point' strategy. Abroad he made his mark at the United Nations Conference on Trade and Development. At home he determined to leave his impress on the statute book. The Minister was determined to appear as a man of drive and energy. His targets were consumer protection and the removal of restrictions on competition. Monopolies, mergers and restrictive practices generally were an obvious target, but the legislation he set in hand could not be put on the statute book before the Election. What he needed was a short sharp piece of legislation to serve as a clear signal of the Government's intentions and his own.

He found it in a subject which at first he had passed over with all the distaste of an erstwhile Chief Whip. The abolition of Resale Price Maintenance was bound to cause trouble on the Tory benches: there were too many small traders and shopkeepers in Conservative constituency associations for it to be otherwise. The introduction of a Private Member's Bill to end R.P.M. forced Heath to define the Government's position. He took the bull by the horns. The Government would legislate itself.

After heated Cabinet discussions he got his way. The public were favourable and the Party furious. Three times Heath faced angry meetings of the Conservative backbench Committee on Trade and Industry, and once he confronted the 1922 Committee. He also met the rebels separately. He was adamant even against pleas for delay. On the second reading, twenty-one Members voted against the Bill and twenty-five others abstained. The Labour Party were in no mood to help. They abstained on the second reading and gave every sign that they might combine with the rebels on specific clauses.

It was the most serious Conservative revolt since Neville Chamberlain had been brought down nearly twenty-four years before. Matters reached a pitch when it was thought, quite seriously, that Heath might have to resign. Time was of the essence. It was now March, no less than seventy Conservative backbenchers had sponsored amendments, and the possibility of a June election was still open. Heath was forced to compromise. The concessions he made did not damage the essential features of the Bill, and it was perhaps not surprising that revolts continued, and that on pharmaceuticals the Government's majority fell to one. Had the vote gone the other way Heath's future and that of the Bill would both have been in doubt.[12]

Curiously the row did little permanent harm to the Conservative Party, although it may have delayed their recovery. Modernisation, however, had not struck the chord the Government wanted. The theme was not dropped, but increasingly the Party turned back to tried favourites, the benefits of affluence and the fears that a Labour Government might undermine them. In part this was because of the difficulty of blending modernisation and Sir Alec into a single image, in part because modernisation aroused more fear and suspicion than eager anticipation. Increasingly, Conservative speeches and broadcasts concentrated on attacking Socialist threats of nationalisation and higher taxation – none more so than the 'documentary-cum-soap-opera' which the advertising agency Colman, Prentis and Varley devised for an August political broadcast. 'We fought it like '59', one Conservative told David Butler, 'not because we wanted to, but by default: we didn't know what else to do.'[13]

Nevertheless it seemed to work. Home's appearances up and down the country put heart into his Party and something of his appeal seemed to spill over to attract support from women generally. In January both he and Wilson began a series of provincial tours. Home was to make no fewer than sixty-four major speeches and one hundred and fifty whistle-stop addresses in a year of office. At the outset he could turn in performances that were quite disastrous: his speech at Swansea on 20 January – which read sufficiently well for the press to call it scathing – seemed to those present to be without verbs, form or even sense. To make matters worse, five days later Wilson delivered a long, detailed and rather heavy speech on his plans for Britain's economic regeneration, but his power and authority were such as to keep his Swansea audience on the boil.

What Home lacked was the time to master his drafts and make them his own. His speechwriters were good, but they never quite got him, and he would not, as Macmillan had done, toss ideas to and fro with his aides before making up his mind what to use. Too often he used material that was not his own, stumbled over phrases, and in general was too well scripted. Often, with disastrous results, he would turn over two pages at once; and the well-meant advice to discard the half-moon spectacles, which the cartoonists had seized upon, proved a mistake. At his best when speaking from his own notes, or off the cuff, Sir Alec now became self-conscious, and his speeches suffered. Not always, however. When he turned to the deterrent or to foreign affairs, a note of confidence and authority showed what he might have done had he spoken less often and in accents more his own. He had a knack for finding homely jokes which went down well with his audiences and his sincere patriotism rang an unfamiliar but not unattractive change over his audiences.

The White House seemed to have become part of the electioneering tour and Home himself visited Washington in February. Once again a parade of world statesmanship as in 1959; but the President was in no mood to offer a public blessing. There were sharp words about Cuba, where British Leyland buses were finding a ready market, and also about American aid to Sukarno's Indonesia. Sukarno was engaged in harassing the Malaysian government, and Home regarded it as an important achievement that, at the end of their talks, President Johnson publicly reaffirmed his support for an independent Malaysia. It was far from being an electoral ace. Nevertheless, Sir Alec was beginning to get across.

By January 1964 the Conservative area agents were agreed that no leader had been more popular and that morale amongst the rank and file had almost completely recovered. 'When Sir Alec was here in November', one area agent recalled, 'he made a wonderfully favourable impression. Everybody commented on how genuinely friendly he was, and how he seemed interested in what people were saying. As far as our people are concerned, he is the best leader we have had in a long time – since Baldwin really.'[14]

If it is difficult to explain the Home phenomenon, there can be no doubt of its effect. In April the Party chairman reported that, whereas in October the Party would have lost an election by 100 seats, this had already been halved. There was some evidence that the swing to Labour in marginals was lower than in other seats and that the Prime Minister was making a distinct impact. In Conservative-held seats the swing was still higher (by about 8 per cent) than it was in Labour seats, but there was evidence that much of this was due to a fall-away of Tory voters and that, by becoming better known, the Prime Minister could halt and reverse the trend.

The evidence, confused as it was, came at a critical moment. The Conservatives had to decide when they were going to fight. Even before Macmillan left the leadership, 1964 had been settled upon and there remained three possible dates, March, May/June, or October. At first sight March had been attractive. Although the economy was strong and there was no need for a credit squeeze – Sir Alec's first act as Prime Minister was to ask whether one was needed – the budget in April would probably have to be mildly deflationary. But the balance of trade was in deficit, and Sir Alec did himself discredit, the day before the February figures were published, when, without the slightest qualification, he said that 'the economy had seldom been stronger'. March was now ruled out completely. It had never really been a runner. The choice between June and October was much more difficult, and Sir Alec's joking references in speeches – 'when the election comes in June . . . (long pause) or October' – began to grate on the nerves of his Cabinet colleagues. The Chancellor favoured the earlier date; the delay might make a 'tight' financial situation later in the year more threatening. But, to the dismay of the younger Ministers who shared his view, he would not press the point. The almost inevitable loss of the first Greater London Council settled matters: Home would not fight with a depressed army. He announced an autumn election and in the event Labour took control of the G.L.C. by sixty-four seats to thirty-six.

The Budget on 14 April was rather less deflationary than the Treasury had wanted, but at no point did Wilson attack him for that; nor did Maudling's public warning of a balance of payments deficit raise a stir. 'This should give rise neither to alarm or dismay . . . it is the predictable accompaniment of a vigorous rate of growth.' Wilson contented himself with spelling out the need for more vigorous governmental intervention to modernise the industrial structure. For some weeks, with industrial production on a plateau, the Chancellor's judgement seemed vindicated.

By mid-summer, however, concern was growing, as exports did not increase and the trade deficit remained ominously high. Maudling asked his advisers whether they advocated fresh measures. The reply was no. The Chancellor was gambling on breaking out from the Stop-Go cycle. He would restrict imports if necessary rather than call off the experiment. Whether he would have succeeded can never properly be estimated – the election was to change certain crucial conditions in mid-experiment – but it came closer to success than most now care to remember.

Maudling had not banked on a simultaneous capital outflow of massive proportions, compounded as it was by the Montecatini oil deal, to which he could not refuse his consent. On 19 August the N.I.E.S.R. predicted a £500 million deficit, and by September there was growing pressure on sterling, in part seasonal and aggravated by electoral uncertainty. Wilson remained publicly optimistic, unwilling to make the matter an election issue. The electorate were untroubled and the Government chiefly occupied with foreign affairs.

Backed by his younger Ministers Home had insisted on a mini-election in May: of the four seats fought, one was lost, but the swings seemed more favourable and that at Devizes (only 2·8 per cent) the smallest since 1961. There was a result almost as good at Faversham in June, and the polls had begun to turn. In August and September the Conservatives led on N.O.P. and were only 5 per cent behind on Gallup. A majority were predicting a Conservative victory. Home had added to his prestige by his skilful handling of the Rhodesian issue at the Commonwealth Conference in July, and the long warm days of August seemed to bring out the nation's sense of well-being. Central Office propaganda returned to the tried theme of affluence, and the recipe seemed to be working. Polling day, it was announced on 15 September, would be Thursday 15 October.

The Labour Party campaign had started three days before at the Empire Pool, Wembley. But the rally which was to launch the Wilson bandwagon was something less than a success. Wilson's speech, journalists said, had 'no headlines in it', a phenomenon which they were to notice again later in the campaign. Their manifesto seemed dull and in places self-contradictory. Sir Alec effectively commented that it was 'a menu without prices'. Wilson made most mileage in these first few days by publicly challenging Sir Alec to a TV debate, but in his appearance on *Election Forum* he seemed ponderous and ill at ease. Home was nervous but on the whole convincing. He had stumbled badly on pensions, however, when he called them 'donations'. Wilson turned this into a most damaging mistake.

On 27 September Gallup put the Tories ahead for the first time in three years. Three days later N.O.P. gave them a 2·9 per cent lead. To make matters worse for Wilson, George Brown seemed to have dropped a brick. Speaking in his constituency he indicated that the interest rate on new mortgages might be cut to 3 per cent. The *Sunday Express* on the 27th splashed this as 'Brown's Bombshell'. The story seemed to have all the ingredients of a political disaster, but Brown was unrepentant. By Tuesday he was almost boasting of the promise, and a Transport House official conceded, 'At least when George drops a brick, it's a golden brick'.

Wilson had made a real gaffe. On the morning of 30 September he blamed an unofficial strike at Hardy Spicer on deliberate political stirring. 'I must say that's a rum one', Maudling commented lightly, 'Tory shop stewards going round sabotaging Mr Wilson's election! Really!' The public laughed with him, but it was the last pleasure the Conservatives got from the campaign. The balance of payments figures for the second quarter were published the same day and provided the best antidote to the Tory lead. Wilson's friend and adviser, Thomas Balogh, urged him to use the figures to savage the Government. Wilson had spoken already of Sir Alec and Selwyn Lloyd as 'Stop-Go and Son', but at Norwich that night Wilson really let rip. He accused the Prime Minister of deceiving the nation and savagely compared him to John Bloom, the washing-machine king, whose financial empire had just collapsed. But it was the Hardy Spicer gaffe that stole the headlines. Not, however, for long. Hardy Spicer's chairman redressed the balance by describing his workers as 'poor dears . . . of pretty poor mentality', and then issued a libel writ which gave Wilson a perfect excuse to remain silent.

It was left to George Brown to ram the message of the balance of payments home in what must be the most hard-hitting and effective television broadcast ever made. Two days later Gallup revealed a 4½ per cent Labour lead, and N.O.P. on 7 October put the Tory lead at less than 1 per cent.

Quintin Hogg enlivened the closing stages of the campaign with a characteristic explosion: 'If you can tell me there are no adulterers on the front bench of the Labour Party, you can talk to me about Profumo.' Against Wilson's wish, the *Daily Mirror* and the *Sun* splashed the story, Hogg reacted angrily, and the subject became front-page news in every paper and a staple topic of conversation. It totally drowned the arguments about the deterrent which Home was deploying, when allowed to by hecklers. Home allowed himself to say, 'The Labour Party must be very hard up if they have to hire these people'. It was a gaffe. Sympathy evaporated in the face of what seemed bad sportsmanship.

The Labour Party was confident and R. A. Butler confessed to George Gale on 9 October, 'things might start slipping in the last few days . . . they won't slip towards us'. It was a miscue. Wilson made his final television appeal on 12 October, and thereafter the Labour Party lapsed into relative inaction. The Conservative counter-attack started on the 11th when the Party chairman took the unprecedented step of calling a press conference on a Sunday. The deterrent, nationalisation, Maudling's estimate of the particular tax increases required to finance Labour's programme were effectively deployed, but the heart of the counter-attack was its weakest point. Home's television address took two days to record and was the work of 'a tone-deaf pianist'. Only the final climactic assault on the folly of relinquishing the deterrent really came alive.

Home missed his final chance too, when he failed to exploit Wilson's inexplicable twenty-four-hour silence before he denounced a London tube strike, and the Liberals made the running instead. Home had done miracles to pull the Conservatives together and bring them to the post as an effective force, but in the campaign Macmillan's shrewdness and experience were badly missed. At the end the master-mind of the Tory campaign, Lord Poole, made his own ruthless calculation. The Tories were going out, perhaps by 30 seats. But at 11.30 on the morning of Friday 16 October it was Wilson who thought he'd lost.[15] Six hours later he was in Downing Street, but the majority was as slim as his forecast, an overall majority of four!

Once it was clear that the Labour Party would have a majority, however small, by which to govern, then Wilson decided that he would govern. He recoiled instinctively from the frustrations and limitations of a coalition, knowing that his party would find it intolerable. If there were compromises to be made, they would be best made in a developing Parliamentary context; and if the experiment of governing failed, no one could blame the Government for seeking a fresh verdict. Whoever forced a dissolution would, in his view, be blamed by the electorate. The critics have tended to class Wilson 'as a superb tactician and operator in the short term, but with a weak grasp for long-term political strategy'. In a Governmental sense, they may have been right – Wilson's visions of the future, his grand design, were trite, almost empty of meaning – but he had a long-term political strategy for his Government. He never lost sight of the need to create the climate for a second, convincing, electoral victory.

It was this which led to his greatest mistake, the decision to ram home the figure of an £800 m. balance of payments deficit and to blame it on the Tories. This was to tie an albatross around the necks of his Chancellor and Government. From the consequences of the decision, neither ever quite escaped.

It has been known for months that Britain would end 1964 with a large deficit, but the figure of £7–800 m. given to Labour's big three on the evening of 16 October was a surprise. Devaluation was promptly ruled out, and instead from the battery of weapons prepared by Callaghan's predecessor for possible use, they selected export rebates and the temporary import surcharge.[16] The economy itself seemed in reasonable shape, and the deficit, so the Treasury forecast, would be halved without any change in policy. The 'Brown Paper' on the economy chose not to reveal this last fact, thus making its announcement much more alarming that it need have been: 'The Government . . . have decided that on this occasion it is right that the most recent estimates should be given to the nation. It is expected when the accounts for 1964 as a whole are available, they will show a deficit on the balance of payments . . . which is most unlikely to be below £700 m. and may well reach £800 m.'

Wilson had determined on a scenario in which a Labour Government, tough, determined, purposeful, would be contrasted with a fractious, irresponsible Opposition who had just bequeathed to Labour one of the largest balance of payments deficits in Britain's peacetime history. His failure was essentially to grasp the multiple audience to which a Prime Minister must address himself, and from the outset there was a glaring gap between the size of the problem he chose to identify and the measures set in train to deal with it. Not unnaturally perhaps, the measures were regarded as inadequate. Few chose to consider the converse proposition, that the problem had been absurdly exaggerated.

In the short term, Wilson's tactics were successful. The Conservatives were thrust on to the defensive and kept there. The Prime Minister asserted his claim to national leadership by portraying the Conservative leaders as unworthy and even unpatriotic.

The first phase of the Labour Government – Wilson's 'hundred days' – was largely dominated by a major sterling crisis. Yet the Labour Government's *Economic Report on 1964* later confirmed that it was in the second half of November that 'a large-scale withdrawal of funds from London began to take place'. The collapse of confidence was not then due to the size of the deficit, nor even to Wilson's reiterated accusations that the Conservatives had concealed the truth of Britain's position. Rather it was the juxtaposition of continued emphasis on the balance of payments problem with the Government's otherwise laudable desire to honour their election promises.

The Labour Government was pledged to increase old age pensions and to abolish prescription charges. For humane as well as political reasons, Callaghan thought it important to take prompt action on these promises, and he was convinced that an autumn Budget which set out the increased taxation by which these measures would be financed would display the Government as a pillar of financial rectitude. Taken together with the advance notice of the introduction of capital gains and corporation tax, the Budget, in Callaghan's view, must help George Brown in his efforts to persuade the trade unions to agree to an incomes policy. This latter forecast was perhaps the only part of the autumn Budget's effect which Callaghan did not miscalculate. Industry was stunned, so too the City and foreign observers. They took it to mean that the Labour Government was giving its social policies priority over the strength of sterling, and the heat was turned on the pound.

The two days after the Budget were marked by 'heavy sales of sterling from Europe and North America'.[17] On Thursday 19 November Bank Rate, which had been expected to rise, was left at 5 per cent. By the weekend the run on sterling had reached such a point that action could no longer be avoided. But the decision to raise Bank Rate on Monday by 2 per cent was taken to be a step born of desperation. Not since 1931 had Bank Rate been raised on a Monday. The sales of sterling accelerated. The answer, Wilson concluded, was to make sterling strong. The Governor of the Bank of England was summoned to Downing Street on 24 November. There was only one solution, he advised, a wage freeze and cuts in public expenditure. After a stormy argument in the course of which Wilson thought both of going to the country and floating the pound, he was able to convince the Governor that the effects on the world financial community would be such that they would pay up to save the pound. Wilson's view prevailed, and by the evening of 25 November Cromer had mounted a $3000 m. credit which for the moment made sterling safe.

The Conservative Opposition, however, found it difficult to take advantage of the situation. The electorate were content to blame them for the crisis; according to National Opinion Polls, only one third even of Conservative supporters were prepared to blame the Labour Government. At the euphoric Labour rally at Brighton Wilson reassured his cheering supporters, 'This is not a return to Selwyn Lloyd. We do not believe, as our predecessors did, that the way to deal with this kind of crisis is to bring the whole economy shuddering to a stop . . .'. George Brown set himself to work to give the words meaning. His unique methods of persuasion, formal and informal, brought both sides of industry together to sign with the Government the Declaration of Intent on productivity, prices and incomes. The Government would set up machinery to review the movement of prices and incomes; management and the unions would try to promote greater efficiency and assist the workings of the new prices and incomes policy. The agreement existed on paper only, but George Brown believed in it with an almost religious fervour.

Then came election shocks for both main parties. Labour's Foreign Secretary, Patrick Gordon Walker, failed to return to Westminster in the

Leyton by-election by 205 votes, while in the Roxburgh by-election on 24 March, a young Liberal, David Steel, captured the seat from the Conservatives. It gave new impetus to Tory discontent with Sir Alec's leadership – a discontent which the Party Whips had failed to still with their announcement in mid-January that Home would not be resigning. The rival promoters for Macleod and Maudling began to manoeuvre for position. The chance of an early election precluded immediate change, but the idea spread that the time for Sir Alec to go would be just before the summer recess.

Callaghan's second budget, introduced on 6 April and intended to be mildly deflationary, raised an extra £323 m. in tax. Corporation tax, capital gains tax, and sixpence on income tax were there as promised, but the Chancellor delighted his supporters by drastically curtailing businessmen's entertainment allowances. Heath delighted the Tories almost as much by the effective way in which he opposed the 226-page Finance Bill clause by clause. The Government was defeated three times – all on the night of 6–7 July, and more than four hundred amendments were made to the Bill, 243 by Callaghan himself.

Tough action was accompanied by soft talk. 'The economic crisis, with the unpopular measures it demanded, is virtually now over', Wilson confidently announced on 4 February. He had some reason for optimism. Maudling's prediction about exports was belatedly coming true. Year on year between 1964 and 1965 they rose by 7 per cent in value, well above the average for the past decade, and throughout 1965 the volume of imports rose more slowly than output. By Conference time, the Conservative leadership had ceased to apologise for 1964 and began to try to take credit. The current account deficit fell by three quarters and the overall deficit by three fifths. There was actually a current account surplus at the end of Labour's first year in office, and they could take some credit for this and for their actions to restrict investment overseas and to reduce Government spending overseas. Between April and June, the credit squeeze was three times tightened, but Bank Rate was reduced, and in June Callaghan announced, 'I think we are round the corner or at least turning the corner'.

Unfortunately for the Government, George Brown's efforts to achieve restraint on prices and incomes coincided with sharp increases in both the price index – tax increases were largely to blame – and in wages. He had set a norm of 3–3½ per cent and appointed a former Conservative Minister, Aubrey Jones, to chair the Prices and Incomes Board. The Trades Union Congress had ratified the new body on 30 April, with only the T.G.W.U.

dissenting. The second half of the year brought some comfort to George Brown on the prices front, where the index rose only 2 per cent in eight months, but a succession of wage offers above the norm pushed wage rates up by 4½ per cent by the end of the year.

The Government's legislative programme was equally slow in taking effect. The introduction of the Rent Act in March and the Redundancy Payments Bill in April saw two important measures begin their successful journey to the statute book. But Labour ran into trouble when it attempted to fulfil its pledge to nationalise steel. Late on 6 May it seemed possible that the rebel votes against the White Paper would lead to a Government defeat. A few conciliatory remarks from George Brown at the end of the debate assuaged the rebels – though incensing the Left. It was clear there was no chance of legislation.

The steel débâcle damaged Labour. By-elections held between May and July registered a swing to the Conservatives, and at the local government elections the pro-Conservative swing was of the order of 6 per cent. From May to September Labour trailed on the Gallup Poll, and only N.O.P. remained to bolster sagging Labour morale. Perhaps the worst blow was the announcement on 15 June that the trade gap in May had widened to £109 m.

There was another heavy burst of sterling sales. The Stock Exchange became nervous. Callaghan blamed it all on the expectation of an early election, and Wilson determined to introduce a note of stability into the situation. At Glasgow on 26 June he gave a categoric pledge that there would be no election that year. The effect was only temporary: the results of the speculative wave were recorded in the gold figures at the end of the month and triggered off a fresh wave. The United States administration was also concerned. It had no wish to force Britain into a 'Little England' posture, but any further loan to prop up sterling must be effective.

The least unexpected result of Wilson's pledge was a fresh leadership crisis in the Conservative party. On 27 June the *Sunday Express* claimed that fully one hundred M.P.s now wished Sir Alec to give way to Heath. Four days later the leadership was discussed at the 1922 Committee Executive; a second meeting on 5 July split the Executive into two halves, although Sir Alec had made it clear to them that he had no intention of going. Heath's supporters headed the revolt, but they were joined by al-most all of the younger Members present.[18] Sir Alec also appeared to have lost ground in the constituencies. Heath's performance on the Finance Bill and in particular the Labour defeats in the early hours of 7 July meant that a credible successor was to hand. The moment of decision had come, but

Sir Alec was undecided. In February, he had set up new procedures to elect a Conservative leader, but he had refused to submit himself to them. His freedom of manoeuvre was thus unimpaired. The consensus in the party was far from complete. A small meeting of backbenchers a week after Heath's parliamentary triumph was still in favour of Sir Alec going on, and during the weekend of 10–11 July he again declared his intention to continue.

But on Tuesday 13 July *The Times* revealed the proceedings in the 1922 Committee. Two days later an N.O.P. poll reported an increase in Labour's lead. Finally on 18 July a long article by William Rees-Mogg in the *Sunday Times* proclaimed it 'The Right Moment to Change'. Sir Alec began to be affected mentally and physically. During a heated debate on Vietnam he had to be prompted by the Chief Whip to speak, and he made a mess of it. A poor performance in the foreign affairs debate on 20 July proved decisive. Sir Alec decided to resign.

The leadership election which followed proceeded smoothly and uneventfully. Maudling and Heath were nominated at once. After some hesitation, Enoch Powell made it a three-way contest. Inside the Parliamentary Party the campaign for Heath was beautifully organised, that for Maudling somewhat haphazard, and on the first ballot, Heath polled 150 votes to Maudling's 133 and Powell's 15. Both his rivals promptly stood down, and Heath at 49 became leader of the Conservative Party.

Almost immediately he was on the attack. On 27 July the Chancellor announced a further stiff package of restrictions, amounting perhaps to £200 m. in a full year, less than a fortnight after he had said that it 'would be an unfortunate thing to do.'[19] There had been a further flurry of speculation, and Callaghan had been convinced by the French Finance Minister that he must cut Government spending and reduce demand to get the economy in order. The new measures cut right across the preparation of the National Plan and convinced many that it ought to be written off even before it was published. To the Conservatives the July measures were a gift from the Gods and they tabled three censure motions as their last salvo before the parliamentary recess.

'Successive British Governments in the 1960s,' Lord Boyle observes,[20] 'had one thing in common; they both found it much less difficult to beat off the parliamentary challenges of their opponents, than to keep the confidence of their own supporters, and the assurance of their continual support.' Adroitly Wilson had taken most of the leaders of the old Left into power where the compensations of administration proved an adequate substitute for the emotional outlet of moral outrage. The afterglow of election victory temporarily sufficed to still the doubts of the remainder, left almost leaderless as they were. Wilson's command of the appropriate rhetoric proved almost as successful in these months as it had in the years of opposition.

The first real trouble came over Vietnam, particularly when bombing of North Vietnam began in February. There were emergency questions in Parliament and a motion signed by fifty backbenchers. Frightened that President Johnson might escalate the war still further, Wilson tried early in February to arrange a visit to Washington and had his ear chewed off. Efforts to involve Soviet mediation proved equally discouraging. Despite further pressure from the Left to declare its inability to support U.S. policy, the Wilson Government stuck to its 'support for the American stand against Communist infiltration into South Vietnam', although this by no means meant that they eschewed frank talking in Washington.[21]

On the economic front, Callaghan's July measures had not immediately killed speculation. Early in August there was a fresh selling wave and rumours of devaluation spread. Wilson was due to go on holiday on the 5th. Two hours before his train left, Callaghan brought a very worried Governor of the Bank of England to see him. Wilson was prepared to go so far as to lay on a contingency trip and a plane to America, but he would not alter his plans. Better for all three of them to go on holiday, he argued: that could only help the pound. He was right. Cromer was prevailed on to leave that weekend for the south of France and the crisis died down.

It had persuaded Wilson, however, that further action was required. George Brown was asked to enquire urgently into ways of strengthening his policy. He was convinced that it was a mistake to underpin a voluntary policy with legal enforcement measures, but reluctantly allowed that it was necessary. On 26 August, after publicly hinting at the need for reinforcing the policy, he confronted representatives of the C.B.I. and the T.U.C. Over six uneasy hours he sought to persuade them to agree to a compulsory early warning system on price rises and wage claims. The Government would take power to refer any price or wage issue to the Prices and Incomes Board, to defer any wage settlement or price increase, while it was under consideration, and to enforce the Board's decisions. Brown explained that he wanted their informal agreement to reassure the United States at what he believed to be a critical stage in negotiations for fresh international support for sterling. Reluctantly the C.B.I. fell into line. The trade unions failed to agree. The Prime Minister was forced to acquiesce in a delay while the two sides consulted their parent organisations.

On 1 September the Cabinet agreed to the new line. Next day Brown swept down on the T.U.C. General Council meeting at Brighton, and after twelve hectic hours was able to announce the plan with official union blessing. Congress endorsed it on 8 September, but by only 5,251,000 votes to 3,312,000.

The ground was now cleared for a massive $1000 m. loan from the central banks which enabled the Bank of England to 'go from the defensive to the offensive'. The speculators made for cover, and the pound was temporarily safe. The Government had bought time to push through its long-term reforms. On 16 September the long-awaited National Plan was published, to be denounced by the Conservative leader even before publication as 'the biggest publicity gimmick' the Government had yet staged. In fact the July measures had already destroyed the foundation on which the statistical groundwork had been laid, and, as more acute observers quickly pointed out, the basis of the exercise was in any case suspect.

By now, Wilson was in buoyant mood. His own speeches at the Conference received massive ovations and optimism was the keynote. 'We are now getting within measurable distance of balancing our overseas payments. The economy is strong. Sterling is strong. Employment is strong . . .'.[22] His standing with the public was also rising sharply and towards the end of 1965 had almost reached the heights achieved by Sir Anthony Eden and Harold Macmillan in their political prime.

The key to this rise is almost certainly to be found in the Rhodesia crisis. The Unilateral Declaration of Independence on 11 November confronted Wilson 'with the severest test of his political skill since he had come to office'. He had already ruled out the use of force. He had now to satisfy the African clamour for immediate action yet keep the problem in British hands, and carry with him the British people.

In the Commons, Wilson was firm. The plan he outlined was to impose sanctions gradually, holding out at every stage the chance of negotiations provided only that Rhodesia returned to the path of constitutional development. On the consequential sanctions which flowed from Rhodesia's act of 'rebellion' the Conservative leadership offered impeccable support to the Government, even on the ban of all purchases of Rhodesian tobacco. Over the days which followed, Heath's tone hardened – an obvious response to the pressures put upon him – and he sought very specific assurances about the use of force. His actions remained studiously moderate, however. As sanctions were swiftly extended the Conservatives either supported or did not oppose them.

The Conservative party was badly divided, and its divisions were exposed to the world in a backbench revolt when, on 17 October, the Government imposed an oil embargo and sought to enforce it with a blockade of the Portuguese port of Beira. Fifty backbenchers defied the Whips by voting against the Government, while thirty-one, led by a frontbench spokesman on Africa, voted for it.

Wilson ignored warnings that his policies would not be enough to bring Smith down, and that even loyal Rhodesians would find it difficult to stand out against him. He was determined to maintain a degree of all-party consensus and confident – as he told the Commonwealth Prime Ministers at their Lagos meeting in January – that economic sanctions 'might well bring the rebellion to an end within a matter of weeks rather than months'. He seemed to relish the crisis and his quasi-Churchillian oratory evoked a marked response from the British people. Heath's popularity, by contrast, had steadily declined and by February 1966 it stood lower than Sir Alec's fourteen months before.

Wilson had reshuffled his Cabinet in December, bringing Roy Jenkins to the Home Office and Barbara Castle to the Ministry of Transport. He was still convinced that the electorate did not want an election but he was being forced to rethink his position. Industrial trouble threatened on the prices and incomes front. Electorally he faced a critical by-election at Hull North which the Conservatives were convinced they would win. There were fears for the health of the Labour Member for the margin seat at Falmouth. Iain Macleod, dealing with his first Finance Bill as Shadow Chancellor, was not likely to be less tough than Edward Heath. Vietnam had not ceased to trouble Labour backbenchers: sixty-eight of them cabled Wilson, while he was in America in December to address the U.N. and secure President Johnson's consent to oil sanctions, demanding that the bombing of North Vietnam should stop. Simultaneously the Government survived a debate on the future of the Territorial Army by one vote. Two measures, the minimum income guarantee and relief on mortgages, had already been postponed, and, although some major Bills had appeared, it was unlikely that any could be on the statute book in time for an October election. Better perhaps to have them in the shop window and go for a decision in March.

Then on 27 January, against most expectations, Labour crushed Tory hopes at Hull with a swing of 4·5 per cent. A week later the M.P. for Falmouth and Camborne died, and that weekend a well publicised Chequers meeting to review policy authorised the drafting of a policy statement for the Annual Conference which, most of them realised, could also be a manifesto.

If Wilson had any doubts about a March election, they were now stilled. An atmosphere of electioneering now pervaded Parliament. Despite all his difficulties, Wilson rode a wave of confidence. By the time of the mass Labour rally in the Albert Hall on 29 January he was quite euphoric: he seemed to have no conception of the abyss which was already visibly opening beneath his Government. In an interim Budget statement on 1 March, Callaghan promised a mortgage option scheme, and said that he foresaw no need for severe increases of taxation. Even the first sign of trouble on the prices and incomes front – the railwaymen's strike against an offer confirmed by the P.I.B. – turned in Wilson's favour, when over beer and sandwiches he settled the strike 'without the payment of any further ransom money'. Deliberately now the Prime Minister set about creating an atmosphere in which his decision to go to the country would seem quite inevitable, and by the time he left for an official visit to the Soviet Union on 21 February, it was quite clear that the campaign was about to begin. The official announcement came on 28 February.

Behind the scenes a row raged over the Labour manifesto, but when it finally reached the National Executive on 7 March it proved to be the mixture as before but at much greater length. The Conservative manifesto, *Action Not Words*, launched two days before, got a rather better press. It had five main themes: tax reform and the economy, Europe, trade union reform, selectivity in the social services, and housing. Heath was to hammer the first four home in the course of the campaign. But the real object of his attack was the threat of inflation implicit in the ratio increase in earnings, prices and production. The Conservatives were aware that they had only one chance, to shock the country into an awareness of the economic situation, with the hope that they would then turn naturally to new measures. There were no new men. Their policy review, their organisational reforms, their new programme of electoral research, were all incomplete. The new Conservative prototype was to be tested before it was really under way.

By contrast, Wilson could afford to fight a subdued campaign, giving no hostages to fortune, and emphasising two simple themes: 'Thirteen Wasted Years' and 'You *Know* Labour Government Works'. He sought to thrust the Conservatives on to the defensive. Labour went into action with a 9 per cent lead and won by the lesser margin of 6 per cent. Few people had doubted that they would win, and the campaign itself seemed a bore to the press, the politicians, and perhaps to the electorate as well. Labour romped home to a 97-seat victory, with their highest poll since 1951. Despite the 1966 victory the glad confident morning of 1964 was gone. Labour had asserted its will to govern, and it had been given the authority it needed to tackle Britain's economic problems.

The election then did not mark an abrupt change, but it was nevertheless crucial for Heath. At stake had been his own reputation and his vision of the Conservative party. He had not allowed himself to lose hope at any stage that he might topple Wilson, but in practice he was as much concerned with staking out the ground for future electoral success as he was with victory in 1966.

His Party had perhaps the most radical programme advanced by any since the war. It represented not just a break with the past but with the past of the Conservative party as well. One of his own major tasks during the campaign was to bring his Party once more into tune with contemporary realities. In doing so he increased his stature within his own Party and the political world.

Hindsight has perhaps painted the 1964-6 Labour Government in rather more roseate hues than it deserves. There had been a record of solid social achievement – increased old age pensions, the 1965 Housing Act and so on – but the crushing success of the 1966 election victory concealed much that had gone wrong and still more that had been shelved. The deficit on the balance of payments in 1965 amounted to £265 m., and although exports stood at nine per cent above their level for the first few months of 1965, the dangers of inflation had been emphasised over and over again during the election campaign.

A month after the election the euphoria still persisted. Gallup showed a lead for Labour almost as large as that in the summer of Profumo. The proportion of the electorate who thought Harold Wilson was doing a good job reached record proportions, and Professor Kaldor's ingenious discovery of S.E.T. enabled the Chancellor to avoid the orthodox deflation the Treasury asked for.

Harold Wilson believed he had a powerful alternative to deflation: an incomes crusade. Here was a cause to which he could devote all his energies. On 11 May, the Parliamentary Press Gallery were treated to a full dress attack on restrictive practices and a call for a 'new spirit of anti-amateurism'. Five days later the National Union of Seamen's strike began. One by one, the ports of London were blocked with abandoned vessels. Exports fell sharply, whilst the foreign bankers thought the unions were out of hand. The London Labour Party decided to back the strikers, and when Wilson attempted to persuade the strikers to accept the Pearson Report over beer and sandwiches at No. 10, the £, as he told them, was already slipping. The seamen would not go back and Wilson was outraged.

In part, Wilson's anger had its effect. The Executive voted for a return to work, and ironically some of the men publicly named as communists by Wilson spent their time persuading reluctant seamen to obey the call. For the first time the Left began to view Wilson with suspicion.

The end of the strike did not bring about an immediate recovery for sterling. Events now came thick and fast. A Bill was introduced to provide advance warning of wage and price increases and to empower the Prices and Incomes Board to defer them while their merits were investigated. Frank Cousins could not stomach the interference with collective bargaining. On 3 July he resigned. The need for stiffer measures seemed obvious, and the choice equally clear – devaluation or deflation? George Brown had no doubt. The National Plan must be served even if it meant devaluation, and he was backed by ministers like Crosland and Jenkins, who were also for devaluation and the Common Market.

Wilson had forbidden any mention of the word. He seemed not to appreciate the gathering storm. On 12 July, the Prime Minister made a full blooded attack on 'the defeatist cries, the moaning minnies, the wet editorials – yes, the Sundays as well – of those who will seek any opportunity to sell Britain short at home and abroad'. The foreign bankers were not impressed, and the Cabinet sharply divided.

Callaghan, by now desperately worried, threatened to join the devaluers, unless he had his way, and the Prime Minister made his choice. He would back the Treasury package; more, he would announce the cuts himself. Even then he made the mistake of forecasting the announcement, and had to advance the cuts to the day after his return from a planned trip to Moscow, which he insisted on fulfilling. While Wilson was away George Brown tried to rally support for devaluation, and at Durham, where he addressed the Miners' Gala, he let it be known he was intent on resigning. But when the Cabinet met on 19 July, the incipient revolt had fizzled out. Callaghan had seen Wilson and had been persuaded to support him. Six members of the Cabinet argued against deflation, but only Brown resigned.

'Where's George?' a Tory M.P. cried when Wilson rose to announce the deflationary package to gasps of disbelief and dismay. The cry turned out to be significant. Brown was considering his position. That evening his supporters arranged a round robin asking him to stay in the Government, and after a long talk with the Prime Minister he told the waiting press that he had decided to stay. Wilson had survived the reversal of a decade of policy pronouncements with his Cabinet intact.

Chief among the pledges Wilson had been forced to reverse was the most recent, from election eve: on a wage freeze. He had told the Commons there was to be a legally binding freeze on wages and prices for six months, to be followed by a period of severe wage restraint. Wilson groped unconvincingly for some difference between his own position and that of the Tory predecessors he had savaged.

The wage freeze aroused most anger. It was hastily incorporated into the prices and incomes legislation, and was given short shrift by the Tories. The Shadow Cabinet had been divided over the milder measure which George Brown advocated. Heath himself, Boyle and Maudling had seen little harm in it, but the 1922 Committee had urged root and branch opposition. There seemed a possibility of trouble among the leadership. The July measures let them off the hook and impaled the Labour Party instead. Having said only ten days before that no elaborate statutory controls were intended, Wilson hastily had them tacked on to the Prices and Incomes Bill, whose passage had been interrupted by the economic crisis. When the Bill came before Parliament on 4 August the Government's nominal majority dropped from 95 to 52, when the Opposition tried to prevent the tack.[23]

There is little doubt that the number of abstentions would have been higher had the dissidents realised that these powers would have to be used. George Brown, who fought the Bill through in Committee with immense skill, said that the Government did not expect that it would have to activate these powers; to do so would require an Order in Council confirmed by a Commons vote; and in any case, he promised they would last no more than a year. But Brown was not to be at his post much longer. Wilson had offered him the Foreign Office, a post which Brown had long coveted. Michael Stewart would exchange offices with him, and Callaghan, who had publicly hinted at his desire for the Foreign Office, would stay at the Treasury.

When he retired to the Scilly Isles on 11 August Wilson was perhaps more satisfied than he should have been. The threat to his position from a Brown-Callaghan axis had been eliminated. The pound was safe again and his dominance over his colleagues seemed unimpaired. He had conceded to his critics a new Cabinet Committee, the Strategic Economic Policy Committee, which would let them into a collective discussion of economic affairs; but this he was to chair himself and the meetings would be irregular.

There were however ominous cracks in Wilson's position. Devaluation, like it or not, was now a possibility in the Cabinet's mind. The freeze had been accepted grudgingly by the C.B.I., and, only after a disputed vote, by the General Council of the T.U.C. Several groups of employees, promised their wage increases before 20 July, persuaded the Courts to uphold their claim that they should be paid. Above all there was Vietnam, especially with the bombing of Hanoi and Haiphong. Wilson's own resilience was further displayed when he chose to address the T.U.C. Annual Congress. Despite Wilson's courage, the T.U.C. was not over-impressed. In a series of conflicting votes, they acquiesced in the Government's policy, perhaps spurred to it by an ill-judged appeal from Edward Heath for them to 'knock some sense into Government by making the freeze voluntary'.

The Labour Party's own conference went unexpectedly well. It began inauspiciously with a demonstration of unemployed car workers, whom Wilson courageously insisted on addressing, and with a Cabinet meeting on the evening of Monday 3 October in the unlikely surroundings of the Grand Hotel, at which it was decided to activate Part IV of the Prices and Incomes Act. But when the T.G.W.U. proposed their resolution opposing wages legislation the following morning, they were defeated by nearly 1½ million votes. Only on Vietnam, predictably, did the Government taste defeat.

Wilson was about to steal some major articles of Conservative clothing, however. As late as March 1966, during the election campaign, he had vented his own hostility to the Common Market, although his formal position remained as always a commitment to entry on the right terms. He was coming to see this as inevitable. The Commonwealth was not the instrument he had supposed it to be as late as 1964, and the strain of defending sterling, perhaps also the French withdrawal from NATO, led him to take his pledge more seriously. Not only was a specific reference made in the Queen's Speech, but a powerful Cabinet Committee under George Brown was set up to consider the implications of joining.

As the balance of Cabinet opinion began to move with him, Wilson suggested a high-level reconnaissance of the European capitals, and this was agreed on the assurance that he and Brown would both go and that a full record of the talks would be circulated. By the time the visits were over Wilson had virtually decided on an application. The Treasury warned of the burdens of sterling and forecast devaluation, but Wilson was no more deterred than he was by warnings from the Paris Embassy that there would be a further French veto.

On 2 May the Cabinet agreed that the application would be made. Time proved a great solvent, there were no resignations – but it was an open secret that seven out of the twenty-one Ministers were hostile, and that three or four might resign.

Wilson had no problems with the Opposition. Heath, Home and Maudling had all blessed his voyage of exploration, and the Conservative leader had, in November, appeared to go a long way towards de Gaulle's position. The importance of this support can scarcely be exaggerated. A warning shot was fired on 21 February when 107 Labour M.P.s tabled a motion recalling the Party's earlier stiff conditions for entry. Three ful - scale Party meetings were given over to the subject, and, with character- istic ebullience, George Brown forecast that it would not be easy for de Gaulle to deliver a veto. Wilson powerfully argued the pro-Market case. The hard-line dissenters were unmoved, but a clear majority of the Parliamentary Labour Party swung into line, and when the issue was at length put to the N.E.C. and Conference in October their backing was substantial and unconditional. With their natural leaders locked up in Cabinet, the anti-marketeers had to rely on veterans like Shinwell, Blyton and even Attlee to take the lead: nevertheless seventy-four Labour M.P.s signed the *Tribune* anti-market manifesto[24] and when Parliament debated the matter thirty-five Labour M.P.s voted against the Government and about fifty abstained. With characteristic candour Heath used a three-line whip to support the Government.

The Government changed course on Rhodesia too. Wilson met Ian Smith aboard H.M.S. *Tiger* in December. Paul Foot in *The Politics of Harold Wilson* has shown quite clearly how, on almost every point, Wilson made concessions to the Rhodesian viewpoint which made 'the *Tiger* Constitution ... more reactionary and more acceptable to the racist Rhodesians' white minority than the Tory Constitution of 1961'.[25] When he returned from the *Tiger* on 7 December he was jubilantly confident that a settlement was within reach, but within a matter of hours the Smith régime had rejected the draft agreement. In the Commons Wilson was passionate; the House sympathetic, but when he chose to endorse the Commonwealth Conference formula, 'No Independence Before Majority Rule', the Conservatives decided on opposition. Wilson saw his chance. He turned the debate into a party battle and branded the Opposition as supporters of the Smith régime. Amazingly he earned himself a standing ovation from his own supporters, many of whom had welcomed the breakdown. Heath bit back just as hard, exposing Wilson's 'hypocrisy', and the debate ended in pandemonium. Ruthlessly Wilson had exploited his one chance to unite his own party, and he found himself compelled to go on to demand international mandatory sanctions against Rhodesia.

On the home front the wage freeze gave way to the 'period of severe restraint' in February 1967. The last quarter of 1966 had seen a heartening balance of payments surplus, and by the end of March nearly all previous Central Bank assistance had been repaid. Wilson was euphoric: he failed to heed warning signs that the removal of the import surcharge the previous November and certain fortuitous factors in world trade had made for a second false dawn. Looking at the trade figures, the wages standstill, and the recovery of sterling, Wilson and his colleagues were convinced that the tide had turned, the victory had been won. He even felt able to rebuke his critics. When they rebelled at the end of February on the Defence White Paper, he told a P.L.P. meeting, 'All I can say is, watch it. Every dog is allowed one bite but a different view is taken of a dog that goes on biting . . . If there are doubts that the dog is biting not because of dictates of conscience but because he is considered vicious . . . he may not get his licence renewed.' It was said in a bantering way, but it aroused fury, which was reflected in press comment. An apparent attempt to muzzle the press a few days earlier by the issue of D Notices gave rise to further hostile comment and an adverse report by three Privy Councillors.

The Government's confidence was no longer shared by the British people. At rock-solid Rhondda West on 9 March the Welsh Nationalists nearly captured the seat, and on the same day the Conservatives took Glasgow Pollok. By-elections at Honiton and Brierley Hill, where the Conservatives handsomely increased their majorities, told a similar tale. On 13 April the Conservatives took the G.L.C. by eighty-two seats to eighteen, the first time for thirty-three years that Labour had lost London, and in the borough elections Labour took only 846 seats, fewer than at any time since the war. The opinion polls followed in the wake of the electorate. Desperately Wilson tried to stem the tide. On May Day he restored history to order. Speaking in Leeds he outlined the three stages of policy which the Labour Government had carefully followed since taking office: Part 1, the battle to save the pound; Part 2, the refit of the economy; and the decks would soon be cleared for Part 3, the 'great leap forward . . . The vision your Labour Government holds out to you is this. That a Britain strengthened by the firm measures of these past two years will be able, as year succeeds year, to move forward at a still more rapid pace into the third major phase of building the New Britain.'[26] Michael Stewart at the D.E.A. had already promised that the compulsory powers under Part IV of the Prices and Incomes Act would lapse at the end of the summer.

Wilson's confidence soon had a rude jolt. On 16 May de Gaulle announced that Britain was not yet ready to join the Six. Wilson retorted that he would not take no for an answer. On the anniversary of Waterloo he bearded de Gaulle in Paris, but the French would not let the British application be tabled. In the end George Brown had to disguise it as a speech to the Western European Union, forty-nine paragraphs delivered at the outset of their July meeting, and the last, the application, right at the close. For once the French were caught by surprise.

At home it was the Government which was surprised by a fresh sterling crisis; they failed to heed the warning Heath gave on 8 July at Carshalton. Afterwards Wilson tried to blame the difficulties on the Six Days' War. In fact the trade gap had widened to an average of nearly £50 m. a month before the Middle East crisis had affected the figures, and the sharp turn-round in the sterling market took place some three weeks before the Arab-Israeli clash. Sir William Armstrong had warned Wilson in April that the existing sterling parity and Common Market entry were quite incompatible. It was this widely-shared view rather than the war or the poor May trade figures that caused the new run on sterling.

In July unemployment reached a post-war record and three-quarters of a million out of work were forecast for the winter. The economy was not growing as predicted and Callaghan hastened to relax the squeeze. He was warned that devaluation was a real possibility, but chose in the economic debate at the end of July to rule it out with passionate conviction. The Prime Minister decided to meet the crisis by intensifying direct physical intervention. On 28 August he took personal control of the D.E.A. Against Treasury advice, hire purchase controls were again relaxed the following day. The decision contributed to a strong consumer boom which had subsequently to be reversed in mid-stream to give devaluation room in which to work.

Devaluation was now a probability, but Wilson would not (and still does not) believe it. At Newport on 8 September he proclaimed that his Government had, at long last, and once again, reached a 'turning point'.

It was a turning point less than apparent to the Trades Union Congress, who passed hostile resolutions on Vietnam, prices and incomes, and unemployment. The Labour Conference at the beginning of October was still more gloomy. On 21 September the Labour Party not only lost Cambridge to the Conservatives, but Attlee's old seat, Walthamstow West, as well – an 18½ per cent swing. Wilson did his best to soften the growing concern about unemployment by delaying the coalpit closure programme, and Callaghan was in his very best form. Conference decided to support the Government's economic policies by 122,000 votes, and they voted down resolutions critical of the prices and incomes policy and of the Government's record on unemployment. Wilson too was in excellent vein and was warmly cheered. The Conference, if glum, was certainly not rebellious. They voted to join the Common Market by a two-to-one majority. But in Europe, the portents for British entry were now beginning to look very gloomy; while at home massive dock strikes at Liverpool and London and another poor set of trade figures created unease. Callaghan had spent little time on the balance of payments when he spoke at Scarborough. He thought it likely that he would be advised to devalue and had personally reached the conclusion that only a long-term credit to reinforce the sterling balances could now save the pound. All that was forthcoming was a small twelve-month loan from the Swiss commercial banks. Bank rate was raised on 19 October, but the decision backfired much as it had done three years before. Couve de Murville's speech on 25 October, damping down European ambitions, could not therefore have come at a worse time and Callaghan was forced into a confident assessment of the overall position when he spoke at the Mansion House dinner the following evening. 'Devaluation not on agenda' was the correct headline for the speech. It was not. The Chancellor was not yet ready to recommend or the Prime Minister to accept it.

Heath's position was awkward. Some of the economists advising his Party had already advocated a change in parity at a Tory economic seminar in July. Heath was passionately against the move, and in any case saw no reason to get the Labour Government off the hook. His Party was growing restless, puzzled by Heath's lack of success in the polls and perturbed by his failure to match the Prime Minister in the Commons. But for its electoral successes Heath might have faced serious trouble at the Brighton Conference. Instead the party tackled his close friend and lieutenant, Sir Edward Boyle, and the education resolution was carried by less than 500 votes. Heath made a first-rate off-the-cuff speech, and won the predictable ovation and a paternal blessing from the Conference chairman that he 'would emerge very fast indeed as the right man'.

There was no such respite for Wilson. On 4 November Callaghan saw Wilson to warn him that the drain on the reserves had intensified and that the Finance Ministers of the Six were preparing to discuss what to do if Britain devalued. Callaghan doubted whether the situation could be held. Over the weekend Wilson decided that there could be no question of a 'political veto', and the Treasury quietly made its preparations. The Cabinet Committee on Economic Policy was told of the situation on the 8th, and the Foreign Secretary reluctantly acquiesced in the possibility the following day. Preparations were being made to devalue on 18 November, but there was still hope of an international package to avert devaluation. By chance over the weekend of 11–13 November the West's banks were meeting. Briefly they toyed with the proposal, then doubts set in. The conditions of a fresh I.M.F. loan would have been too onerous for the Government to accept. When no package emerged, confidence weakened, and on 13 November, after the Prime Minister's speech at Guildhall, Wilson and Callaghan took the decision to devalue. A small ministerial group was brought into the preparations next day, but the Cabinet was not told until the 16th. It was while the Cabinet was in session that they were told of a private notice question based on reports of an international loan which the newspapers that morning had splashed.

Callaghan insisted on taking it himself. There was no attempt to get the question postponed. It proved to be a costly mistake. At first Callaghan was at his best, playing the bowling with the deadest of dead bats. Macleod was helpful, Jeremy Thorpe rather less so, but it was a Labour back-bencher, Stanley Orme, who specifically pressed devaluation. Callaghan's reply had been worked out on Wilson's advice at the Cabinet that morning: 'I have nothing to add to or subtract from anything I have said on previous occasions on the subject of devaluation, and in any case it does not arise from my original answer.' Within minutes the speculators went mad. The question and answer cost Britain over £300 million. The actual announcement of devaluation was almost an anticlimax when it came late on the evening of 18 November. Inevitably it was seen as a major defeat, not least for Wilson himself. Sensing this, he allowed himself to be persuaded, against his own better judgement, into representing devaluation almost as some brilliantly conceived panacea. On television he used a reassuring and easily remembered phrase for which the Tories were to pillory him: 'Devaluation does not mean, of course, that the pound here in Britain, in your pocket or purse, or in your bank has been devalued.' Generally overlooked, even at the time, was the rest of the paragraph when 'higher prices over a period for some of our imports, including some of our basic foods' were mentioned. Perhaps this is because most people do not automatically link import prices and shop prices. Much more open to criticism was his mention of a 6 per cent growth rate in 1968 at a meeting of the Parliamentary Labour Party. 'If this had been attempted, it would have meant frittering away most of the benefits of devaluation in a domestic boom', Samuel Brittan concluded,[27] and the idea, if it was ever a reality, was soon abandoned.

Heath made a bitter and effective television broadcast in reply to the

Prime Minister, and opened himself to a scornful attack in the House of Commons, which remains the best measure of Wilson's euphoria:

> As I told the House last Thursday . . . that is before devaluation . . . we could look forward to a substantial increase in production over the next year – well above the five per cent which we had envisaged earlier . . . Now of course with the opportunities of export-led expansion resulting from devaluation, it is right to tell the House that the problem which we shall be facing in a year's time is far more likely to be not deflation and unemployment but expansion to a scale which might lead to labour shortages in many areas.[28]

In sober hard fact unemployment did not fall, and in 1968 a 3·5 per cent growth rate was achieved.

The Prime Minister's most pressing problem was to find a new Chancellor. The Tories were howling for Callaghan's blood, but he defended devaluation with considerable dignity in the few days left to him. Privately he insisted on resigning; Wilson was able to persuade him to consider an exchange of offices instead. He would have preferred Crosland to Jenkins at the Treasury, but the latter had a considerable following on the back benches. Callaghan wanted the Home Office if he was going to stay. A straight swap seemed the simplest way out, and on 29 November it was announced that Roy Jenkins would be the new Chancellor.

There was to be one more bitter disappointment. Wilson had made his proposals for a new European Technological Community the centrepiece of his Guildhall speech. He hoped still that Britain might join the E.E.C. But the day before the exchange of ministerial posts, de Gaulle in his half-yearly press conference gave a resounding 'Non' to British entry. It had little immediate impact in Britain, nor did Wilson's reply distract the press from news of the reshuffle; but the combination of a collapsed parity with a bankrupt European strategy proved a severe blow to national morale. The Opposition's reaction to devaluation did little to help. Their suppressed venom burst out, not only in a justified attack on the Government's ineptitude but in an attack on the policy itself at a time when this was the only right course.

Wilson's attitude was strikingly different and almost equally misguided. Callaghan had prepared a series of moderate restraints to accompany the devaluation decision, but the Cabinet refused to contemplate the comprehensive programme, designed by the Treasury to restrain the home market, cumulatively, as the rise in exports gathered strength. Callaghan was not prepared to force it through, believing that this was a matter or his successor.

Jenkins was immediately subjected to a baptism of fire. There was acute concern in the House about the conditions the I.M.F. had imposed as part of the stand-by arrangements. With Wilson's agreement the Chancellor decided to publish the letter which his predecessor had addressed to the I.M.F. on 23 November. The day before it was published, however, Jenkins rashly told the House that 'the Fund has not attached conditions to their credit' and he added that the policy set out in the letter involved no new deflationary policies. It was hard to reconcile these words with the Government's promise in the letter to cut home consumption by £750 m., as Macleod pointed out in an emergency debate on 5 December. Nigel Birch was caustic: 'to tell a fib when one is bound to be found out within ten minutes is pathetic, childish'. Eighteen Labour M.P.s voted against the Government, and probably as many abstained. There were press stories that an attempt would be made to change the tenancy of No. 10. The Tory lead on Gallup, $7\frac{1}{2}$ per cent before devaluation, was now standing at $17\frac{1}{2}$ per cent. In these threatening circumstances Wilson was glad to find technical reasons for delaying the imposition of further cuts. By Christmas there were still no new limits on consumption despite a sensational pre-Christmas boom. Nor was devaluation backed by temporary import controls. By December 1967 there was a renewed outflow of foreign exchange. There was a real fear of a second devaluation.

Wilson's political position was safeguarded by private assurances from the Left, and was curiously strengthened by the row which followed a decision by the Cabinet's Defence and Overseas Policy Committee to re-examine the decision not to supply arms to South Africa in the light of the far-reaching review of public expenditure which the new Chancellor had set in train. The decision was a victory for those like George Brown who wanted the ban relaxed, at least to allow the export of naval equipment. Wilson claims that he made his opposition clear, but his remark that, if exports were to be the only criterion, then the possibility of East European trade must be considered despite Foreign Office deference to the United States, probably contributed to a widely-felt sense that his mind was still open. Certainly Brown had that impression. Callaghan, who had not been at the meeting, told a Labour backbench group that the arms ban could not be sacrosanct. The news leaked into the press, and two young backbenchers tabled an early day motion which attracted 140 signatures. The Chief Whip encouraged signatures and his team suggested that they would suit the Prime Minister. Wilson put the question to the Cabinet on

14 December. The Foreign Secretary was in Brussels stranded by fog, and Wilson told the Commons that afternoon that this was the reason why the matter had not yet been considered. He may not have intended to rebuke Brown, but that was the way the remark was taken. When the Cabinet met on Friday Brown led a powerful but numerically inferior group, which included Callaghan, Gordon Walker, Crosland and Gunter. After an acrimonious discussion the Cabinet Committee's decision was upheld. That afternoon the press was briefed. Wilson was reported next day to have been defeated on the issue, and both *The Times* and *Evening News* suggested that he had lost all authority and might be replaced. The Sunday press was as hostile. Wilson would not allow any counter-briefing, but called a sudden Cabinet meeting for Monday 18 December. The position was intolerable, he said, and he must have the Cabinet's permission to repudiate the stories. He did not press for a decision on the substantive question, despite pressure from those who favoured the ban and sensed that the sensational press briefing had swung opinion in their favour. But one of those who had favoured arms sales now intervened: 'the matter should be decided at once and for his part he felt that we had no alternative but to maintain the embargo'. Sheepishly, with the exception of Brown, the rest of the Cabinet chimed in and Wilson was able to tell the House that the ban remained firm and unequivocal. An ironic footnote to the row was provided by Government-inspired press stories that the Americans had vetoed the sale of Beagle light aircraft to South Africa to safeguard the sale of their own Cessnas, which were being used there for internal security.

Wilson had secured his control of the Parliamentary Party but dissatisfaction in the Cabinet reached new heights, checked only by the absence of an agreed successor and an uncomfortable feeling that only Wilson had the cheek, the resilience, and the political abilities to get the party out of the mess in which it found itself.

A useful side-effect of the controversy was the way in which it eased the passage of the cuts in public expenditure announced on 16 January 1968. The immediate withdrawal from the Persian Gulf, a speedier leave-taking from South-East Asia, and the cancellation of orders for the American F111A strike aircraft were bound to be strenuously resisted by the Defence Minister and Foreign Secretary. The restoration of prescription charges and postponement of the school-leaving age would be a formidable task to get through Cabinet. Cabinet cohesion was at a low point. There were ten days of bitter semi-public wrangling in which Wilson found that 'views were so evenly divided that any attempt to express a consensus or, indeed, a majority view, would have been challenged. It was the only time in six years that colleagues seemed to be keeping their own tally of the "voices".'[29]

Jenkins was adamant. A set of bilateral meetings with the Chancellor and a series of Cabinet meetings left no doubt that cuts had to come, and, although the Cabinet remained almost evenly divided on the Far East and defence, in the end the package went through with only one resignation, that of Lord Longford. The result was a ruthless massacre of prejudices and election promises which fanned the growing discontent of the Labour Party to the point where twenty-six Labour backbenchers abstained, two of them in protest against 'permissive whipping'. When the House of Commons voted on prescription charges in May no less than forty-seven Labour members voted against.

There was now a further two months' delay before the Budget of 19 March introduced the next instalment of post-devaluation measures. In the interim there was a dangerous international currency crisis bred by the shortage of world liquidity. In the end the pressure on gold became so great that a Bank holiday was declared while its future was discussed and fresh arrangements were made to safeguard the world monetary system and the existing price of gold. There were fresh rumours of devaluation and a resignation to alarm the public. George Brown was not at the special meeting of the Privy Council early on 15 March which closed the foreign exchange market. He refused to believe that he could not have been traced to be told about it, and when he learnt of what was going on, he rang the Prime Minister at 1 a.m. to say that a number of the Cabinet had assembled in his room. Would the Prime Minister come over? Wilson would appear to have agreed, then sensed this would seem like a court martial, and asked them instead to come to No. 10. There is dispute about the events of that meeting, but eventually Wilson and the Chancellor were able to satisfy their critics, all but George Brown who resigned. When Jenkins made an emergency statement to the House, which was still in session, Brown seated himself ostentatiously at the end of the second bench. This time there was to be no reconsideration, no round robin begging him not to resign. Michael Stewart became Foreign Secretary. In his resignation statement Brown complained of the way the Government was run: almost certainly he had in mind the South African arms affair as well as the latest row, but his accusations of quasi-Presidential government were a little hard to take from one who a few days before had urged the Prime Minister to defer less to his Cabinet.[30]

The summer recess brought not only respite but recovery. The Conservative lead fell from an average 20 per cent in June to only 8½ per cent in October. But there was no sign of recovery in the balance of payments, and the chances of improvement were hampered by a series of strikes that undermined the incomes policy. It seemed possible that this was aggravating the very inflation it sought to stem: certainly, coupled with the surge in the cost of living since devaluation it was a major cause of strikes. The 1968 T.U. Congress voted by 7·7 million to one million against the Government's wages policy, with the engineers, freed from 'Carron's Law', joining the other left-wing unions: the T.U.C.'s own voluntary incomes policy scraped through by only 34,000 votes. All that Wilson could do was to advance the clash at the Labour Conference to the beginning of the week, and follow it with his keynote speech – 'This is the Conference they will look back on and say, "That was when Labour came back fighting"'. Predictably enough incomes policy went down heavily, by a vote of nearly 5 to 1: less predictably the rest of the conference went smoothly and Wilson's own speech was a triumphant success. 'Wilson resurgent' was the *Daily Telegraph*'s headline. But there were sharp reverses for the platform on Rhodesia and Nigeria, wholly expected but hardly palatable.

On Rhodesia Wilson was ready for a fresh settlement and his soundings in Salisbury had given him some hope that a basis might now exist. In any event he must try. A hard-line segregationist constitution was on the way, which he felt he must try to avert if he was not to attract widespread criticism. In any case an honourable attempt which failed would bury the issue as a matter of inter-Party dispute, at least until after the election. Early in October Wilson met Smith at Gibraltar, and their talks upon the *Fearless* were in part successful. They ended with a fresh offer from the British Government which both the Opposition and the press thought fair. Further discussions followed and a Cabinet minister visited Salisbury: as late as the following spring there were still desultory exchanges, but the chances of a settlement steadily slipped away as the Salisbury régime embarked on a new constitution and on policies which had less and less in common with the six principles.

The close of 1968 was as gloomy as it was possible to be. Sterling's difficulties had been accentuated towards the middle of November by speculation about the revaluation of the mark. While Roy Jenkins was dressing for the annual dinner of the National Export Council, he was called to a hastily-summoned conference in Bonn at which the cracks were papered over. A series of border taxes in effect upvalued the mark by 3 per cent. While he was in Bonn, Wilson pushed through the Cabinet a fresh series of restrictions. Jenkins hastened back to London to announce them on 22 November. Hire purchase controls had already been tightened so he acted on credit, used the regulator to increase consumer taxes and imposed a temporary import deposit scheme. Confidence was not restored, even though the trade figures could be shown to have improved with every passing month. Early in December a fresh wave of rumours swept the City. A mood of near panic developed in which some newspapers even felt moved to call for a National Government.

The November trade figures published on 12 December offered Wilson a favourable trend to comment on, and he attacked the speculators. However, the persistent weakness of sterling and the worsening industrial situation strengthened Barbara Castle's determination that the legislation she was preparing to implement following the Donovan Report must contain teeth. The more she became bogged down in the incomes morass and the more exasperated she became with those trade union leaders with whom she came into contact, the more inclined she was to accept departmental arguments that Donovan had not gone far enough. There is no evidence that Wilson was pushing her, although his mind had moved in the same direction.

A November weekend at Sunningdale, where Barbara Castle talked with union leaders, employers and industrial relations experts, finally convinced her that penal sanctions must come, and her civil servants were told to include them in the White Paper which was to precede legislation. A strike at Girlings brake factory early in November which affected over five thousand car workers prompted thoughts of a conciliation pause; the inclusion of strike ballots and fines was prompted equally by the Government's recent experiences with disputes.

The draft White Paper was to go to the Cabinet early in January. Because it was known that Callaghan would be opposed to the measure, the Cabinet committee on industrial relations, to which he belonged, was bypassed. Mistakenly, however, as Wilson himself later admitted, it was shown to the T.U.C. on 30 December, before the Cabinet had seen it. The Cabinet on 3 January was not altogether happy, and Wilson, while he wrestled with the Commonwealth Prime Ministers assembled in conference from 7 to 15 January, fitted in further meetings for his colleagues to consider the matter.

The Prime Ministers' Conference ended in agreement; there would be no showdown on Rhodesia and no immediate withdrawal of the *Fearless* proposals. The Cabinet too had reached agreement: Barbara Castle's White Paper was to be published on 17 January. They had been placed in an almost impossible position, as Richard Crossman later pointed out, and there were many who doubted the wisdom of the proposals. The toughest opposition to the White Paper came from Callaghan and Marsh, but they had support from both Crossman and Crosland, who saw no reason to divide the party in the year before an election. Callaghan was particularly worried about the flow of funds into the party coffers, but the trade unions with their usual self-abnegation continued to contribute as much as usual.

The opposition to Barbara Castle's proposals was mirrored on the back benches. There the rumours that she intended to impose cooling-off periods and compulsory ballots and to promote the law to enforce collective agreements were at first received with incredulity. The Left could not believe that Barbara Castle would lend her name to such proposals. But when the White Paper appeared, they were included, together with a formidable package of increased power for the Minister and backed by the threat of criminal sanctions. There was an immediate outcry from the unions and Labour back benches. However, as motions hostile to the White Paper began to flood into Transport House, the N.E.C. began to wheel its heavy artillery into position.

The White Paper was not to be debated until March and before then the Government unveiled further defence cuts and two major measures – Dick Crossman's earnings-related superannuation scheme and the reform of the House of Lords.

A most improbable coalition developed against the latter led by Michael Foot and Enoch Powell. It was composed of Conservative backbenchers who were determined not to erode the power of the House of Lords and Labour backbenchers who wished to abolish it, and to them were joined all those who resented the great extension of Prime Ministerial patronage that the Bill represented.

On 18 February Robert Sheldon filibustered for over two hours, the longest speech for fifteen years, and on 2 April the Government were forced to abandon the debate at 10 p.m. because their Chief Whip lacked enough support from his own side to be sure of maintaining the House. By the Easter recess, the House had taken nine days in committee on the first five clauses. Faced with the total dislocation of their parliamentary programme, the Government decided to abandon the Bill.

The Government's White Paper on Industrial Relations was debated on 3 March. The Conservative Party thought many of the proposals were inadequate and some of them quite wrong. Nevertheless Robert Carr, for the Opposition, welcomed the Government's acceptance of the need for radical reform, and in the circumstances the Shadow Cabinet decided to

abstain from voting against the White Paper. Almost certainly those circumstances included the fact that there were others prepared to do so.
The House of Commons approved the White Paper as a basis for legislation by 226 votes to 64. The minority included fifty-five trade union
M.P.s, and at least another thirty deliberately abstained. As one trade
union M.P. earlier put it 'the trade union group of M.P.s has already taken
as much as it can'.[31] The Government were determined to restore their
authority. They were also deeply concerned about the pound. The strike
record of British industry was growing worse and in February there was a
lengthy and damaging strike at Fords. In the circumstances the Government determined not to wait to bring in the industrial relations legislation
but to bring in a short Bill before the summer recess.

The economic situation was far from healthy. The confidence outflow
of funds from London had spent itself and there were some signs of
gathering strength for sterling, largely as a result of the firm clamp-down
on credit expansion and a further rise in interest rates. On 27 February the
Bank Rate was raised again to 8 per cent, a decision which was sharply
attacked by Heath because it might lead to industrial bankruptcies. The
Government protested that the rise in interest rates was world-wide but
their critics were unmoved.

The short-term monetary inflows did not deceive Roy Jenkins. He was
not prepared to use them indefinitely to finance a basic deficit. If that had
not been cleared by the autumn of 1969, he would consider floating the
pound – downward. His Budget introduced on 15 April was deliberately
low-key and designed to buy further time to allow devaluation to work.
There were attractions in waiting for the autumn. Once the German
elections were over in September, the mark might be revalued, and a
further devaluation could be masked by an international realignment of
currencies. Nevertheless taxation was increased by £340 m. The largest
single increase was to S.E.T., but the net effect was calculated only to take
some £200–250 m. out of demand, appreciably less than the Treasury
wanted.

The Budget was received more favourably than Jenkins expected. The
public seemed relieved that the rise in taxation was so small. Built into the
Budget speech was the announcement that the Government proposed to
introduce immediately a Bill based on the White Paper. The prices and
incomes powers were being dropped at the end of the year, Jenkins
explained. New curbs on unnecessary damaging disputes were therefore
essential. Barbara Castle was no less determined the next day although she
made one concession to the mutinous mood in the Labour Party: she

would not take powers to order strike ballots.

There seemed little doubt of the Government's courage and determination. They were acting in defiance of both the T.U.C. and the Labour Party's National Executive Committee. On 26 March the N.E.C. voted to inform Mrs Castle that they could not agree to support legislation on the suggestions in the White Paper. Wilson was not present: he was on his way to Nigeria in an attempt to mediate in the Nigerian civil war. Jim Callaghan had moved a somewhat obscure amendment, which he explained was an attempt build bridges, but he had also voted for the N.E.C. motion which had been carried by a majority of more than three to one. He did not resign from the Cabinet. A few days later Wilson let it be known that he had reprimanded him during a Cabinet meeting. Even before the Cabinet's decision to go ahead was announced, Wilson had confronted the T.U.C. on 10 April to hear their objections to the proposed legislation. Wilson invited them to deal with the two major problems of inter-union disputes and unofficial strikes but he did not encourage them to think that this would enable legislation to be postponed. 'If the Government stood on one side and did nothing, it could be destroyed economically and politically', he told them. 'We cannot just fold our arms and say because the T.U.C. does not like it we will do nothing about it.'[32]

A week after the Budget announcement, the General Council decided to call a special Congress of the T.U.C., the first since 1920, to consider the amendment of rules 11 and 12. It was not enough. Interviewed on B.B.C. television on 20 May, Wilson said 'I have got to ask for something a little more definite than that . . . I believe that the life of the country is at stake on all these issues. . . .' Next day he told the T.U.C. General Council that the changes to the rules proposed in the T.U.C.'s *Programme for Action* did not go far enough and they must tighten up their procedures for dealing with unofficial disputes.

Behind the scenes, there had been a series of meetings with the trade union leaders to persuade them to agree to specific procedures of intervention where a dispute took place and a return to normal working while negotiations went on. There were six hotly disputed meetings of the P.L.P., at which Barbara Castle vehemently defended her proposals. Meanwhile, the opponents of the Bill had begun to organise against it. Eric Moonman had called a meeting of the 113 Labour M.P.s who had either abstained or voted against the White Paper. Seventy of them attended and elected a committee which sounded out backbench opinion. By the middle of May they had the names of sixty-one Labour M.P.s who would vote against the Bill and a further thirteen who would abstain. The figures were passed to the Whips and to the Chairman of the P.L.P., Douglas Houghton. The Trade Union Group of Labour M.P.s, nearly 130 strong, began to urge the Government publicly to drop the penal clauses.[33]

Wilson had already made his dispositions. His Chancellor's concentration on S.E.T. had disenchanted Labour's Co-operative Members and they were joined in the lobbies by one or two left-wingers and, more seriously, by several right-wing disciplinarians, anxious to expose the weaknesses of John Silkin's liberal régime. Labour's majority fell to 28. Silkin singled out some persistent rebels for treatment: the selection seemed oddly arbitrary and some rebels annoyed that they were not for burning. Wilson decided to replace him with Bob Mellish. Silkin and he exchanged posts, and the letters of suspension already sent out were withdrawn. At his first P.L.P. meeting Mellish said bluntly that failure to carry the Industrial Relations Bill would mean a dissolution. In his diary Wilson recorded, 'all hell was let loose. The left was inflamed by Bob Mellish. Meanwhile the professional W[ilson] M[ust] G[o] group was also at work.'[34]

This much smaller group of M.P.s almost certainly cared less about the Industrial Relations Bill than about the general shortcomings of Wilson's leadership. They were certain that they could use the Bill to force him from the leadership, could they but agree on a successor. Callaghan had opposed the Bill and had been dropped from Wilson's inner Cabinet (the 'Parliamentary Committee') as a result. But he was unacceptable to both the Left and the 'Radical Right', and in his opposition to the Bill he lacked the support of any of his senior colleagues. Jenkins was equally unacceptable to large sections of the Labour Party who were not prepared to break Wilson to make him king. Without any concerted opposition to him, especially from within the Cabinet, Wilson seemed secure.

In addition to the loyalty of Douglas Houghton, Wilson's greatest strength was that the Left, while hating the Bill, were disposed to prefer him to any alternative leader. Knowing this and realising that no serious revolt was possible without an agreed successor, Wilson determined to press on with a reform that he believed to be both desirable and popular with the electorate. Publicly he had identified himself more than once with the Bill. It seemed inconceivable that he could retreat. It was equally impossible that the Bill should go through in the teeth of opposition from the trade union M.P.s and with the Conservative Party unready to facilitate its progress by allowing the Government to remove it from the floor of the House.

The General Council of the T.U.C. had published their Programme for Action on 12 May, and it was in the knowledge that this was to be put to a special congress at Croydon on 5 June that the Government decided to defer the introduction of the Bill. Wilson had told the T.U.C. that their proposals did not go far enough on the question of unofficial strikes, and Barbara Castle warned that without specific mechanisms for action their proposal 'could at best be regarded as a pious hope'. The General Secretary, Victor Feather, replied that it was a fallacy to think that the imposition of automatic sanctions would solve disputes. He remained anxious, however, to find a way out and made modifications to the text of the trade unions' proposal which still did not seem to go far enough. That, as we have seen, remained the position when Wilson met the General Council on 21 May, and when Wilson had informal talks at Chequers with the T.U.C. chairman, Vic Feather, Jack Jones and Hugh Scanlon, he got no further. At Croydon the T.U.C. proposal was overwhelmingly approved, and their opposition to compulsory legislation and statutory financial penalties reaffirmed.

The following week saw three meetings between Wilson, Barbara Castle and the General Council; after the third of these on 12 June Victor Feather said that 'progress was virtually nil'.[35] The same day Wilson formally confirmed that the Government 'were prepared to drop those parts of the legislation which they found controversial if they would agree to a rule change', something which the T.U.C. General Council believed to be beyond their power. The Government felt that an official decision had to be taken on 17 June and in Cabinet Wilson 'gave it as his judgement that the credibility of the Government required it to legislate if the T.U.C. would not legislate through its own rules'.[36] The previous evening he had received a letter from the party's liaison committee which warned the Prime Minister 'that there was no chance of the Government carrying in the Commons a strike-curb bill containing any penal clauses . . . not even if the Commons were kept sitting well into August would there be any chance of the Bill getting through'.[37] Immediately after Wilson had finished speaking the Chief Whip intervened to state that there was not a hope of the measure passing. Minister after Minister now declared their opposition. Callaghan, Crossman, Crosland, Mason and Marsh found themselves joined by such figures as Peter Shore and Judith Hart. The meeting was then adjourned until after lunch. In the morning Wilson and Barbara Castle had been virtually isolated, but the lunchtime period of reflection had given the Prime Minister leeway. The afternoon meeting was by no means so critical. The difficulty was the deadline, a meeting at

7 p.m. with a very anxious group of trade union M.P.s. At five to seven the dissidents attempted to get an immediate decision in favour of shelving the legislation. That was rejected. Wilson concluded that he would again tell the General Council that, in default of a binding change in their rules, legislation would be introduced.[38]

Wilson knew he spoke for a badly divided Cabinet, but the T.U.C. could not have guessed it from his demeanour. That night he told Vic Feather that he held the proxies to carry the Cabinet, and next morning he offered the General Council a straight choice between legislation and a change in Rule 11. In an interval of the talks an official suggested to Wilson that the Government could agree to a suggestion from the T.U.C. to print in its rules the Government's draft change as a note of interpretation. Wilson killed the suggestion. It may, however, have focused Wilson's mind for what was to follow. The General Council would not budge on a rule change. Fred Hayday suggested they would enter into a solemn and binding undertaking to abide by the Government's draft as an interpretation of Rule 11. Jack Jones claimed that this could have the same effect as a rule. Over lunch Barbara Castle gave the proposal her support, and Wilson determined to give in. So long as the undertaking was unanimous he would recommend it to the Cabinet. The Cabinet was relieved and ready to accept any compromise. There is little doubt that the Government's decision to accept this compromise cost them dear.

As late as May 1969 the trade figures still brought unmitigated gloom. The Treasury was now deeply anxious that there was no sign of a revaluation of the Mark. Sterling was again under pressure. In these circumstances the I.M.F. agreed to re-finance their credits but in return they extracted a fresh Letter of Intent in which a £400 m. ceiling on domestic credit expansion for 1969–70 was laid down. Any failure to observe the agreed terms required consultation before the standby could be drawn. Regarding such 'banana republic' conditions as being politically unacceptable, Harold Lever flew to Washington and negotiated regular quarterly consultations to which no such stigma attached. Even so the Letter of Intent still provoked anxious debate. However, during the final agonies over the Industrial Relations Bill, almost unnoticed, the May trade figures were published showing that the trade deficit had fallen to £14 m. More significant still was the news that exports had been under-recorded and invisibles were already providing the basis for a surplus. A few prescient observers including Peter Jay of *The Times* announced that the corner had at last been turned. The Chancellor remained anxious and most voices were still sceptical. At the end of June Roy Jenkins publicly announced that he expected a balance of payments surplus for the year as a whole of £300 m. The tide had begun to turn.

Labour's new-found unity and determination were demonstrated when the Government refused to alter constituency boundaries before the General Election. Forced by High Court action to introduce the proposals, Callaghan asked his party to vote them down, and fewer than ten Labour M.P.s refused to do so.

Soon, the Government was benefiting from a rapid turnround in the economic situation, despite a last speculative flurry in August. Appropriately enough Roy Jenkins had just opened the Export Services Exhibition at Earls Court on 8 September when he heard the figures for August. They made it quite clear that sterling was back in the black. At a single stroke the political situation was transformed.

The Government were also benefiting from Callaghan's firm but understanding handling of the situation in Ulster, where fighting had broken out in Londonderry in August. Northern Ireland appeared to be 'a working example of Labour's claim that it was more than a match for the Conservatives in terms of its responsibility and still more its humanity'.[39] It was Labour's ideals that Transport House's publicity machine sought to emphasise in a £100,000 campaign which they launched at the end of August. 'Labour's got life *and* soul', advertisements and posters proclaimed, but the message seemed to convince few. Labour's recovery was much more linked to the economic situation. The Conservative lead, which had averaged over 19 per cent in July, was down to 12½ per cent in September. The National Executive Committee had prepared a new policy document, *Agenda for a Generation*, for discussion at the Labour Party Conference. Their economic strategy was elaborated in a further document which spoke of planning to be enforced by 'comprehensive surveillance' of the economy by a whole range of state bodies, a national investment board, more state ownership, statutory price control and by new tax proposals including a wealth tax. Macleod sharply attacked the document as 'resurrection pie'.

Courageously, Wilson defended his policies at the Trades Union Congress in September. Predictably he got a chilly reception. At the end of the month he was at a relaxed and more friendly gathering. The Labour Party Conference had decided to work for victory. In two sparkling speeches Wilson brilliantly created an image of excitement and achievement. When the Conservatives assembled at Brighton on 8 October they were confronted with an O.R.C. poll showing the Conservative lead down to 4 per cent. For the first time in two years there were doubts about the inevitability of victory. The Conservative leaders found themselves in a tactical dilemma. To blur the tax-cutting image by announcing the details of their tax package might prove electorally damaging, but if they did not do so their credibility might be damaged and Labour's task in taking over some element of their proposals eased. In the end, both Macleod on taxation and Carr on industrial relations went into considerable detail. The virtues of value-added tax were canvassed but there was no formal commitment. The only serious difficulty the leadership faced was on immigration; a disastrous performance by Quintin Hogg meant that the official line was approved by a majority of under 400. More predictably a hard-line capital punishment amendment was carried against the platform. By contrast the party's approach to the Common Market was passed by three to one.

Robert Carr had given fresh details of the proposed reform of industrial relations, and, more tentatively, Iain Macleod had taken further wraps off the Value Added Tax proposal. A major paradox was becoming apparent. The Conservatives, stack full with policies, were having to be cautious about the targets they offered for attack. Wilson by contrast had clearly decided that the best means of defence was attack. Increasingly from now on he recaptured his best opposition form. By treating the Tories as an alternative Government, almost as the Government, he might yet bring his ship home to port. The remainder of the autumn must have been a disappointment to him. Heralded by an exceptionally effective attack in the House from Edward Heath, and by his speech at Croydon on election eve, the five by-elections on 30 October saw a swing to the Conservatives of $10\frac{1}{2}$ per cent. Swindon was their only gain. The polls suggested that Labour was closing the gap with the average Conservative lead falling to $7\frac{1}{2}$ per cent in December.[40]

The Government's programme for its final session was scarcely dramatic, although the Bills to nationalise the ports and make comprehensives compulsory were calculated to cheer the Left, while that on superannuation and social insurance was thought to be an election winner, a perennial delusion of Crossman's which foundered in a welter of incomprehension and suspicion. The Labour Party was still rebellious: in December the indiscipline seemed to have become endemic. On 8 December forty-nine Labour M.P.s voted against the Government on Vietnam, and, the following day, twenty-four again defied the Whips on Nigeria. There followed 'a week of desperate appeals for Party loyalty and all the strains of the most intense whipping the Labour Party has known since the 1966 General Election'.[41] The Government was to reactivate Part II of the

Prices and Incomes Act as a prelude to further legislation which would merge the P.I.B. into a new Commission for Manpower and Industry. There had been the clearest indications of 'mass revolt . . . even forecasts of the Government's defeat', as Wilson recalls.[42] Heath made the decision the subject of a major attack, perhaps worried by suggestions from Central Office that an immediate election could result in a Labour victory. Labour's Chief Whip wrote to his flock to warn that anyone failing 'to vote for the Government is voting for the Tories and will be judged accordingly'.

Over the Christmas recess Heath flew to Australia, when he skippered *Morning Cloud* to victory in the Sydney–Hobart race. Confidence revived, he drew further comfort from the polls which swung back towards the Conservatives. In February they still led by an average of 10½ per cent and Labour's burst of publicity, tentatively planned for the spring, was postponed. Starting, however, at Swansea on 10 January, Wilson began to campaign. Perhaps significantly he made little effort to slow the wages explosion. Settlements averaging 12 per cent were made in the public sector, and it became a matter of speculation whether opinion would move faster towards the Government than inflation would in eroding the higher wage levels.

At the end of January the Shadow Cabinet gathered at Selsdon Park in Surrey. Publicity was not the object of the exercise, rather an attempt to fit the elements of policy into a coherent frame. Both privately and publicly the Conference was a huge success, and a series of speeches by Sir Keith Joseph on the Conservative concept of 'civilised capitalism' received a good deal of attention.

At first Wilson was worried by the publicity: his own trip to see President Nixon had by contrast been quietly received. Then his tactical sense took over. He seized on the Tory emphasis on law and order, took up battle on behalf of the trade unions, and tried to pin Toryism back to its thirties image. The Friday after Selsdon, 6 February, he launched his assault at Nottingham, accusing the Tories of not just a lurch to the right, but of an atavistic desire to reverse the course of twenty-five years of social revolution. Wilson had refound himself, the caustic, aggressive leader of opposition. Heath's reply was a strongly worded but dignified repudiation of this description of Tory policy, although Quintin Hogg wildly blamed Wilson for presiding complacently over the century's biggest crime wave.

Wilson was in his element. 'Selsdon Man' became his particular target. Meanwhile, Europe, too, seemed to have become the subject of party political manoeuvre when the Government published their White Paper on the possible costs of entry. By now the Superannuation Bill was in

Committee, and the session was taking a predictable course. There was an ill-tempered clash over reports that the Conservatives had a private emissary in Rhodesia. Almost petulantly Heath challenged Wilson to prosecute him. Ulster continued to concern the House deeply, particularly when a detainee died of a heart attack. In the country a Tory tide was still running but the pace was slowing. At Bridgwater on 12 March the swing was only 8½ per cent, and at South Ayrshire a week later it is possible that for the first time since Hull North, four years before, the swing was the other way. The pressures on Roy Jenkins to have an electioneering Budget doubled and redoubled. Wilson was reported to be pressing him hard, particularly when the County Council elections between 6 and 11 April still showed a 9–10 per cent swing to the Tories.

On 14 April Jenkins presented his third Budget, brave but rather unimaginative. His mind was set on the Foreign Office and his mien responsible. He gave away rather under £200 millions, almost entirely concentrated on those at the bottom end of the income tax range. These concessions did little more than offset the effects of inflation bringing people into the tax range, and then only to an extent which would be undone by the price rises of a single month. In the Commons the Chancellor concluded his speech with near silence from his own backbenchers. His own colleagues were far from happy, a perfect example of Macleod's law that the first reaction to a Budget was invariably wrong. The public liked Jenkins' restraint, and by the date of the municipal elections, Labour was in the lead.

By now, many supposed the election to be on, and the borough results appeared to give Labour a first-rate chance of victory. The swing was one of the largest ever recorded in local elections over a twelve-month period. Gallup on 12 May had shown a 7 per cent Labour lead. Wilson had already made up his mind, he claimed, four years before, and certainly by 13 April. He did not consult his senior colleagues until May. By then there was really no choice left. The pressures to go in June were irresistible. On 18 May the election was finally announced.

It was an election to make any politician schizoid. In the constituencies there appeared to be a groundswell, sometimes massive, in favour of the Tories right from the outset of the campaign. Only in London, and, to some extent, Scotland, was this not true. The press nevertheless carried polls which daily told a different story. Puzzled friends phoned one another, sometimes across Party lines, and in the end many of them decided to trust their own senses. Conservative strategists found it still more puzzling. Their own polls told a rather different tale. The campaign itself had followed an unusual course, the first issue, the fears of violence over the South African cricket tour, vanishing from the headlines as soon as it was called off at Callaghan's specific request. The Conservative manifesto had long been prepared, the Labour Party's had a more chaotic birth, but from the first Wilson's emphasis was on his own personality and his afternoon and evening walkabouts. Heath was serious, careful, with well-prepared speeches hammering at the issues. But it was Wilson who captured the press, so much so that Heath seemed to be stumbling courageously towards defeat.

Labour had, however, given hostages to fortune. They refused to grant the doctors their promised pay rise, and Crossman was reported to have said the country was 'in extreme economic peril'; Callaghan on 3 June refused to promise there would be no wage freeze. Heath was slow to seize on the economic theme, his advisers were divided, and it was not until an unofficial council of war at the Albany on 7 June that it was decided to press the theme home.

In the meantime the campaign made headway with the housewives, hit hard by rising prices. The most effective television piece of the election showed a pair of scissors snipping away at the pound. The press however preferred to concentrate on Enoch Powell – that is when they were not coping with the strike that shut them down on 10 June. Wilson's successful efforts to get the newspapers back on the streets were perhaps ill-requited, for in Central Office careful preparation had been made for the various economic indicators that were going to appear before polling night. For them Powell was a distraction, even a dangerous distraction. He had decided to make immigration a key issue and that in itself could have made life difficult but for the indiscreet and intemperate 'Dachau' attack made by Wedgwood Benn. [For Powellism, see pp. 193–5.]

Meanwhile, three of the indicators picked out by the Tory strategists duly came up, the latest strike figures, the monthly cost of living index, and on polling day, the record number of jobless. But it was the fourth, the unknown, the monthly trade figures that provided decisive ammunition. There was a deficit of £31 millions. The purchase of two Jumbo jets had led to a jumbo-sized scare, Wilson promptly replied, but the damage was clear. People were reminded, at a critical moment, of past turning points that had come to nothing. At the close of Heath's press conference on 16 June a carefully worded and detailed economic brief was handed to the press to substantiate Heath's charges. It had one un-covenanted benefit. Buried in the text was the argument that if Labour policies were pursued, another devaluation would occur within four years. It was hardly short-term scaremongering, but Wilson took it as such. His sharp attacks, unluckily backed perhaps by Callaghan's detailed refutation of the 'devaluation smear', enabled Heath to return to the theme effectively in the closing stages of the campaign.

It was 18 June, however, that proved to be Waterloo for the press, the polls and Harold Wilson. From the first result at Guildford the writing was on the wall: by midday on the 19th it was quite clear that Edward Heath would be the next Prime Minister. For five years he had struggled to hold the Conservative Party together in the face of continual doubt about his ability and popularity. Unlike any other leader his poll rating had always trailed that of his party, even at the moment of their by-election triumphs. But his own chief concern had been with policy, the necessary adjustments to take Britain into a new decade and a new world, that of Europe. Major reforms of taxation, of industrial relations, of housing subsidies, a new approach to industry, above all a restructuring and a new style of government, were his promises to the electorate. There was little about short-term policies to deal with immediate difficulties, no obvious answer to inflation, and it remains ironic that in a sense his victory was written in terms of the rising prices that he could do little to stop. But in a sense too, it was appropriate that a man who saw Britain's problems as deep-rooted in past history and past attitudes should try to take her from the decade of disillusion into Europe. Harold Wilson had promised much the same, had in more vivid ways talked of the same need for structural reforms. His answers had been tried in a difficult economic climate and found wanting. In a still more threatening economic world, it remained to be seen whether Heath's sense of the strategic could prove a more sure recipe for Britain's troubled discontents.

NOTES

1. *Steering the Economy* (Penguin ed.), p. 234.
2. In addition there were party committees on monopolies and mergers, consumer protection, and industrial relations.
3. 12 June 1961
4. The swing to the Liberals was of the order of 31·7 per cent.
5. Cf. *Spectator*, 27 July 1962.
6. *Listener*, 28 July 1966.

7. Lord Butler, *The Art of the Possible*, p. 236.
8. *Daily Express*, 12 July 1963.
9. Quoted Irving *et al.*, *Scandal '63*, p. 178.
10. 20 June 1963.
11. Cited in A. Howard and R. West, *The Making of the Prime Minister*, p. 104.
12. B.B.C. Television interview with Heath, 20 January 1967.
13. Cited by Butler and King, *The British General Election of 1966*, p. 93.
14. Butler and King, p. 84.
15. King and West, p. 225.
16. This was designed to save £300 m., which, taken with the Treasury forecast that the balance of payments deficit would be halved without any change of policy, would have corrected the position by the end of 1965.
17. *Bank of England Bulletin*.
18. *Sunday Times*, 'Insight on the Tory Leadership', 25 July 1965.
19. *Hansard*, 15 July 1965.
20. Reviewing the Wilson memoirs in the *Sunday Times*.
21. *Hansard*, 1 April 1965, cited by Paul Foot, *The Politics of Harold Wilson*, p. 214.
22. Labour Party Conference Report, 1965, p. 156.
23. *The Times*, 30 July 1966.
24. *The Times*, 8 May 1967.
25. p. 267.
26. *Daily Telegraph*, 8 May 1967.
27. In *Steering the Economy*, p. 364.
28. *Hansard*, 22 November 1967.
29. *The Labour Government*, p. 481.
30. Cf. *The Labour Government*, p. 512.
31. *Sunday Times*, 5 January 1969.
32. *Financial Times*, 12 April 1969.
33. *Financial Times*, 21 May 1969.
34. *The Labour Government 1964–70*, p. 646.
35. *The Labour Government*, p. 655.
36. Peter Jenkins, *The Battle of Downing Street*, p. 152.
37. *Daily Telegraph*, 17 June 1969.
38. *The Labour Government*, p. 657.
39. *The British General Election of 1970*, p. 120.
40. On 4 December, on a swing of under 10 per cent, the Conservatives took Wellingborough.

41. *The Times*, 18 December 1969.
42. *The Labour Government*, p. 736.

Part Two

THE ISSUES

1 The Liberal and Nationalist Revival

CHRIS COOK

The eleven years from 1959 to 1970 constituted a decade of lost opportunity for the Liberal and Nationalist Parties. On separate occasions, each of the three smaller Parties seemed set to achieve a major political breakthrough – the Liberals at Orpington in March 1962, Plaid Cymru with the triumph of Gwynfor Evans at Carmarthen in July 1966 and the Scottish National Party when it swept to victory in the hitherto Socialist citadel of Hamilton in November 1967.

The high hopes engendered by these victories soon faded. The Liberal tide had receded by the autumn of 1963. Indeed, the Party emerged from the General Election of June 1970 with its parliamentary representation more than halved and with the constituencies that symbolised resurgent Liberalism – Orpington, Cheadle, the Colne Valley and Birmingham Ladywood – all lost. The results of June 1970 similarly destroyed Nationalist aspirations. Plaid Cymru lost Carmarthen to Labour; Hamilton likewise reverted to its old allegiance.

However, despite the failure of the Liberals and Nationalists to maintain a sustained revival, these parties played an important – and at times dramatic – part in the politics of the 1960s.

The Liberal revival after 1959 brought Britain nearer to three-party politics than at any time since 1929 or even 1924. This Liberal upsurge was, essentially, the product of a double opportunity. First, there was the opportunity provided by the fratricidal warfare which engulfed the Labour Party after its third successive General Election defeat. Secondly, the Liberals were able to exploit the economic difficulties in which the Conservatives increasingly found themselves after 1961. If two events symbolise the start of the Liberal revival, then the Scarborough Conference of 1960 and the 'pay pause' announced by Selwyn Lloyd in July 1961 provide convenient dates.

To this extent, the Liberal revival owed little or nothing to its own strength – even though the party proclaimed a series of attractive policies and possessed in Jo Grimond a vigorous and popular leader. Essentially, the Liberal revival was dependent on the weakness – temporary as it proved – of its Conservative and Labour opponents. The rise and fall of 'Orpington Liberalism' has to be seen within this context. When Wilson succeeded Gaitskell as Leader of the Opposition, finding Party unity and a technological revolution in the process, and when the Conservatives gathered morale after the débâcle of the last days of the Macmillan era, the Liberal tide was already fast ebbing.

The Liberal upsurge after 1959 had, it is true, been preceded by marked signs of hope before the General Election. The by-election triumph of Mark Bonham Carter at Torrington in March 1958 (the first by-election victory since Holland-with-Boston was gained in 1929), together with earlier encouraging performances at Hereford (February 1956) and Rochdale (February 1958), were better results for the Party than at any time after 1945. The momentum of this advance, however, failed to carry over into the General Election. If the 1959 results showed a perceptible advance, it was hardly dramatic:

	1955			1959		
	Votes	*M.P.s*	*% Vote*	*Votes*	*M.P.s*	*% Vote*
Con.	13,286,569	344	49·7	13,749,830	365	49·0
Lab.	12,404,970	277	46·4	12,215,538	258	43·0
Lib.	722,405	6	2·7	1,638,571	6	5·9
Others	346,554	3	1·2	255,302	1	2·1

The Liberals had increased their share of the total vote from 2·7 per cent to 5·9 per cent and in 46 constituencies the party had polled over 20 per cent of the votes cast – but this remained the sum total of its achievement. The significance of 1959 was not how well the Liberals had done, but how badly Labour had fared.

The date at which the Liberals first began to attract significant support after 1959 can be seen in the graph on the next page.

The first real indication – in parliamentary terms – of the Liberal revival came with the by-election in April 1961 at Paisley (Asquith's old constituency). A spirited campaign by John Bannerman brought the Liberals within 2,000 votes of victory.[1]

In the space of the next ten months, the Liberals managed to secure second place in eight by-elections in constituencies in which the Party had been third in 1959. Similarly, in the municipal elections, the party improved its base in May 1960 (with 130 Liberals elected) and in May 1961 (with 196 Liberals elected).

In the autumn of 1961, this increase in support gathered momentum. It was particularly evident in by-elections in Oswestry and in the Moss Side division of Manchester.

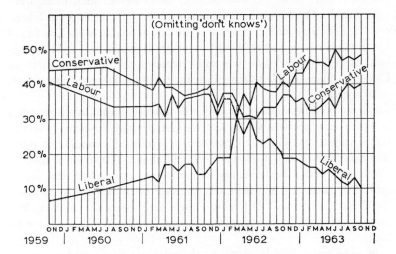

(Omitting 'don't knows')

This trend continued early in 1962. In March, a sensational revolt came from the normally true-blue Conservative seaside fief of Blackpool North. In the face of a strong Liberal challenge, the Conservatives retained the seat by a mere 973 votes. Compared to 1959, the figures were:

	By-Election	1959 General Election
Con.	12,711 (38·3)	25,297 (57·8)
Lib.	11,738 (35·3)	8,990 (20·6)
Lab.	8,776 (26·4)	9,440 (21·6)

The result was a portent of greater things to come. The following day, when polling took place in Orpington, a middle-class Kent commuter suburb, a Conservative majority of 14,760 was overturned into a Liberal majority of 7855. The Conservative share of the poll had fallen by 22 per cent to give Eric Lubbock a resounding victory. There was little doubt that Orpington had proved to be the most sensational by-election since East Fulham in October 1933.

For the Liberals, after a generation in the wilderness, the promised land seemed at last to have arrived. Indeed, for a fleeting moment, the

Daily Mail National Opinion Poll (published on 28 March 1962) showed the Liberals to be the most popular Party in the country (the figures were: Liberals 30 per cent, Labour 29·9 per cent, Conservatives, 29·2 per cent).

On the same day as Orpington, the Liberals forced the Conservatives into third place at Middlesbrough East. Other by-elections, though not repeating the Orpington victory, indicated the force behind the Liberal revival. The Party took 27 per cent of the poll at Stockton-on-Tees (April 1962), 25 per cent in Derby North (also in April), whilst the Liberal strong-hold of Montgomeryshire was easily retained following the death of Clement Davies. In West Derbyshire, the party missed victory by a mere 1220 votes.

Despite these near-misses, probably the most significant by-election was in North-East Leicester. On 12 July, the Conservative candidate (who had polled within 1431 votes of victory in 1959) finished a humiliating third. The Liberals ran only 1948 votes behind Labour. The result of this by-election convinced Macmillan (if he needed any convincing) that drastic action was necessary. The next day, seven of the twenty-one members of the Cabinet were axed. As Jeremy Thorpe aptly remarked of Macmillan, greater love hath no man than this, that he lays down his friends for his life.

In addition to these by-elections, the most impressive evidence of the Liberal advance was to be seen in the May 1962 municipal elections.

The size of the Conservative débâcle could not be disguised: in such safe home counties territory as Aldershot, Finchley, Kingston and Maiden-head, the Conservatives lost every seat they were defending. Outside this 'Orpington' territory, however, Liberal progress was less substantial. In the Midlands and North (except for such towns as Leicester and Bolton) their gains were very much smaller. In the seaside and spa towns, the Liberals made heavy inroads.

However, much the most disquieting aspect of the Liberal upsurge was that virtually no gains had been made at the expense of Labour. Even in the commuter suburbs, the Liberals secured very few seats in the Labour-controlled boroughs – none at all in Acton, Watford, or Mitcham.[2] The Labour strongholds emerged unscathed from the Liberal attack.

The result of the by-election triumphs was predictable. The Party achieved a publicity it had not known for a generation. Even the finances improved and the Party treasurer, Colonel Gardner-Thorpe, was able to raise the target for income for 1962 from £100,000 to £150,000. Among the recruits to the Liberal ranks were Sir Frank Medlicott (National Liberal M.P. for Norfolk Central from 1951 to 1959) and three other former M.P.s – one Conservative and two Labour.

After the climax of North-East Leicester, it was evident by the autumn of 1962 that the Liberal tide had begun to recede. By October those intending to vote Liberal had dropped below 20 per cent in the opinion poll; thereafter, the decline in support was steady and uninterrupted.

Although the May 1963 local elections rather disguised the fact (since the Liberals were contesting seats last fought in 1960), Liberal support in the boroughs was ebbing fast. Thus in Leicester, where in the local elections of May 1962 the Party had won five wards, the position was as follows:

	1962 Votes	Seats	1963 Votes	Seats	1964 Votes	Seats
Con.	27,452	2	25,806	4	31,052	6
Lab.	27,407	9	33,348	12	33,376	10
Lib.	25,941	5	18,074	—	12,666	—

As 1963 ended, the political climate moved progressively against the Liberals. In the Luton by-election (November 1963) the Liberal failed to save his deposit. The following month, in Sudbury and Woodbridge, the party actually polled a worse percentage than in October 1959. A by-election in Dumfries produced yet another lost deposit.

Similarly, in the Greater London Council elections in April 1964, the first for the new authority, the Liberals failed to win a single seat, although polling well in such suburban areas as Bromley. Another setback came in the May borough elections, when the party could win only 149 seats, compared to 255 in 1963 and 454 in the wake of Orpington.

Meanwhile, the parliamentary by-elections and opinion polls went from bad to worse. In May, in the last three by-elections fought by Liberals under the Conservative Government, the results proved depressing. By June 1964, support for the Liberals in the National Opinion Poll was down to 9 per cent.

The polarisation towards the major Parties continued during the summer. Labour's lead over the Conservatives in the Gallup Poll fell from 8 per cent on 3 July to 6½ per cent on 7 August and to 5 per cent on 13 September.

It was against this background that the Liberal Party faced the General Election.

Before the election campaign proper was under way, Grimond delivered a major speech (on 20 June 1964) on the theme 'Charter for New Men',

It was a major appeal for a classless, dynamic society, emphasising greater promotion opportunities for the young technologists and executives, a reduction of the burden of income tax on earned incomes, a ceiling on mortgage rates, and so on.

This appeal provided the basis of the 1964 Liberal Manifesto 'Think for Yourself, Vote Liberal'.

Although sadly short of money, the Party fought a vigorous and enthusiastic campaign in October 1964. In particular, Jo Grimond's television appearances were unanimously praised. And yet, when the results came in, the Liberals had little tangible comfort.

The result of the election (the closest in post-war British history) was:

	Vote	Percentage	Seats
Con.	12,002,906	43·4	303
Lab.	12,205,779	44·1	318
Lib.	3,101,103	11·2	9
Others	367,094	1·3	—

In terms of seats gained, the 1964 results were disappointing. The Liberals gained only four seats: Bodmin in Cornwall, and Inverness, Caithness and Sutherland, and Ross and Cromarty in Scotland, losing Bolton West and Huddersfield West where Conservatives fielded candidates for the first time since 1950. At least, the Liberals had the consolation in 1964 that all their nine M.P.s had been elected in three-cornered fights, whilst the marginal victory won in North Devon by Jeremy Thorpe in 1959 was now secure with a 5136 majority.

The real Liberal success in 1964, however, was not in seats won but in votes polled. The Party, with 365 candidates in the field, polled 3,101,103 votes and forfeited only 53 deposits. The Liberal share of the poll was 11·2 per cent compared to 5·9 per cent in 1959. In the seats contested by Liberals, each candidate polled on average 18·4 per cent, and in the seats contested in both 1959 and 1964 this percentage rose to 20·6 per cent.

Although the seats won had been in the 'Celtic fringe' the Party polled well in many parts of Britain. In the South East area, in addition to Orpington, which was retained with a reduced majority in the face of a massive Conservative challenge, the Liberals took over 25 per cent of the poll in such home counties seats as Finchley, South Buckinghamshire, East Surrey and Farnham, together with such coastal resorts as Southend West, Hastings and Eastbourne.

Similarly, in the North West, the Party polled well in such Manchester commuter suburbs as Cheadle (which recorded the highest Liberal vote in the country). In all, there were sixty-eight seats in which the percentage gap between the Liberals and the winning Party was less than 25 per cent. However, the irony of the 1964 election was that, in the best performance by the Party since 1929, the Liberals returned only nine M.P.s – all of whom, with the solitary exception of Eric Lubbock, were elected in the 'Celtic fringe'.

As in 1959, however, the real significance of the election lay not in how well the Liberals had done, but in the cardinal fact that, by however small a margin, Labour had narrowly snatched victory from the Conservatives.

Nor could the size of the Labour victory have been more harmful to the Liberals – because, whilst the Party never actually held the balance of power, it had come as near as made no difference.

Twice since 1918 the Liberals had held the balance of power – in 1923 and again in 1929. On neither occasion had the Party cause for pleasant memories. And so it proved after 1964.

Between the General Elections of 1964 and 1966 very few things went right for the Liberals. Almost the only exception was the victory of David Steel in the Roxburgh by-election of March 1965. Even this victory, however, though giving a boost in morale to committed Liberals, had little wider impact. Except in the earlier by-election in East Grinstead (February 1965), where the Party pushed up its percentage of the poll to 31·5 per cent, the by-elections told a depressing story. In three-cornered contests in the seven other by-elections fought by Liberals up to the summer of 1965, the percentages were: Leyton, 13·9; Nuneaton, 16·2; Altrincham and Sale, 19·4; Salisbury, 12·9; Saffron Walden, 11·9; Birmingham Hall Green, 16·4; and Hove, 16·7.

Behind these uninspiring by-election results lay more fundamental troubles. The narrow Labour victory in 1964 had effectively destroyed the cherished Liberal hope of replacing Labour as the alternative to the Conservatives. The Liberal Party, after 1964, had lost both its sense of purpose and its sense of direction. The Liberal dilemma took a new twist when Grimond gave an interview to the *Guardian* in which he quite clearly indicated that he would be prepared to contemplate coming to terms with Labour if the Parties could agree on long-term policies and aims. Whatever Grimond intended to produce by these remarks, he must have been considerably pained by the instant hostility aroused in the Party. The idea was shelved, but the future role the Party should play remained as undecided as ever.

The divisions within the Liberal hierarchy did nothing to improve the image of the Party.

The by-elections in Erith and Crayford and the Cities of London and Westminster in November 1965, in which the Liberals polled 7·2 per cent and 6·3 per cent of the poll respectively, were further evidence of the slump in Liberal fortunes. In both seats, the result was a worse performance than even the 1950 General Election.

This pattern of a 'squeeze' on Liberals in third place was repeated in the crucial Hull North by-election in January 1966. The Liberals could poll only 6·3 per cent in the by-election, compared with 15·9 per cent in the preceding General Election. As one correspondent wrote, the Party had been ground to fine powder beneath the upper and nether millstones of Government and alternative government.[3]

The result in Hull North, with its tonic for Labour morale of a 4·5 per cent swing in their favour, was widely interpreted to herald an early election. The speculation was soon proved correct.

Facing a second election within two years was not a happy prospect for the Liberal Party. By late February, the Liberals had only 251 prospective candidates ready – significantly, 175 of these in Conservative-held seats and only 72 attacking Labour constituencies.

Not only was the Party relatively short of candidates. It entered the election against a triple disadvantage: there was a quite clear 'squeeze' on the Party in every constituency in which it was not the 'alternative' Party;[4] the 1964–6 Parliament had ensured a quite distinct loss of identity for the Party and almost inevitably in the tightrope parliamentary situation after October 1964 – only in the debate on steel nationalisation had the Liberals really made a distinctive, constructive contribution. Finally, and linked to these factors, was the definite loss of unity at the top that had accompanied the decline in fortunes – in particular, criticism of Grimond's leadership had mounted after the episode in which he had openly discussed his future as leader.

It was against this background that the Party entered the 1966 election. The party manifesto *For all the People* emphasised the moderating role which, it claimed, the Liberals had played; and committed the party to major defence cuts, entry into Europe and a new approach to industrial relations.

When nominations closed, the Party fielded 311 candidates, 54 fewer than in 1964. This reduction, however, disguised the fact that the Party entered the fray in 33 constituencies which had not been contested in 1964

but withdrew from 87 seats fought at the previous election.
Compared with 1964, the results of the election were as follows:

	1966			1964	
Lab.	13,064,951	363	Lab.	12,205,779	318
Con.	11,418,433	253	Con.	12,002,906	303
Lib.	2,327,533	12	Lib.	3,101,103	9
Others	452,689	2	Others	347,094	—

Although, with a reduced field of candidates, the Liberal vote had fallen
by more than 750,000, the Party had emerged with its representation
increased to twelve. On the 'Celtic fringe' the Party lost two seats
(Cardiganshire, unsuccessfully defended by Roderic Bowen, and Caithness
and Sutherland, involving the defeat of George Mackie) but gained North
Cornwall and West Aberdeenshire. The most encouraging gains were
Cheadle, a Manchester residential commuter seat, won by Michael
Winstanley, and Colne Valley, won by Richard Wainwright.

It was ironic, however, that the election which produced the largest
Liberal contingent for over twenty years also marked the end of the road
for the 'Orpington-style' Liberalism.

Whichever way the position of the Party was reviewed, the underlying
fact was that the hopes of the Orpington era had been finally shattered.

This was particularly true of the seats in which the Liberals had been
the major challengers in 1964. Then, the Party had finished second in
fifty-five constituencies: by 1966, this total had fallen to twenty-nine.
Even these twenty-nine seats (largely confined to safe Conservative suburban or remote agricultural seats and equally safe Labour-held industrial
backwaters) were hardly promising territory. In only eight constituencies
throughout Britain were the Liberals within 5000 votes of victory. Despite
the victory in Cheadle, 'Orpington man' was a declining force. In every
seat adjacent to Orpington itself, the Liberals failed to achieve even second
place.

The convincing Labour victory in the 1966 election, however, soon
provided the Liberals with another opportunity. Labour's popularity
vanished as the economic difficulties of the country mounted. The Labour
Government moved from crisis to crisis, and the voters vented their disillusion in increasing numbers. By 1968, support for Labour in the opinion
polls had slumped from the 47 per cent of 1966 to only 26 per cent.

The great paradox of the years from 1966 to 1970 is that, at a time of
unparalleled electoral adversity for Labour, and with the Conservatives

led by an unpopular leader, the Liberals, in this most perfect political vacuum, got precisely nowhere.

What had happened to the Party in these years? The first and most obvious change was the resignation of Jo Grimond on 17 January 1967. Grimond had decided that, with the Labour victory of 1966, it was time for the Liberals to start again – and Grimond clearly wanted it to be under someone else. In the election for a new leader, Jeremy Thorpe received six votes, Eric Lubbock three and Emlyn Hooson three.

The period of Thorpe's leadership proved an unhappy time for the Liberals. Morale in the constituencies was low. There was a sharp decline in the number of really active associations. The numbers of delegates at the Party Assembly went down from 1400 at Brighton in September 1966 to 900 at Brighton three years later. By April 1970, the Party had only seventeen constituencies with full-time agents.

The performance of the Party in by-elections was equally unencouraging. In twelve of the twenty-eight seats contested the party lost its deposit. The only by-election triumph the Liberals enjoyed was in Birmingham Ladywood, where Wallace Lawler had built up a massive local following through pursuing a policy of community welfare. The luck of a by-election in this seat produced a satisfying Liberal gain – but this constituency easily reverted to Labour in 1970. The Liberals seem unlikely either to succeed in re-electing Lawler to Westminster or to make a breakthrough elsewhere in Birmingham.

If Ladywood provided the Party with a moment of optimism, elsewhere there was a variety of storm-clouds. Discontent with Thorpe's leadership produced a clumsy and abortive revolt in May 1968. Meanwhile, both in Wales and Scotland, the upsurge in Nationalist support produced considerable anxiety as to the likely effect on Liberal fortunes. In Scotland, Grimond together with other Liberals urged some form of alliance with the S.N.P. – but this proposal merely produced further splits in the Liberal ranks and produced little response from the confident Nationalists.

Added to these problems was the challenge faced by the old-style Liberals from the 'Red Guards' – the militant Young Liberals within the Party – together with a financial crisis.

Back in 1966, these Young Liberal 'Red Guards', intent on rebuilding and reforming the party, descended upon an unsuspecting Liberal Assembly. The aim of the Young Liberals was clear. They wanted a movement committed to securing popular democracy at constituency level. To achieve this end, the conventions of the system could be flouted.

The elders of the Liberal Party reacted none too favourably. As David Ridley, a former editor of *Liberal News Commentary*, declared:

> ... The Liberal Party reacted much in the fashion of an elderly bachelor confronted by a putative son. There was pride at the thought of not being sterile; fear of public opinion if convention were flouted; and doubt about the child's true paternity.[5]

Many older Liberals thought the Young Liberals were anarchist, Trotskyist or even Maoist. Grimond himself seemed to accept the Red Guards wholeheartedly.

Whatever contribution the Young Liberals made to radical political discussion, however much they harnessed the disenchantment of youth over the shortcomings of the Labour Government, whatever success they achieved (as in the Stop-the-Seventy-Tour campaign), their effect on the electoral fortunes of the Liberal Party was probably almost wholly damaging.

The financial crisis had been brewing for some time. In 1967, faced with the increased expenditure arising from the Smith Square headquarters and the lack of progress in the 'Million Fund' appeal, the adverse balance had reached £70,000.

By the autumn of 1969, with a General Election at most eighteen months away, and with the party by now £100,000 in the red, the *Liberal News* (its own future in doubt) carried in large black type the headline CRISIS on 14 October. The noun was appropriate.

The result was a fundamental review of finances. A small committee was established under the chairmanship of Philip Watkins, which shortly afterwards proposed drastic economies. At the same time, Jeremy Thorpe launched a scheme calling on 8000 Liberals to subscribe £25 a year to the party.

The response to the appeal was immediate; by the end of 1969 over £25,000 had been received. By spring 1970, the deficit was halved. Meanwhile, on 2 December 1969, a standing committee was appointed to plan the long-term evolution of the Party; simultaneously, a Finance and Administrative Board was established under the chairmanship of Philip Watkins.

One result of the sudden improvement in Party finance was that the Liberals were able to field 332 candidates for the June 1970 election (although the Party Council in 1968 had endorsed a total of 500). Despite Liberal efforts, however, the election campaign received relatively little publicity. Wilson and Heath (to say nothing of Powell) were the headline stories. Thorpe was an also-ran.

Although the Party had entered the election without any great hopes, the actual result was worse than any Liberal had supposed. The Party secured 2,117,638 votes, compared to 2,327,533 in 1966. Its share of the total vote fell from 8·5 per cent to 7·5 per cent. Even worse, Liberals lost no fewer than seven seats – Ladywood and the Colne Valley to Labour; Orpington, Cheadle, Bodmin, West Aberdeenshire and Ross and Cromarty to the Conservatives. Thorpe retained North Devon by a mere 369 votes; David Steel was in at Roxburgh by only 550. With six M.P.s, and not a really safe seat amongst them, the Party had come full circle to its parliamentary representation of 1959. For even the elders of the National Liberal Club, there had rarely been more depressing nights.

What was the explanation behind the failure of the Liberal revival? Why had the political opportunity of 1959 faded, and why had the political vacuum of 1966 similarly not been rewarding for the Liberals?

At the heart of the failure was the fact that the Party hopes had always depended less on its own strength than on the weakness of others. Once the unilateralist debate within the Labour ranks subsided, the ground was removed from underneath the Liberals. The Liberal failure was not so easily explained.

As Professor King has written:

... in retrospect, one suspects that the Liberals always pitched their hopes too high. Even in Labour's darkest days, there existed a large volume of sympathy for Labour waiting to be activated by some reversal of public fortunes. The Liberals' bargaining strength was always limited by their lack of a solid voting bloc in the country which could be delivered to one of the other parties.[6]

Linked with this failure to replace Labour was the attempt by the party to portray itself as the Party for the 'new middle class'. Professor Vincent has written of this strategy:

... The Liberals have been obsessed for ten years by the belief that they, like the Congregational Church, have a vocation to serve the 'new' middle class. This is market research gone mad. It has got the party precisely nowhere.[7]

In addition to these crucial weaknesses however, a whole variety of further factors ensured the failure of the Liberal revival. The Party lacked both money and organisation. In the wake of Orpington, when money and recruits flowed into headquarters, the resources of the Party had been hopelessly over-extended. This had left the Party with such burdens as a prestige Smith Square headquarters which could not be maintained.

The Liberals (like the Nationalists after 1966) suffered also from lack of a secure press outlet. No major national popular newspaper gave the Liberals persistent support during the 1960s. The vehicle which might have played this role (the *News Chronicle*) had died in October 1960.

A more important reason for the extent of the Liberal failure concerns policy. Whilst the Liberal Party had done at least as much to define policy as its main rivals (and in the 1959–62 period was the leader in progressive thought), it was equally true that no issues really identified the Party in the public mind. The Party possessed different policies, but not a distinctive image. Similarly, Alan Watkins makes the important point that such M.P.s as Sydney Silverman (on the hanging issue) have made as much impact as the whole Parliamentary Liberal Party.[8]

There is also truth in the strong attack launched by Richard Lamb (the erudite Liberal editor of *New Outlook*) on the failure of the Liberals to develop their policy after the success of Orpington. Lamb correctly argues that the Liberals suffered from an innate conservatism after the spectacular success of 1962. The Party remained content to rest on its policy laurels instead of moving ahead (especially in the 1964–6 period) to a further comprehensive radical policy. Linked to this must be criticism of the Grimond leadership's policy first of waiting for Gaitskell in 1960–1 and then – an even more invidious task – waiting for Wilson in 1964–6.

After the watershed of 1966, the failure of the Liberals to advance was for rather different reasons. In the difficult and unpromising position after 1966, the Party became increasingly introspective, engaging in a soul-searching scrutiny of its constitution. Admittedly, the Party could boast a fine record on social reform and immigration; elsewhere, however, the Liberals made little impact.

As David Butler wrote in the Nuffield 1970 Election study:

> ... Of the most distinctly Liberal policies, co-ownership remained but stirred little public interest. The flag of devolution was being waved much more vigorously by the Nationalists, and that of Europe by the Labour Government. The Liberal M.P.s, with Lord Byers, Lord Beaumont and others in the Lords, took up various causes, but at no point seemed to engage the attention of the nation ...

Above and beyond this failure of policy, however, went a wider failure: the leadership of Jeremy Thorpe. Despite (or perhaps because of) having one of the most brilliant minds in British politics, Thorpe has not proved the type of leader the Liberals require. Whatever range of talents he can boast of, he has never been able to harness the disillusion of the British electorate to the Liberal Party.

However, when all the reasons and possibilities why the Liberal revival after Orpington collapsed so rapidly are exhausted, it is important once again to put that period into perspective. The Liberals only won one seat from the Conservatives during the Macmillan Government of 1959–63. No seat was won from Labour. Even at the height of Liberal popularity, in the *annus mirabilis* of 1962, in the municipal elections of that year the Party won only one in nine of the council seats at stake.

Nothing that has happened since June 1970 has in any way altered the bleak outlook facing the Liberals. On the eve of the 1970 general election, David Steel wrote in the *Guardian*/Panther election guide:

> The Liberal Party has a vital and possibly influential role to play in the 1970s. It is a role essentially different from that of the other two parties: if it did not exist, it would be necessary to invent it.[9]

Whether the electors share that view is becoming increasingly doubtful.

In many ways, the nationalist revival bore outward similarities to the Liberal saga. To the critics, the victories of Carmarthen and Hamilton constituted, like Orpington, acts of protest at an unpopular government. And, the critics argued, the municipal rise and fall of, for example, the S.N.P. almost paralleled the municipal progress of the Liberals after Orpington.

Electorally, at least, the parallels were closest between the Liberals and the Scottish Nationalists. From the Party's foundation until the Hamilton by-election of November 1967, the Scottish Nationalists had only once returned an M.P. – elected in April 1945 in a by-election at Motherwell. This seat had been lost in the succeeding General Election. Otherwise, they had achieved only isolated successes – the election of Compton Mackenzie as Rector of Glasgow University in 1931 and the attention aroused by the million-signature 'Covenant' in 1948.

Not surprisingly, at least after 1950, the political pundits had consigned Scottish Nationalism to an early death. For many years it seemed they were right. However, after 1959, the unpopularity of the Conservative

Party, the divisions within the Labour ranks and the mounting unemployment in Scotland all aided the Nationalists. This combination of factors enabled the Party to put up a creditable performance in the by-election in Glasgow Bridgeton in November 1961. The Nationalists polled over 3500 votes, 18·7 per cent of the total poll, and finished only 400 votes behind the Tory. Although Bridgeton was a Labour stronghold, clearly years of apathy in the local Labour Party (turnout dropped to 41·9 per cent) and a typically unexciting candidate played a part in the Nationalist vote.

A further opportunity for the Nationalists came in a by-election in West Lothian in June 1962 – three months after Orpington, at a time when Conservatism in Scotland was hitting rock bottom. Several factors played into the Nationalist hands; the threat to the local oil-shale industry was a theme which the Nationalist candidate, William Wolfe, had campaigned on for some time; Tam Dalyell, the Labour candidate (and far removed from the ideal candidate for such a constituency) gave the issue one line in his election address.[10] Furthermore, the Conservative Government announced the withdrawal of tax relief on home-produced shale oil during the campaign. All these factors (plus a Liberal standard bearer in a constituency last fought in 1924) produced a startling result:

1962 By-election			1959 General Election		
		%			%
Lab.	21,266	50·8	Lab.	27,454	60·3
S.N.P.	9,750	23·3	Con.	18,083	39·7
Con.	4,784	11·4			
Lib.	4,557	10·8			
Comm.	1,511	3·6			

By any standards the result was sensational; the Conservative candidate's percentage of the poll fell from 39·7 per cent to 11·4 per cent, the Nationalist took nearly 10,000 votes and 25 per cent of the poll. Significantly the Liberals, in this seat clearly the weaker protest Party, lost their deposit.

Despite this Nationalist upsurge, the remaining by-elections of the 1959–64 period provided little comfort. The S.N.P. polled 11·1 per cent in Glasgow Woodside (November 1962); 7·3 per cent in Kinross and West Perthshire (November 1963); 9·8 per cent in Dumfriesshire (December 1963); and 7·4 per cent in Dundee West. In the Rutherglen by-election of May 1964, the S.N.P. actually reversed its earlier decision and declined to contest the seat.

In the 1964 General Election, encouraged by the support received in by-elections, the Nationalists fought on a wider front than hitherto – fielding fifteen candidates. Although the Party averaged only 10·9 per cent of the vote in the seats contested in certain areas the Nationalists made definite progress. In West Lothian – the great S.N.P. hope – a concentrated effort and a spirited campaign produced a Nationalist vote of 15,000 and more than 30 per cent of the total vote. The S.N.P. also began a perceptible advance into such Labour-held seats as West Dunbartonshire (12·0 per cent) and Stirlingshire and East Clackmannanshire (12·2 per cent).

The 1964 seats, even if encouraging in a few areas, gave no indication of the definite advance that was to come two years later. The General Election of 31 March 1966 produced the first signs of a distinct Nationalist upsurge. The S.N.P. fought twenty-three of the seventy-one Scottish seats, polling an average of 14·5 per cent in the seats contested. Compared to 1964, the votes cast in Scotland were:

	1964	%		1966	%
Lab.	1,283,667	48·7	Lab.	1,273,916	49·9
Con.	1,069,695	40·6	Con.	960,675	37·7
S.N.P.	64,044	2·4	S.N.P.	128,474	5·0
Lib.	200,063	7·6	Lib.	172,447	6·8
Others	17,070	0·7	Others	16,868	0·6

In 1966, the S.N.P. managed to save thirteen deposits, although not a single deposit was saved in the four largest towns of Glasgow, Edinburgh, Dundee and Aberdeen. The most noticeable feature of the Nationalist progress was the increased support received in the industrial Labour-held seats of central Scotland – in addition to West Lothian, the Nationalists polled well in West Stirlingshire, West Dunbartonshire, Midlothian, Dunfermline Burghs and Kirkcaldy.

It was a paradox that, at a time when Labour predominance in Scotland had never been greater (the party elected forty-six M.P.s with 49·9 per cent of all the votes cast) and the Conservatives were down to twenty seats and 37·7 per cent of votes cast, the Nationalists were making most headway in Labour strongholds. In 1966, the S.N.P. contested none of the Highland crofting seats and few rural seats. In other areas where Liberals were strong (as in Roxburgh, Selkirk and Peebles), the S.N.P. made no progress.

The results of the 1966 election gave the S.N.P. a new impetus and sense of purpose. Recruits – particularly young people – flocked to join the local branches. The central organisation of the Party was built up by

Ian MacDonald – National Organiser of the Party since 1962. The results of such activity were impressive: the S.N.P. could claim 486 branches by 1969, compared to a mere forty in 1963. The Party gave an image of youth, energy and activity that contrasted with the sterility of Labour and the lairdly respectability of the Conservatives.

The result of all this was displayed when a by-election occurred in the Pollok division of Glasgow on 9 March 1967. The omens did not appear favourable for the Nationalists. The Party had not fought the seat before, whilst the constituency was also highly marginal. The result, however, was a sensation.

	By-election	%	1966	%
Con.	14,270	36·9	19,282	47·6
Lab.	12,069	31·2	21,257	52·4
S.N.P.	10,884	28·1		
Lib.	735	1·9		
Comm.	694	1·8		

Although the Conservatives took the seat from Labour, the S.N.P. had come within 3500 votes of victory. It was a tonic whose effect was felt throughout Scotland and whose impact on the burgh elections was immediate and dramatic. The votes cast in the Scottish burgh elections for the S.N.P. are set out in the following table:

Year	S.N.P. Votes	S.N.P Candidates	Gains	%Vote
1964	13,670	32	1	—
1965	18,540	30	4	—
1966	34,330	58	4	4·0
1967	144,952	159	23	15·6

It was significant that, at the same time that the S.N.P. vote was soaring upwards, turnout also increased. Turnout in the burgh elections rose from 41·6 per cent in 1966 to 45·0 per cent in 1967 and 48·5 per cent in 1968.

Between the burgh elections of 1967 and those of 1968 there occurred the Hamilton by-election of 2 November 1967. In the second safest Labour seat in Scotland (the Party obtained 71·2 per cent of the votes cast in 1966), Mrs Winifred Ewing was able to wrest the seat from Labour. The result was: S.N.P., 18,397 (46·0 per cent); Labour 16,598 (41·5 per cent); Conservative 4,986 (12·5 per cent).

Viewed against what was happening in by-elections south of the border, this result was less dramatic than it appeared. On the same day as Hamilton, South West Leicester was lost to the Conservatives on a 16·6 per cent swing, while in September 1967 West Walthamstow went Conservative on a 18·4 per cent swing.

Even if, in many respects, Pollok was a more impressive Nationalist achievement than Hamilton (since Hamilton was a constituency dominated by one Party), the impact north of the Tweed was dramatic. Membership of the S.N.P. rocketed upwards: by 1968 the party claimed 125,000 members.

In the burgh elections the Party swept the board in many large towns. Unfortunately for the S.N.P., no further parliamentary by-elections occurred until the Glasgow Gorbals vacancy in October 1969 and South Ayrshire in March 1970.

Neither was the kind of seat in which the Nationalists particularly hoped to do well. This pessimism was proved correct. The Party polled 25 per cent of the vote in the Gorbals and only 20 per cent in South Ayrshire. This clear decline in S.N.P. support (reflected also in the opinion polls) was similarly demonstrated in the 1970 burgh elections. The S.N.P. vote in the burgh elections fell from a peak of 343,000 (30·1 per cent) in 1968 to 221,500 (22·0 per cent) in 1969 and a mere 131,300 (12·6 per cent) in 1970. The net result was that, at a time when Labour morale was rapidly rising, the S.N.P. entered the General Election as a Party clearly in decline. The election campaign itself did nothing to restore the fortunes of the Party. It was symbolic that the Party, attracting little attention in the press and less on television, switched its attack to opposition to the Common Market.

The result of the election was a total rout for the Nationalists. No fewer than forty-three of the sixty-five S.N.P. candidates forfeited their deposits. Whilst the Party polled over 300,000 votes (11·4 per cent of the total poll in Scotland) a more significant figure was the decline in the average percentage of seats fought in 1966 and 1970 from 14·5 per cent to 12·2 per cent.

Ironically, the Party actually won a seat in a General Election for the first time in its history – capturing the remote Western Isles division from Labour. Whatever local factors produced this electoral aberration, elsewhere S.N.P. support was nowhere near giving them victory. Interestingly, the Party made nil impact in the industrial areas where its revival had occurred, but instead polled quite respectably in the Highlands and in the North East (to some extent at the expense of the Liberals). After the elation of Hamilton, the vessel of Scottish Nationalism had seemed set

fair to sail. The 1970 election showed it to be a latter-day *Marie Celeste*.
Since the General Election (as with the Liberals) little has gone right.
The local elections in May 1971 were calamitous – every retiring S.N.P.
councillor in Glasgow, for example, suffered electoral defeat. The
electoral future seemed as bleak as the windswept moors of the Highlands.

The reasons for the Nationalist failure bear many parallels with the
Liberal decline. The new support attracted by the Party (much of this
from previous non-voters) faded with the revival in the fortunes of the
larger Parties. Once again, the Nationalist revival was dependent on its
opponents' weakness. Interestingly, where the other possible protest
parties had local strength (such as the Liberals in Greenock), the Nationalists made no progress. Virtually all the factors harming the Liberals –
problems of policy, of finance, of publicity in a General Election campaign – harmed the Nationalists. Fundamentally, the Nationalist revival
owed its strength to the anti-Labour sentiment that could not easily find
expression in Conservatism. The Nationalists also suffered – as well as
gained – from their decision to enter local politics. The S.N.P. burgh
victories in 1968 and 1969 soon exposed not only the inexperience and
low calibre of many S.N.P. councillors, but also the lack of thought-out
Nationalist policy on such bread-and-butter issues as rents, rates and
education.

However, when all the reasons for the S.N.P. decline have been assembled, it is arguable that the Nationalist revival did at least achieve
the positive result of inaugurating a debate on the place of Scotland within
the United Kingdom, not only spotlighting the constitutional case for a
Scottish Parliament, but also bringing much-needed attention to the social
and economic conditions that have given Scotland a lower standard of
living and a higher level of unemployment than exist south of the border.
The paradox of the rise of Scottish Nationalism is that (in 1972) the
Scottish economy is suffering more severely from the hands of a London
Government (as with the fate of U.C.S.) than it has for a generation.

It is in many ways misleading to compare the rise and fall of Welsh and
of Scottish Nationalism, for in many vital respects Plaid Cymru is very
different from the S.N.P. Although the Plaid has attracted less attention,
it is arguable that Welsh Nationalism will retain an importance and
influence far more than the S.N.P., because its cultural and linguistic
roots are planted in firmer ground.

As a political party, Plaid Cymru is essentially more homogeneous than
its Scottish counterpart. It is also decentralised and radical in the true

Welsh tradition. This radicalism enables the party to encompass quite strong syndicalist, pacifist and Nonconformist elements.[11]

A corollary of this was that, throughout the Forties and Fifties, the majority of the party activists were lecturers, teachers and ministers – that mainstay, since the days of David Lloyd George, of Welsh radicalism.

Another difference between the Plaid and the Scottish Nationalists has concerned electoral strategy. The S.N.P., despite its lack of electoral progress between 1945 and the revival after 1960, never really questioned the necessity of fielding parliamentary candidates. The Plaid, however, as recently as 1962, seriously doubted whether to continue what seemed a forlorn electoral battle.

The victory of Gwynfor Evans, the very able President of the Welsh Nationalists, at Carmarthen in July 1966 banished those doubts. This by-election, rapidly followed by very strong Nationalist votes in Rhondda West and Caerphilly, transformed the political climate in Wales. The Plaid went on to fight the 1970 General Election on a broad front – with thirty-six candidates. Although none was elected the Party pulled 175,000 votes. Significantly, its best performance was in the traditional rural Welsh-speaking part of North Wales. The Plaid finished within range of victory in Caernarvon and Merioneth in addition to polling strongly in Carmarthen (although Gwynfor Evans lost the seat), Cardigan and Anglesey. In the valleys, the Plaid took over 10,000 votes in Aberdare and Caerphilly, proving that there is clearly still a reservoir of protest votes to be polled.

Whilst the social and economic factors behind the rise of the Plaid have been the same as with the Scottish Nationalists, it is hard to deny that the success of the Plaid, and indeed the whole atmosphere of its resurgence, are akin to a religious revival. For this reason, and because of the strength of the Welsh language and the whole cultural heritage of Wales, the Plaid is likely to be a longer lasting force than the S.N.P., though possibly this force will not be seen only in electoral terms.

Interestingly, the success of the Plaid between 1966 and 1970 changed the character of the Party. The hard core of the Plaid was joined by a new influx of working-class supporters – men uncertain of their future in the declining heavy industries of the South. This influx has created its own problems. For example, the language issue has been of little interest to the newcomers from the South. Their aims (symbolised by Party Vice-President Phil Williams) were much more an economic nationalism. This dilemma of priorities and aims within the Party has still to be solved.

The eventual electoral failure of the Plaid, however, was due less to these divisions, or even to the adverse publicity which reflected on the Party from the activities of the 'Free Wales Army', than to the recovery of morale in the Labour Party. Despite its stronger roots, the Party suffered, like the Scottish Nationalists, from the nature of the 1970 General Election. Temporarily, at least, Welsh Nationalism has been forced again into the shadows.

Possibly, both the Nationalist Parties should take comfort from the complete failure of the other minor Parties during the last decade. Despite some brief and ugly manifestations in local elections (as in Huddersfield) anti-immigration extremists have failed to win electoral support. The Communist Party has again demonstrated that its future lies as firmly behind it as ever. The Democratic Party, which was founded by the enigmatic Desmond Donnelly in April 1969, has not exactly succeeded in producing its aim of national regeneration. Its founder has now joined the Conservative Party.

However, despite all this, it must have seemed to Liberals and National- ists on that evening of 18 June 1970, as the Liberal seats fell like wickets on a wet day at Old Trafford, that some traumatic nightmare was under way. They were wrong. It was only the end of an impossible dream.

NOTES

1. The figures were: Labour 19,200 (45·4 per cent), Liberal 17,542 (41·4 per cent), Conservative 5597 (13·2 per cent).
2. See David Butler, 'Liberals Build Their Council Base', *Sunday Times*, 13 May 1962.
3. *The Times*, 28 February 1966.
4. By the end of 1965, Liberals in by-elections had shown an average drop of 3½ per cent in places where they were third, but a rise of 7 per cent where they were second (*Observer*, 14 November 1965).
5. *Tribune*, 29 August 1969.
6. *Observer*, 4 September 1966.
7. *New Society*, 26 January 1967.
8. See Alan Watkins' excellent study, *The Liberal Dilemma*, pp. 110–11.
9. David McKie and Chris Cook, *Election '70*, pp. 161–4 (London, 1970).
10. I. McLean, 'The Rise and Fall of the Scottish National Party', *Political Studies*, XVIII no. 3, September 1970.
11. See Alan Butt Philip, 'Plaid Cymru', *New Society*, 9 January 1967.

2 The Economy – a Study in Failure

PETER SINCLAIR

For the British economy, the sixties were years of bitter disappointment. The real failure of Governments lay not so much in their economic policies as in their extravagant claims of omnicompetence. A credulous public was led to expect El Dorado, found only plenty, and became understandably dissatisfied. Some of the economic problems were found to be intractable. Others could be disposed of, like the heads of the hydra, only at the cost of creating more numerous and more horrifying new ones. Each of the problems became more serious as the decade wore on. The traditional instruments to deal with them seemed less and less effective. The battery of new devices rarely improved upon the old.

The decade opened in hope and closed in disillusion. Much vaunted economic expertise failed to bring home the goods that some Governments were foolish enough to predict. Measured by the standard of history, Britain's economic performance was not discreditable. But the spread of information ensured that the international comparison was seen as more relevant than the historical one. On this test, the record was rather abysmal. And when measured by the standard of absurd Government claims and predictions it was even worse.

The problem that came to override all others was growth. Fullish employment had been continuous in Britain and elsewhere since the early forties. The ghosts of the thirties had been laid. Economic theorists and policymakers began to turn their attention to the 'long period'. What had preoccupied specialists in the fifties became the popular watchword of the sixties. The sheer arithmetic of growth was its most eloquent advertisement. An economy growing at three per cent per year will, for instance, raise its national income nineteenfold in a hundred years. Raise the growth rate to six per cent, and national income will be raised 340-fold.

It became clear by the late fifties that the large gap between the growth rate of much of Continental Europe and that of Britain was hardly narrowing at all. The familiar explanation was that Germany, Italy and

Japan had suffered disproportionately from the war and that faster growth rates could be expected of them until they had, at least, regained pre-war levels of output. But this argument was wearing thin.

There are three ways of looking at the growth of real gross domestic product: total; per caput; or per person employed. In Britain, between 1952 and 1959 (the years are selected for their approximately equal degree of unemployment of resources) the annual growth rates under these three headings were: 2·7 per cent, 2·25 per cent, and 2·2 per cent. ('Real' means that price changes have been allowed for.) While this performance differed little from those of the U.S.A., Canada and Belgium, the total national income in most of Western Europe grew at 4·5 to 5·5 per cent per year between these years. Germany and Japan grew considerably faster still. Those concerned with developing countries argued about 'take-off'. For Britain the appropriate aeronautical metaphor was 'landing'.

Growth is a mysterious and widely misunderstood process. How much an economy produces depends upon the quantity, efficiency and distribution of the resources it employs. If resources are badly distributed or unemployed, we can raise output in the first case by improving their distribution within or between industries, in the second by reflation. But once these two types of waste are gone, we meet a barrier. How fast the economy can grow beyond this point depends primarily upon two things: what happens to the size of available resources, and to their combined efficiency.

Grave theoretical and practical problems crop up when one tries to value resources. But it is safe to say that an economy's growth rate will go up if labour input grows faster, if investment grows faster, or if technical progress accelerates.[1]

What happened to growth in Britain in the sixties? For the first four years, it rose only slightly. Between 1959 and 1963, gross domestic product (G.D.P.) rose in real terms at an annual average rate of 3·3 per cent in total; 2·5 per cent per caput; and 2·4 per cent per person employed. But between 1963 and 1970, the three rates were respectively 2·6 per cent; 2·15 per cent; and 2·6 per cent. This apparent rise in the growth of productivity (that is, output per person employed) over the decade was at first sight far from unimpressive. However, most of the rise occurred in 1964 and, under the impact of devaluation, in 1968. And it took place against the background of a reduced rate of increase in the working and unemployed population between 1963 and 1966 and also a large protracted fall of half a million between 1966 and 1970.

This was the first such decrease since immediately after the First World

War. Under normal circumstances, when the size of the labour force grows more slowly, productivity will grow more quickly. What is more, S.E.T. and squeeze combined to drive into enforced leisure many part-time and marginal workers whose productivity was low and who often failed to register as unemployed. Because of business cycles, the years between which to measure actual growth must be chosen carefully. It would, for example, be quite misleading to compare the 2·1 per cent annual growth of actual total G.D.P. between 1964 and 1970 with the 2·8 per cent annual growth achieved in the thirteen previous years, let alone to treat this as any kind of yardstick upon which to judge the Wilson Government.

Unemployment was so very much higher when the Labour Government left office than when they entered it. Unemployment figures suggest that 1952, 1959, 1963, and 1970 are reasonably comparable years between which to identify the changes in the underlying rate of growth of output. Because unemployment grew faster between 1959 and 1963 than in the other periods, the growth of capacity or potential output was rather higher than that of actual output between these years. And because unemployment may have risen faster than the figures suggest between 1963 and 1970 (later school-leaving, lower net immigration, university expansion, earlier voluntary retirement and changes in the age-sex profile of the population do not completely explain the fall in the total working and unemployed population), the growth of potential output in total and per caput may have been a little faster than that of actual output.

All in all, the sixties were rather a dreadful decade for growth in Britain. Real productivity growth at least held up; the growth of total productive potential seems to have accelerated slightly in the early sixties, only to fall back later. The British performance looked particularly poor when compared with that of the U.S.A. – where real gross national product grew annually at 4·55 per cent and potential output at probably 4·2 per cent between 1960 and 1969 – and also when compared with those of Italy, France, Holland, Germany and Japan, all of whose total national incomes grew faster or much faster than 4½ per cent per year.

Why did Britain continue to do so badly? The two ways of raising growth temporarily are bringing unemployment down, and making better use of existing resources. Britain has had almost full employment since the War, and we have measured growth between years when unemployment was approximatly equal. It has even been suggested, unconvincingly, that a looser labour market could have helped growth.[2]

Could better use be made of existing resources?

There was one source of growth in most other European countries which Britain lacked: a large pool of agricultural labour on which industry could draw. The move from the land had really been a nineteenth-century phenomenon in Britain; 13 per cent of the total working population was engaged in agriculture, forestry and fishing in 1901; by 1950, 5·3 per cent; by 1960, 4 per cent; by 1970, 2·7 per cent. By contrast, much of the rest of the developed world employed as much as a quarter of its labour force in agriculture as late as the early fifties. In the fifties and sixties, France, Italy, Germany and Scandinavia enjoyed a transfer of labour out of agriculture between three and ten times as large (as a share of the total labour force) as that which occurred in Britain. One series of estimates points to the conclusion that about one quarter of the difference between Britain's growth rate and those of France, Italy and Germany between 1955 and 1962 is attributable simply to this.[3]

The self-employed people are another class whose labour is often considered to be under-productive. Whether underused or not, this British reservoir has again been smaller, and has been drained more slowly, than its equivalents elsewhere. But even if one assumes that those who cease to be self-employed are one quarter as productive as those hired to replace them, Britain could not have raised its growth rate between 1955 and 1962 by more than one fifth of one per cent per year, even if it had been able to reduce self-employment as much as the rest of Western Europe did.

What did Governments do, in the sixties, to improve the distribution of resources?

The greatest single innovation was the much-maligned Selective Employment Tax, hurriedly revealed to the world in the Callaghan budget of 3 May 1966. Like every major fiscal change introduced under Wilson, it was due entirely to the ingenuity of Professor Nicholas Kaldor. It was designed to have many effects. In some ways it was conceived as a second-best policy – second-best to the act of devaluation, which the Labour Government, like its Conservative predecessors, had ruled out. In another way, S.E.T. was to counteract a moderate distortion of market prices: excise duties were levied on many consumer goods but not, directly at least, on any services. Furthermore, its introduction was hurried forward and refashioned so that it could act as a powerful weapon of short-term deflation which left income tax rates and public spending unchanged. But the major object of the new tax was to raise the *level* of output and, in the meantime, the observed short-term rate of growth.

In manufacturing industry, there seemed to be a close relationship between the growth rate of output and the growth rate of productivity (output per employee). One possible explanation for this, which Kaldor favoured, was that manufacturing was exhibiting economies of scale. The service sector, on which evidence was usually scanty, was felt to have lower levels and growth rates of productivity and to lack economies of scale. Output growth unexplained by input growth was found, under several neutral assumptions, to have been one per cent lower per year in services (including distribution) than in manufacturing in Britain between 1948 and 1962 (but about three per cent lower per year between 1924 and 1957).[4] Britain in the middle sixties was suffering from a tight labour market, particularly in manufacturing. Employment in manufacturing was lower (in level and in rate of growth) in Britain than in most other industrialised countries.

The British economy, Kaldor argued, was mature, or senescent:[5] people's tastes had moved towards services. We could raise output only by checking and, if possible, reversing this trend. S.E.T. was in fact an application of the old Cambridge concept of Ideal Output, achieved by taxing firms producing under increasing cost and subsidising those with economies of scale. The tax was therefore to be a way of raising output, and *not* a way of raising the permanent rate of growth.

So S.E.T. was born. All private sector employment was taxed at £1.25 per week (less for women and youths). Manufacturing later received a refund and a premium of 37½p. on top; services, including building, were refunded nothing; agriculture received the refund but no premium. The rate of tax was later virtually doubled in two stages (1968 and 1969); in November 1967, the premium for manufacturing was abolished for firms outside the development areas and multiplied five times for firms within them.

Did it work? The Reddaway Report[6] looked just at the effect it had on shops during the first two to three years. The authors felt it had succeeded in raising productivity, but found it very difficult to allow for the delayed effects of Heath's abolition of Resale Price Maintenance in 1964, and for the general trend towards supermarkets.

But did it achieve its major purpose of transferring labour out of service industries into manufacturing? Apparently not. The decline in manufacturing's share of total civil employment accelerated, as did the rise in employment in most services, if not selling. What can be said about the effects that the tax had on growth is that they clearly cannot have been startling, and that five years of fairly severe recession may not, perhaps, have been a long or appropriate enough period on which to judge the effectiveness of the measure.

Two further points must be made. First, S.E.T. is (or was) a very blunt instrument. Presumably some service industries enjoy economies of scale; presumably some manufacturing firms or industries don't. There is no guarantee whatsoever that the simple classification of industries into manufacturing and service was the best that could be made. Furthermore, depressingly little was done to differentiate the effects of S.E.T. by region or by age of employee. It might well have been more sensible to place a high tax on the employment in service industries of fairly young (and therefore mobile) men, especially in areas where manufacturing was particularly short of labour; and to leave other labourers untaxed. No amount of taxation of middle-aged waiters in Torquay will turn them into fitters in Smethwick.

Secondly, there are two other explanations, besides Kaldor's, for the finding that productivity growth and output growth tend to be closely correlated. One is that the engine of growth is really that neglected (if suspect) input, capital; the other, that productivity growth causes output growth, and not vice versa.[7] If either of these hypotheses is correct, S.E.T. cannot perform any useful function.

S.E.T. was not, of course, the only attempt to search out areas where productive efficiency could be increased. If the British economy really did have a soft underbelly of under-used labour, it consisted in the tragic overstaffing of many traditional industries – shipbuilding, textiles, railways, coalmining and the docks. Railways and coalmining, under the adroit leadership of Beeching and Robens, managed to shed nearly half a million men over the decade, mostly by natural wastage. The textile industries went through the same kind of process under the impact of the Cotton Industry Act of 1959. But this so-called restructuring has been painful, and many local communities suffered terribly. Government policies towards shipbuilding and the docks, on the other hand, merely tinkered with peripheral issues. The temporising loans, the pig-in-the-middle games over ownership, and the overdue changes in the archaic systems of wages have been no substitute at all for the immediate provision of alternative productive employment.

Various measures have been taken to get labour moving more easily from place to place and from job to job. Small removal and travel grants are now paid to a few jobless workers, and to some key workers with firms migrating to development areas. Local authorities have been encouraged (though neither generously nor successfully) to provide immediate council housing for new arrivals. By the beginning of the seventies there were six times as many places in Government retraining centres as there were in 1963. Joseph Godber's justly famous Industrial Training Act of 1964 which set out to subsidise, reorganise and improve technical training in industry, led to greater homogeneity of schemes and so to greater mobility. But comparison with, for instance, Sweden, where by 1970 more than one-tenth of the average worker's life was spent retraining, was revealing. The medieval English guild brother would find much that was perplexingly novel in twentieth-century Britain. But he would have no difficulty recognising some things. The apprenticeship system; the wonderful labyrinth of wage hierarchies; the canny devices with which the aristocracies of labour contrive to protect themselves – all this would be familiar.

There were other continuing obstacles to labour mobility: pension rights could rarely be transferred from one job to another, and the costs and delays involved in moving house were formidable.

Britain's three applications to enter the Common Market had as their main economic purpose the net reduction of the misallocation of resources brought about by tariffs. But the real object of the application was emotional. Macmillan's liquidation of Empire and the increasing aware-ness of the country's poor economic performance left Britain like a neuro-tic widow approaching the menopause. Remembering Dakar, Suez and Nassau, de Gaulle vetoed Macmillan's 1961–3 application. In March 1966, Wilson chastised Heath for being prepared to 'roll over like a spaniel' on the Common Market issue if de Gaulle gave encouragement. Within a few months, however, Britain had reapplied: now Labour was 'going at the hell of a pace' and 'not taking "no" for an answer'. De Gaulle's new pretext for a veto was the state of sterling and the weak British balance of pay-ments situation at the time. Sir Roy Harrod was now joined by increasing numbers of economists in opposing British entry. Among politicians of both the big Parliamentary Parties, the anti-Market group won more and more adherents. Opinion polls moved sharply in sympathy.

This new Agoraphobia had a variety of forms and origins. Some urged a North Atlantic Free Trade Association (NAFTA); others sought closer links with Comecon (Russia and her European satrapies); yet others accepted the economic case for entry but disavowed the political unity towards which the Community was thought to be heading.

But for most it was emotional. The menopause had arrived; the widow became reconciled; she was suddenly self-sufficient in her memories, independence and desire for privacy. Whatever the effects of entry[8] on the balance of payments and the distribution of income (which were and are utterly unpredictable because of the plethora of political unknowns and can only be serious if British Governments are unwilling or unable to counteract them by devaluation or fiscal redistribution), its effects on the distribution of resources would be small but probably beneficial. Yet the claim that entry would permanently raise the rate of growth merits profound scepticism. EFTA (invented as a consolation and a temporary expedient) seems to have had rather little effect on anything.

The only method of raising the rate of growth permanently is to increase permanently the growth of the size and efficiency of inputs. In the sixties, Governments came to see that it was consumption per head over time, and not total national income, that should be maximised; and that faster labour growth probably works against this.

One major input – the volume of the labour force – was growing at a slower rate than before. Emigration rose; immigration was checked; the post-war baby boom had fallen away. There are two ways of increasing the level of the effective labour force without reducing the level of income per head. One is by encouraging women and the old to work; the other, by inducing people to work longer and harder. The number of women working has continued to rise in the sixties, though not as fast as in the fifties. (The proposal in the Barber Budget of 1971 to let husbands and wives choose separate tax assessment was long overdue.) The proportion of men over sixty-five staying on at work fell steadily, but this was partly because so many more of the over-sixty-five population nowadays are in their seventies and eighties. No Government acceded to requests to abolish the earnings rule for old age pensioners.

Getting people to work harder and longer is more difficult. The British people have always been agreeably deaf to the sort of insolent cant that totalitarian régimes are wont to emit about the value of hard work. Both Conservative and Labour Governments worried about the disincentive effects on work of high marginal rates of taxation on earned income. The only change that occurred in the standard rate throughout the sixties was a rise from nearly 6s 0½d to 6s 5d in the pound shortly after the 1964 election. That the Wilson Government should never again have resorted to raising this rate (as opposed to allowing inflation to reduce the real level at which this and higher rates became operative) is very significant; particularly so when one remembers the dreary succession of deflationary packages that inevitably came to characterise the Chancellorships of Callaghan and Jenkins. Presumably they were inhibited by political considerations: but much was made of the alleged disincentive effects.

Were they right? There is no satisfactory evidence on whether leisure and other goods are complements or substitutes – that is to say, whether rises in the *average* rate of tax on income raise or reduce the supply of effort. What about a rise in the *marginal* rate? It is just possible (but rather unlikely) that an individual may react by working longer hours. But that a society will on average react like this can be safely dismissed as preposterous. In fact, people who neither moonlight nor employ themselves are rarely in a position to choose how many hours to work.

So much for labour. What about other inputs? Investment (the addition to the 'stock of capital') and technical progress (output growth unexplained by the growth of inputs) are always thought of as absolute essentials for growth. Governments in the sixties set out to encourage them – for they are often indissolubly linked – in three ways: direct subsidy; planning; and vigorous reflation.

First, subsidies. In 1959, a system of tax allowances for investment was reintroduced. It brought down the effective price of plant and machinery, for firms that made profits, by about one fifth. In January 1966 this scheme was replaced by another – on the whole, fractionally more generous: cash grants. The major argument for this change was that some businesses had been discovered to ignore tax rates if and when they assessed the profitability of possible projects. Virtually all service industries were to get no subsidy; but manufacturing in development areas was to buy its plant and machinery at nearly half-price. The cash grants were cut back slightly in 1968, and wound up by the Conservatives in 1970. They were replaced by a system of accelerated tax-free depreciation, but the effective subsidy implicit in the scheme was much the same.

Planning in Britain in the sixties was an entirely different affair from the system of physical controls established temporarily in Britain towards the end of the first war, and again in the early nineteen-forties. It was even further removed from the various types of direction practised in many totalitarian and developing countries. Planning in the sixties in Britain was *indicative*.[9] It was initiated by Macmillan.[10] A National Economic Development Council was set up in 1962: Macmillan saw it as an important and timely creation, part of the historic process of Government intervention which was well under way in the last quarter of the nineteenth century. Its duties were, among others, to project feasible rates of growth; to study the implications for the balance of payments and the required distribution and growth of resources; and, by raising expectations and reducing uncertainty, to induce the extra investment which might turn the original projection into a self-fulfilling prophecy.

This kind of planning was seen by Macmillan as the belated implementation of Keynesian economics. An unplanned liberal economy contained no *futures* markets, for tomorrow's goods as well as today's. Resources were insufficiently interchangeable. Firms and households were mercurial, ignorant and nervous about the future; they over-reacted to random events. The workers and the wealthy were haunted by memories of particular prices in the past. The economy would fail to adjust; there would very probably be short-term instability and periodic unemployment. Macmillan felt profound scepticism about the invisible hand, about the capacity of the unguided economy to look after itself. He thought (more controversially) that it would always waste opportunities for growth.

Planning was also an appetising programme for Labour. It titillated a taste for direction which had been for so long on the palates of the more cerebral of British Socialists. It provided a sort of continuity with the Attlee period. And it also appeared an essential part of the technical professionalism which Britain was thought to lack, and which Wilson was anxious to display. His experience of Government economic statistics in the war, and as President of the Board of Trade from 1947 to 1951, turned him *dirigiste*. The impression brilliantly conveyed to the electorate in 1964 was that some undefined negative attitude implicit in 'stop-go' and some unspecified kind of governmental amateurism were all that had deprived Britain of rapid growth in the fifties and early sixties. Purposive and dynamic government would suddenly restore her rightful rate of growth.

Under Wilson, the system of Little Neddies – Economic Development Committees at industry level – was developed. A Department of Economic Affairs was set up. Wilson felt that the Treasury had sacrificed long-term growth for short-run solvency. Only a powerful new institution could fill the gap. The tension between the two Ministries might be creative. Brown and Callaghan, his rivals for the Leadership eighteen months before, were cunningly made their respective heads.

The culmination of all this was the 1965 National Plan. It consisted of little more than the printed replies to a questionnaire sent to industries about their estimates of inputs and outputs on the assumption of 25 per cent real growth by 1970. The hope was that this stated assumption would justify itself by encouraging business to create the additional capacity required to make its 'prediction' come true. Conventional wisdom has it that balance of payments crises were responsible for the Plan's early abandonment and obvious under-fulfilment. The truth is that its targets could not conceivably have been achieved. But accuracy in forecasting is not the right criterion by which to judge it; for although inaccurate predictions are dangerous in themselves – they make industry less ready to believe prediction and future indicative planning less effective – the real test is whether the Plan actually raised the growth rate of capacity output. Unfortunately one cannot isolate its effects on growth from other influences. But it would be most surprising if they were either significant or unfavourable. Even if subsequent actions by Government had not dispelled any of the optimism and increased certainty which the Plan tried to instil, its contribution to additional growth would probably have been both low and temporary. The Little Neddies did succeed in identifying a few bottlenecks; and they (and the ill-fated Prices and Incomes Board) made some scattered contributions to improved utilisation of resources, project evaluation and productivity. But all in all, indicative planning failed miserably when judged against the extravagant claims made for it. In fact, the real growth of capacity may well have slowed down. Disillusion grew; and the D.E.A. (under Stewart, then Wilson himself, and finally Peter Shore) withered away unnoticed and unaneled.

The third policy of encouraging higher growth through investment consisted of 'running the economy at full capacity'. The argument here was that high demand and high growth in the past bred high growth in the future. The links in this virtuous circle were provided by business expectations and investment; and sometimes by exports by manufacturing industries thought to exhibit economies of scale. For Britain, the argument ran, the circle was vicious: poor growth bred poor growth. A similar argument was that growth had been throttled by policies of 'stop-go', which was held to make industry uncertain and pessimistic about future sales, choke off investment, and so reduce future levels of output.

The 'all out for growth' experiment started with Maudling's major reflation of demand in 1962. This differed little from the preparation for the two previous Conservative pre-election booms. The wild and pious hope was that if go-go replaced stop-go, the full capacity constraint and the balance of payments deficit into which the economy would run might be self-eliminating, given sufficient investment and time. If only the Government could ride out the balance of payments storm and keep demand up for long enough, the economy might emerge with a higher-capacity growth rate. This kind of sloppy wish-think naturally appealed to many politicians; the Treasury was more sceptical.

Interestingly, the election in October 1964 did not stop the Maudling experiment; history did not repeat itself. For Labour subscribed to the same optimism about growth. And with a parliamentary majority of five, to fall to three after the Leyton by-election in January 1965, it had no choice. Such acts of deflation as there were remained fairly mild until after the election of March 1966, when a majority of 100 at last gave Wilson the opportunity to be less myopic politically and more realistic economically. The then bipartisan policy of rapid growth in public spending, launched by Macmillan, continued from 1964; indeed, the spending rate rose still faster.

So how did these three policies – incentives, planning, and high demand – affect investment and growth? Investment rose rapidly in the early sixties, much more slowly in the second half of the decade. Fixed capital formation in Britain, gross of depreciation, rose from 10·27 per cent of G.D.P. (1955–9 average) to 15·22 per cent (1960–4) and 17·3 per cent (1965–70). In the same period, gross fixed investment in manufacturing industries rose from 4·26 per cent to 4·52 per cent to 4·65 per cent, and declined, irregularly, as a share of total investment. The reasons for the reduced rate of growth of investment in the 1965–70 period are simple enough: faster rises in interest rates; a severe prolonged slump; investment incentives roughly constant in level throughout the sixties having been withdrawn for two years in the late fifties.

The effects on growth are difficult to assess. One of the conclusions of an important article by J. R. Sargent[11] was that the effects of higher investment in the early sixties had negligible consequences for the underlying growth of productivity. All the incentives did, his assessment implies, was to goad firms into undertaking projects which would otherwise have been rejected, quite rightly, as unprofitable. In fact, since the end of the period studied by Sargent, the share of national income going to profit-takers has continued to fall and the rate of growth of investment has slowed down. By 1970, the profit share was about one third below its 1964 level. The obvious explanations – prices lagging behind wages, higher contributions by employers to national insurance, low demand depressing profits because labour is hoarded, the impact of S.E.T. on margins in the service industries – do not account for all of this.[12]

Not nearly enough research has been done to give a clear answer. But it does seem that raising investment is a much more painful and much less effective way of raising even the short-term growth rate of the British economy than had previously been thought. So in fact, all three experiments ended in disenchantment: enthusiasm about investment incentives can at most be lukewarm; planning ended the decade in perhaps rather more disgrace than it deserved; and the 'all out for growth' experiment failed abysmally.

So what about that much employed and much abused remedy, 'stop-go'? Despite the social misery and economic waste involved, in the form of periodic unemployment, stop-go had little effect on the rate of growth. Firms continued to believe (at least until the very late sixties) the pious protestations of Governments about their commitments to full employment. The experience of mild trade cycles (which Government actions slightly amplified)[13] also kept investment fairly insensitive to levels of and changes in demand. In fact, Britain's rate of growth and share of investment in output have varied much less from year to year than those of most countries whose economies have grown faster.[14]

It is difficult to escape the depressing conclusion, therefore, that there is no feasible way of substantially raising the long-term growth rate of capacity in Britain.

Governments were, and are, virtually powerless. The growth-optimism of Macmillan, Maudling, Wilson and Brown proved groundless. Raising investment, reducing uncertainty, encouraging the exploitation of economies of scale and improving the use of resources are all difficult, and in any case, they are only ways of raising levels of output rather than ways of raising the long-term rate of growth. Their effects are static, not dynamic. Raising the growth of labour merely reduces incomes per head; raising the growth of other inputs seems to encounter sharply diminishing returns. Technical progress appears to be harder to achieve than enthusiasts had imagined. All Britain has for consolation is the knowledge that Germany's growth rate has been falling recently and that Italy's and Japan's may well do the same; and also that many of the improvements and innovations which must have been made elsewhere must at least be capable of imitation. Fortunately, the decade closed with a general feeling that growth had anyway been over-emphasised as an economic objective.[15]

The second big problem in the British economy in the sixties was the balance of payments. Britain emerged from the cocoon of exchange controls in February 1955 when the Bank of England decided to support the £ in the black markets for non-transferable sterling. As time went on, it became increasingly clear that we were facing three separate kinds of balance of payments problem: acute crises of the current account; acute crises of the capital account; and a chronic deterioration in the full employment balance – that is to say, Britain's balance of payments when employment was full was going further and further into the red.

The acute crises on current account occurred in 1960, 1964–5, 1967 and 1968, while the acute capital account crisis years were 1961, 1964, 1965, 1966, 1967 and 1968.

The current account crises of 1960 and 1964–5 (deficits of £256 m., £395 m. and £77 m. respectively) were caused by fluctuations not in exports, which grew very steadily, but in three categories especially of visible imports: manufactures; semi-manufactures; and raw materials. The last group rose at the end of booms and fell back later. The first two tended to jump at a rate of 30 to 40 per cent per year in money terms for about fifteen months at the end of each boom, and then to remain constant for the next three years or so.

The 1967 and 1968 crises were rather different. In 1967 there was a very atypical though small fall in exports in money terms and a large rise in imports. Reasons given at the time were the closure of the Suez canal, the Arab–Israeli war, and the end of the 1964 import surcharge. But probably more important than any of these was the simple fact that the subsequent devaluation was anticipated by traders. There was an enormous rise of £253 million in imported manufactures, although consumer and invest-ment expenditure were rising more slowly than usual. 1968 was an equally poor year for the current balance (£319 m. as against £312 m. in 1967). The major reason for this was that in the months before the devaluation of November 1967 began to have sizeable effects, the imme-diate impact on the trade balance was inevitably adverse.

The capital account crises were due chiefly to two things – speculation and arbitrage (exploiting price discrepancies to make a riskless profit). There were, of course, years when it was thought likely that the Deutsch-mark would be revalued: 1957, 1961, 1968 and 1969. It was not really until 1970 that the foreign exchange market had any solid confidence in the £ vis-à-vis the $. At various times in several years (1961, 1964, 1965, 1966, 1967 and 1968) this lack of confidence was particularly marked. On occasions, speculators would sell spot sterling. They did this when they thought there was a decent chance of imminent devaluation of sterling or revaluation of other currencies, for instance the Deutschmark. But much more often, speculators sold sterling forward. This they did by contracting to provide sterling at a given time a number of months ahead, in return for a promise of a specified sum of foreign currency, again to change hands on the agreed date.

These transactions did not themselves show up in the balance of pay-ments accounts, for they did not involve spot currency. But they had a big indirect effect. By bidding down the forward price of sterling, the speculators induced an actual outflow of capital. By selling holdings of short-term British Government debt in London, buying a particular foreign currency spot, acquiring equivalent holdings of that country's

Government's short-term debt, and selling that foreign currency forward
in return for the now cheaper forward sterling, one could assure onself of
an effectively riskless profit. In the process, capital would leave Britain,
albeit perhaps only temporarily.

Two further factors contributed somewhat to the capital account crises.
In some years, particularly 1964, there was heavy long-term direct investment overseas by British companies. And, especially in the first half of the
decade, when it was much easier to do so, British citizens tended to acquire
shares and property abroad. All in all, the total annual (non-Government)
net outflow on the capital account of the balance of payments averaged
£446 m. in the six crisis years of 1961 and 1964–8. The year 1964 showed
the lowest deficit and 1966, 1967 and 1968 the highest. By contrast, there
was an average inflow of some £28 m. in the remaining five years of the
1959–69 period.

But it was the third balance of payments problem, the chronically
deteriorating trend of the full employment balance, that was really the
most serious one. Tolerably full employment (unemployment running at
about $1\frac{1}{2}$ per cent) had been consistent with a small surplus on current
account in the mid-fifties; some twelve years later, unemployment at this
rate would have led to a deficit of some £400 m. per year.

How did Governments react to these problems as they developed?
The acute crises on current and on capital account were rarely permitted
to reduce the gold and convertible foreign currency reserves deposited
with the Bank of England. These reserves were so low that they averaged
about double the average *annual* outflow on capital account for the six
crisis years, 1961 and 1964–8. The deficits were financed by Government
borrowing from international and foreign institutions, largely the International Monetary Fund and foreign central banks. This borrowing was
accompanied, involuntarily and anyway unavoidably, by deflation at
home.

Deflation took many forms. Tax rates were raised, the planned growth
of public expenditure was cut, the growth of the supply of money and
credit was restricted. The decade opened with a general disenchantment
with monetary policy.[16] There were grave doubts about the manner,
speed and size with which spending reacted to a change in monetary policy
in general, and to the use of specific monetary instruments in particular.
Fiscal policy (changing taxes and public expenditure) was thought to be a
more effective way of controlling demand. The decade closed with the
boot very much on the other foot. Monetary policy was powerful, if
slow; the effects of fiscal policy were thought to be no faster, in general,

and ambiguous in some ways (particularly for the level of prices). Money was previously thought powerless because, it was said, changing the supply of money would hardly affect bond and share prices, and spending would hardly react to any change in share and bond prices. This has now been seen to be both theoretically unsound, except under restrictive and inapplicable assumptions, and empirically false.

The surprising thing is that the mix of deflationary packages was almost unaffected by these changes in opinion about the relative efficiency of the various instruments. Consumer durables were the favourite target, and the least difficult one to hit. Initial deposits and minimum repayment periods on hire purchase agreements, together with purchase tax changes, were the favourite weapons. In 1961, fiscal policy was liberated from the shackles of the annual spring budget: a new device called the 'regulator' permitted the Treasury to alter tax rates by up to ten per cent whenever the Chancellor liked. The opportunity this gave of pushing up purchase tax rates, or increasing the duty on alcohol, tobacco and petrol, was not missed.

The traditional monetary instruments were Bank Rate, and the Bank of England's open market operations in Government debt. Their use was supplemented by increasingly specific ceilings on lending by the banks, and by a scheme of special deposits. Banks were forced to lodge these with the Bank of England, and to exclude them from the minimum percentage of their assets (fixed from 1962 at 28 per cent) to be held in liquid form.

Monetary and fiscal deflation was employed invariably to right the balance of payments and protect the reserves. Reflation was resumed eventually when it was thought that the balance of payments could stand it, in order to bring down unemployment, often in preparation for an impending General Election.

How effective was deflation in curing balance of payments problems? The acute crisis deficits on current account did prove curable. But improvement took time. The lags were long enough as it was, and they seemed to be lengthening. Most of the impact on imports was felt between six and fifteen months after each package. Often, these packages were sold politically as the only available formula for 'making room' for exports – that is to say, forcing manufacturers into the export market as it became more and more difficult for them to sell at home. With the exception of the special case of 1968–9 (after devaluation) the evidence shows this argument to be wholly specious. Exports in aggregate were virtually insensitive to deflation, except in a very long-term sense. Deflation worked by cutting the growth of demand, output and imports.

The general criticism of the deflations of the sixties is that there was rather too much, far too late. The Conservatives delayed in 1960 and 1964. The deterioration in the current account was visible and predictable, but no substantial measures were taken until the crises broke later. The 'all out for growth' wild goose chase restrained Maudling from deflating on the scale required. The same is true of Callaghan. Labour resorted in 1964 to a temporary surcharge on many categories of imports, in defiance of EFTA and GATT, and in the face of a Conservative opposition made hollow by Maudling's admission that he might well have used it too. The surcharge proved fairly effective but it could not last. The 1966 election over, Labour was at last able to deflate, but chose to defer really serious action until the grave crisis of July 1966 forced its hand. Except for devaluation, Labour's only departure from the previous current account policies consisted of stopping and reversing the previous rapid expansion of overseas aid, together with a quite astonishingly delayed decision, in 1968, to make drastic cuts in overseas defence spending.

The acute crisis deficits on capital account responded more quickly, but less predictably. Here the impact of the deflationary package was psychological. It was hoped that holders of sterling assets would be persuaded that the Government meant business and would fight to preserve the exchange rate. If it worked, this would raise the price of forward sterling; cut arbitrage outflows; and make speculators less anxious to dispose of spot sterling. The Government could use two other devices: Bank Rate was often raised at the same time as the introduction of deflationary measures, and sometimes earlier, in order to induce inflows of short-term capital. Then, in the mid-sixties, the Bank of England began to buy forward sterling in massive amounts. This involved promising to deliver dollars at some point in the future. The purpose was to prop up the price of forward sterling, and thereby stem or reverse the arbitrage outflow of capital. Both these policies usually worked well. But there were occasions, as in November 1964, when the Labour Government foolishly delayed a large rise in Bank Rate from the conventional Thursday to the following Monday; this, if anything, increased uncertainty about the future price of sterling. Forward market intervention was effective, but profitable and advisable only when the authorities were in fact able to hold the existing exchange rate parity. The 1967 devaluation was to lead to a gigantic exchange loss of over £350 m. purely because the Bank of England had to honour nearly £3000 m. worth of forward commitments in now more expensive foreign currency, undertaken before devaluation to prop up the forward rate.

The general criticism of Government handling of the acute capital account crises of the sixties is not simply lack of foresight and early remedial action: it is that, given the inhibiting commitment to a fixed exchange rate, not enough was done to deal with the fundamental weakness of sterling. This weakness of sterling sprang from the disturbingly large ratio of liquid liabilities to liquid assets. The familiar analogy is a bank with enormous but untouchable illiquid assets and negligible liquid assets facing large short-term debts and large deposits which can be and often are presented for immediate payment. Runs on the bank are inevitable.

In the sixties the ratio of liquid assets to liquid liabilities varied between 1:4 and 1:6 depending on the year and the method of computation. Intrinsically it need not have been dangerous. Only when accompanied, as it was, by large fluctuations in the ratio of external payments to receipts, and by a seriously deteriorating trend, did it acquire the character of a nightmare. There were obviously three solutions: raise liquid reserves; reduce liquid liabilities; or raise international liquidity or lines of credit so that the size of reserves no longer mattered.

One way of raising liquid reserves – selling off illiquid assets – was ruled out. These were owned privately by firms and individuals. To force them to part with these assets was held to be politically out. In fact, the Treasury sold some £50 m. of Government holdings of shares in American companies in 1967, while from 1965 various controls brought the outflow of capital exports by individuals down to a trickle. A more obvious but more difficult way of raising liquid reserves – running a continuous balance of payments surplus – was ruled out by the twin commitments to a fixed exchange rate and fullish unemployment.

What about reducing liquid liabilities? This was easier said than done. They were often misunderstood, thought of on the Left as some kind of post-imperial albatross which could be disposed of at will, and on the Right as the sacrosanct embodiment of the international role of sterling, inseparable from the invisible export earnings of the City. They could be divided into three components, which at the end of the decade stood about equal in value: short-term debts to the I.M.F. and others; sterling balances held largely by Commonwealth Governments in London; and sterling held by foreigners to finance international trade. They represented nothing but the accumulation of past balance of payments deficits. Paying off these debts by running balance of payments surpluses would have been excessively masochistic and quite unnecessary. The correct policy was to attempt to fund them, possibly protecting parts of them (the sterling balances) against exchange rate changes by guaranteeing their dollar value, along the lines of the Basle Agreement of 1968. This policy should have been pursued earlier and much more vigorously than it was.

The third solution was to increase international liquidity and develop extensive lines of credit to supplement the reserves. Significant moves were made in this direction: the General Agreements to Borrow, the Swap Agreements, and, in the late sixties, the elaborate negotiations which were to lead in time to the functioning of Special Drawing Rights, for all of which American officials like Robert Roosa must claim most credit. These were supplemented by frequent *ad hoc* loans (in the middle and late sixties) from other central banks, in which America, Germany, Italy and Switzerland features prominently with France a notable absentee. The French alternative – a rise in the dollar price of gold – would have benefited South Africa, Russia and to some extent France, but not Britain. The major objection to all these arrangements was that, while admirable in themselves, they became an excuse to avoid or delay changes in exchange rates for which they could be no substitute.

The only fundamental solution lay in changing the increasingly unrealistic parity of $2.80: that this was done so late is the strongest indictment of the economic management of the Governments of the sixties.

Why did the basic trend deteriorate? The simple answer is the slow growth of exports. Between 1952 and 1966 exports grew at an annual rate of 3½ per cent in volume and 4½ per cent in value, while world trade grew at much faster rates. Britain's share in the total exports of manufactures by the industrialised world fell fairly regularly from two-ninths in 1952 to less than one-eighth in 1967. In 1970, despite devaluation, it was down to little more than one-tenth.

The suggestion that Britain was concentrating on slow-growing products and slow-growing markets is not satisfactory.[17] There is better justification for putting the blame on the slow overall growth of capacity. Exclusion from the E.E.C. is sometimes said to be a further reason. But the relatively small rise in members' penetration of each others' imports markets suggest that this argument is not particularly well founded.[18] Other suggested explanations dwell on factors other than price: poor advertising and distribution, bad after-sales service, lack of market research, and so on. There is no statistical evidence to help one here, but, in this quagmire of uninformed waffle, some case studies of firms and products tend to support this view.

But the real explanation lies in inflation. Britain somehow could not avoid inflating at an annual rate usually at least one per cent faster than

Germany. For most of the decade, Japan and America inflated more slowly; occasionally faster inflation (as in France in 1968–9) was followed by devaluation. The relatively high inflation in Britain was all the more serious in view of the high sensitivity of export demand to export prices. An important American study[19] using slightly less primitive econometric techniques than many previous attempts found that a one per cent rise in prices of British exported manufactures against constant prices in the rest of the world would eventually reduce demand for these exports by 2 to 3 per cent.

British export prices rose at about one per cent a year, compared with general domestic inflation of about $3\frac{1}{2}$ per cent per year, between the early fifties and 1965. This suggests what other evidence has often confirmed: a falling rate of profit on export sales, as opposed to sales at home. British export producers found themselves unable to raise export prices fully to reflect rises in costs. So faster inflation in Britain than elsewhere explains why the balance of payments should have been not merely weak, but also deteriorating.

Faced with this situation, Governments had two choices. They could reduce domestic inflation; or they could reduce the external value of the £ by devaluation or depreciation. It was with the greatest reluctance, and several years too late, that the easier second course was taken. From 1964, Wilson chose the first course, with a prices and incomes policy of greater severity than any that had preceded it in peacetime. Unfortunately there was no immediate or dramatic change in the rate of inflation.

In retrospect, bringing Britain's rate of inflation down to an international average looks quite impossible; and this makes the ostrich-like refusal to contemplate devaluation more tragic. In 1964, of course, Labour did introduce a rebate for indirect taxation paid on exports; the effective rate of subsidy was $2\frac{1}{4}$ per cent and it was very welcome; but it could not deal with the scale and dynamic aspect of the problem, and three more years of inflation eroded it.

Slow growth in exports explains much, but not all, of the deterioration in the crucial statistic: *the basic balance of payments at a constant level of unemployment.* The other villain of the piece was Government invisible imports (mainly overseas aid and defence spending abroad). This category of imports quadrupled in money terms between the early fifties and the late sixties.

It is not possible to gauge the net impact these imports had on the balance of payments, for without them, exports would have been rather lower; and, since tax rates would have been lower, imports would have been a little higher. It may be assumed that had Government invisible exports been held at 2½ per cent of total current account receipts, the speed of the deterioration of the current account at a constant level of unemployment would have been reduced by about one third.

Clearly then, the main blame for balance of payments deterioration must fall on the fixed exchange rate policy and higher than world average inflation, with – partly as a result – slow growth of capacity in producing for export.

With hindsight, it is clear that we should have devalued earlier – probably as soon as 1961. The trend was reasonably evident as soon as that. Labour can be excused for not devaluing in 1964: a majority of five forbade it. And with overfull employment at that time, any gains from devaluation would have been gobbled up by inflation, all the more so because any significant deflation would have been politically impossible. The biggest mistake was the refusal to devalue in May–July 1966. Wilson felt that Labour's devaluation in 1949 had cooked its electoral goose for 1950 and 1951. He decided that if ever devaluation proved inevitable, the electorate would pardon a Government only if it was clearly seen to have been forced into it. As it was, he hoped that savage deflation and wage control would do the trick. They did not. Speculative crises continued, involving ever larger flights of funds from London. The current account improved briefly, only to deteriorate very sharply in 1967. At long last, in November, the inevitable occurred. But the huge crisis that preceded it was almost a repetition of 1931. France's elegant and unprovoked devaluation twenty-one months later was an object lesson, and utterly refuted Wilson's case that an electorate will forgive rape but nothing else.

The extent of the devaluation (14·3 per cent) was chosen carefully and intelligently: enough, it was hoped, to dispel fears of recurrence, but not enough to induce retaliation by major competitors. But the delays before the essential accompanying acts of deflation were nothing short of amazing. One cannot quarrel with the two months it took Wilson to prepare and announce £800 m. cuts in the planned future growth of public spending. But most of these cuts were quite understandably not to take effect for at least a year.

Devaluation was itself accompanied by fairly minor (though again mostly delayed action) deflation of £400 m. But rises in taxation (although widely expected, as can be seen from the large consumer boom in the winter) did not occur until March 1968 (£920m.) with further increases in November. And a seriously restrictive monetary policy was not introduced until the middle of 1969 – more than eighteen months after the devaluation.

The Government was not helped by a rather antedeluvian attitude towards devaluation on the part of some leading Conservatives, who appeared to believe that it was an act of dastardly treachery towards the holders of sterling balances. The truth was that the bulk of these balances had been held in the form of Treasury bills (short-term Government debt) upon which substantial danger money was paid. The danger money took the form of interest rates usually substantially higher than those that could be obtained on comparable assets in other financial centres; and about ten years' accumulated danger money more than compensated for a devaluation of 14·3 per cent.

The devaluation worked very well. There was a massive £700 m. improvement in the current account between 1967 and 1969. Certainly some of this was due to the colossal, if tardy, deflations of 1968 and 1969, and to the rapid expansion of world trade. But without devaluation, improvement on this scale could never have occurred. The only difficulty was that it took at least a year to have maximum impact. In the meantime (during which the current account position actually deteriorated) doubts were expressed about its success. Later events quickly dispelled them. The decade closed with the balance of payments at last in substantial surplus. One head of the hydra had been cut off; a head that had been menacing the country, increasingly seriously, since 1960. But just as this head came off, two more emerged, more threatening than ever. These were inflation and high unemployment; for the first time in recent history, they actually accompanied each other.

The post-war inflation had slowed down to a fairly gentle pace of about 3½ per cent per year since 1952. But from 1965, it accelerated to 5 per cent, and after 1969 it was moving towards 8 per cent.

Most of the fifties and sixties were preoccupied with a lacklustre debate as to whether it was demand or cost which led to inflation. Econometric studies were far from conclusive but did provide some tentative findings. Wage rates and earnings rose fast when unemployment (gross or net of unfilled vacancies) was low and falling. Wage rises both preceded and followed price rises. Price rises came fastest in years of slow growth because of lags and the brevity of business cycles and because firms, hoping for better times ahead, hoarded labour and found their unit costs rising faster than usual. Monetary expansion was one way (but not the only way) of raising demand, reducing unemployment and thereby, eventually, adding to or creating inflation. Wage inflation unaccompanied by monetary expansion raised interest rates and eventually, painfully, petered out in higher unemployment.

There were three theories of inflation in popular currency. The first was the so-called Phillips curve. This predicted that the lower the rate of unemployment, the faster would be the rise in wages and subsequently in prices. The implication was that price stability could be won only at the cost of throwing men out of work. The Government's job was to steer the least unpopular course between these two evils.

The second, which was rather vaguely stated, drew on the metaphor of a spiral staircase. Wages and prices chased each other up. One could attribute neither priority nor cause. The origin of inflation was probably sociological; it merely registered incompatible claims by groups on the national income; its effects were merely redistributive. The job of Government was probably to squash it, by statutory controls if necessary.

The third theory rested upon the correlation of money with prices. It was brought back into the prominence it had lost since Keynes by Milton Friedman's torrent of sometimes lucid logic and often muddy statistics. The job of Government, if it wished to avoid inflation, was simply to restrict the expansion of money to the rate of the growth of output.

The Macmillan Government subscribed to the Phillips theory and in smaller measure to that of the spiral too. Enoch Powell, Nigel Birch and their superior Peter Thorneycroft were exponents of the third theory; but their resignation from the Treasury had already taken place by October 1959. No one bothered much about inflation during the interregnum of Sir Alec Douglas-Home; they were all too busy fighting an election and purusing the chimera of growth. Callaghan, Wilson's first Chancellor, came when in office to accept a cross between theories one and two – in so far as he followed any theory. The early Jenkins continued on the Callaghan course; the late Jenkins turned to theory three, under the welter of monetarist injunctions which the I.M.F. began putting out in 1969.

Wilson himself clearly realised that the consent or acquiescence of the unions was essential for the success of what is blandly described as incomes policy, but he was a firm believer in the spiral theory, with the implication for imposing controls which that carried. Experience of the seamen's strike in 1966 and the dock strike in 1967, coupled with the emergence of new militants (especially Scanlon of the Amalgamated Engineering Union and Jones of the Transport and General Workers) made him increasingly impatient with the unions. He seems, for instance, to have accepted the widespread but quite erroneous[20] view that working days lost through strikes were consistently higher in Britain than on the Continent. The Donovan Commission reported in 1969. Its dislike of legal solutions was disregarded. Only the probability of a defeat in the Commons by dissident backbenchers, and Callaghan's challenge to Wilson's leadership,[21] forced Wilson to abandon his proposed Industrial Relations Bill (with its draconian curbs on the unions). This and other considerations led to the formal burial of the incomes policy a few weeks later.

Why did inflation suddenly accelerate in the mid-sixties? The simplest and most cogent explanation is simply that people came to expect it.[22] In the fifties, one might argue, the rate of inflation expected was low, for there had been long periods of peace (1873–98 and 1920–35) which had witnessed continuing falls in the level of prices. But as time wore on, and the actual rate of inflation turned out to be relatively high (due as much as anything to the high level of demand) the rate of inflation which people expected for the future began to go up. The Vietnam war, American capital exports, and the recent rises in international liquidity have also, obviously, played their part in raising inflation everywhere.

While unemployment was held at a low level, inflation could be expected to rise at an increasing rate. On top of this there was a rapid expansion in public spending, initiated by Macmillan and accelerated by Wilson; and a very low level of unemployment for two years (mid-1964 to mid-1966) which was attributable to the 'dash for growth' policy and to covert electioneering.

In July 1966, Wilson moved to curb inflation by applying a statutory wage freeze: the byzantine Prices and Incomes Board, set up in 1964, was at last given sharp teeth. Selwyn Lloyd's unpopular voluntary pay pause five years earlier looked mild as milk by comparison. Six months of statutory freeze was followed by successive periods of severe restraint, but by 1969 political pressure had become uncontainable and the policy was dropped.

Meanwhile, the rate of inflation continued at its new faster rate of five per cent per year, dropping a little in 1967. There were three reasons for this in 1966 and 1967. In 1965 there had been a large shortfall of price rises behind wage rises with no accompanying rise in productivity – so that prices were bound to catch up. The 1966–7 period also saw output growth ($1\frac{1}{2}$ per cent per year) considerably below capacity growth ($2\frac{1}{2}$ per cent per year); so, because labour was hoarded, producers' unit costs went up even if wages did not. The third reason was the increases in indirect taxation (purchase tax, S.E.T., and excise duty) brought about by the Government in its attempts to deflate demand. By 1967–8, the rate of rise of wages (rates and total earnings) was fully back on trend, quite unaffected, apparently, by the fire and brimstone of the P.I.B.

The Government was anxious to encourage wage rises for the lower-paid and for those workers who increased productivity. In fact, the distribution of wage rises was quite general and did not reflect either of these favoured criteria. There was increasing suspicion about several so-called productivity agreements; for one thing, increases in productivity were often simply reflections of more capital-intensive techniques. Lower-paid workers had slightly above average rises in pre-tax earnings, but probably slightly below average rises in post-tax earnings.

On top of all this came the devalution of November 1967. This led, inevitably, to sharp rises in the sterling price of all goods traded internationally. The subsequent deflationary measures leant heavily on indirect tax rises, which raised the cost of living, for direct taxes were thought to be quite high enough already.

Did incomes policy help? A recent major study[23] suggests that it reduced wage inflation when unemployment was low, but raised it at high levels of unemployment. The authors argue that incomes policy set a norm, and thereby reduced the sensitivity of the wage bargain to the state of the labour market. So if a government wishes to minimise inflation, the argument runs, it should use incomes policy only when the pressure of demand is, or has recently been, high. The conclusion looks reasonable, but there are two problems with this study: a failure to identify changes in the intensity with which incomes policy was or was not applied; and a failure to deal with the dynamic role of expectations in raising the trend of inflation in the course of the sixties. Much of the apparent tendency of incomes policy to raise wage increases when demand is low is explained by the fact that inflation was faster anyway in the middle and late sixties for all the quite different reasons we have seen; and incomes policy was applied in more frequent steps and more continuously in this period than in previous years. Furthermore, their econometric estimation techniques were inadequate.[24]

But while the freeze did little if anything to contain the growth of real wages, it unfortunately conveyed the impression that it was doing so. A deep well of resentment was sunk. People felt deprived (although it was difficult to show that they really were). The brilliant oratory of Iain Macleod, the Shadow Chancellor, and the baleful comments of press and television made things worse. By 1969, the resentment could no longer be contained; Labour began to look carefully at the next election. Enormous wage demands followed. It could be argued that, had there been no incomes policy, the long-run rate of inflation might have been lower. But without any attempt by the authorities to contain inflation between 1966 and 1969, the rate of inflation between these years would probably have been higher.

So much for direct controls: what happened with monetary restraint? There is no doubt that, had the kind of monetary policy pursued for a time after mid-1969 been applied much earlier, there would have been less inflation. But the rate of inflation would have fallen slowly at first. And the rise in unemployment, in the medium term, would have been quite unacceptable. The Friedmanite objections to the Phillips curve (that there could be no trade-off between inflation and unemployment in the long run because expectations adjust) appears not to be valid for any period less than three to five years. The monetarist prescription for stopping inflation is socially intolerable and, at first at least, rather ineffective.

So we are left with the conclusion that, with inflation as with growth, the authorities did about as well as they could be expected to have done. Both problems were intractable; the mistake was that Governments (or to be more accurate, Parties fighting elections) made claims for their ability to influence the economy which events have shown to be lamentably exaggerated. The one area of solid success in economic management was the improvement in the balance of payments position. But this success was deplorably belated. And devaluation is not a permanent cure for a balance of payments deficit. For in the long run, price readjustments and expectations will make it a rather neutral instrument. But *if* one is committed to a régime of fixed exchange rates, it is by far the least ineffective way of correcting over-valuation. The tragedy of the sixties is that sterling became increasingly overvalued, and that the myopia and false optimism of successive Governments condemned the country to unnecessary suffering.

NOTES

1. How much it will in fact go up by is obviously governed by the extra output that each new input permits, the interchangeability of resources (both within and between industries) and the extent of any (dis-)economies of scale.

2. E.g. F. W. Paish, *Studies in an Inflationary Economy* (London, 1966), pp. 309–32.

3. Edward Denison, *Why Growth Rates Differ: Post-war Experience in Nine Western Countries* (Brookings Institution, 1967), p. 327.

4. R. C. O. Matthews, 'Some Aspects of Post-war Growth in Relation to Historical Experience', *Transactions of the Manchester Statistical Society*, session 1964–5, Table IV, p. 17. See also G. D. N. Worswick and C. G. Fane, 'Goods and Services Once Again', *District Bank Review*, March 1967, pp. 3–22.

5. N. Kaldor, *Causes of the Slow Rate of Economic Growth of the United Kingdom* (Cambridge, 1966).

6. *The Effects of the Selective Employment Tax: First Report on the Distributive Trade* (H.M.S.O., 1970).

7. See, in this connection, J. N. Wolfe, 'Productivity and Growth in Manufacturing Industry: some Reflections on Professor Kaldor's Inaugural Lecture', *Economica*, May 1968.

8. Readers interested in haruspication are referred to the two White Papers (February 1970 and July 1971) and to N. Kaldor, *New Statesman*, 12 March 1971; M. Miller, *National Institute Economic Review*, 1971; P. Oppenheimer, *National Westminster Bank Review*, 1971; D. Swann, *The Economics of the Common Market* (London, 1970), and Williamson and Botterill, *University of Warwick Research Papers in Economics*, 1971.

9. See J. E. Meade, *The Theory of Indicative Planning* (Manchester, 1970) for an exhaustive theoretical treatment.

10. The Rt. Hon. M. H. Macmillan, *The Middle Way* (London, 1938). This book provides a deeper understanding of many of the decisions taken under his premiership. His views were influenced by economic conditions in his then constituency of Stockton-on-Tees.

11. J. R. Sargent, *Economic Journal*, 1968.

12. See Andrew Glyn and Robert Sutcliffe, *New Left Review*, 1971.

13. See R. C. O. Matthews, *Economic Journal*, September 1968, and 'Post War Business Cycles in the U.K.' in M. Bronfenbrenner (ed.), *Is the Business Cycle Obsolete?* (1970); also G. D. N. Worswick, in Sir Alec Cairncross (ed.), *Britain's Economic Prospects Reconsidered* (London, 1971), pp. 36–60.

14. See T. Wilson, 'Instability and Growth' in D. Aldcroft and P. Fearon (eds.), *Economic Growth in Twentieth-Century Britain* (London, 1969). This conclusion is weakened a little when the later 1960s are included, and after quarterly interpolation and normalisation.

15. E. J. Mishan, *The Costs of Economic Growth* (Staples, 1966), had a big impact. For output statistics ignore leisure, and growth statistics

ignore the consumption of scarce natural resources (like beauty and peace), possible satiation, reductions in choice, etc.

16. The Radcliffe Report, *Report of the Committee on the Working of the Monetary System*, Cmnd. 827 (1959), reflected and added to this.

17. *Board of Trade Journal*, 1965; *National Institute Economic Review*, 1967.

18. N. Kaldor, *New Statesman*, 12 March 1971.

19. Junz and Rhomberg, *American Statistical Association 1964*, and *IMF Staff Papers 1965*.

20. H. Turner, *Is Britain Really Strike-Prone?* (Cambridge, 1969).

21. P. Jenkins, *The Battle for Downing Street* (London, 1970).

22. For an analysis of the effects of expectation on inflation, see Sir John Hicks, *Banca Nazionale del Lavoro*, September 1970; R. M. Solow, *Price Expectation and the Behaviour of the Price Level* (Manchester, 1969); Milton Friedman, *American Economic Review*, 1967; and David Laidler's article in H. G. Johnson and A. R. Nobay, *The Current Inflation* (London, 1971).

23. R. G. Lipsey and J. M. Parkin, *Economica*, May 1970.

24. See L. Godfrey's article in H. G. Johnson and A. R. Nobay, op. cit., pp. 99–122.

3 Britain and the World

LESLIE STONE

For much of the 1960s, Britain suffered from an acute identity crisis, uncertain of its position and status in the world, unsure of its current power and future direction. The former United States Secretary of State, Dean Acheson, summed up the British predicament in his famous speech to the cadets of the Military Academy at West Point on 5 December 1962. His final verdict, the conclusive punch-line, has become drearily familiar over the years. Britain, he assured his audience, had lost an Empire and not yet found a role. Yet, at the time, Acheson's analysis was vigorous and fresh – and to some people deeply wounding. One passage in the West Point speech still bears repetition:

> Britain's attempt to play a separate power role (said Acheson), that is, a role apart from Europe, a role based on a 'special relationship' with the United States, a role based on being the head of a Commonwealth which has no political structure or unity or strength and enjoys a fragile and precarious economic relationship – this role is about played out. Great Britain, attempting to work alone and to be a broker between the United States and Russia, has seemed to conduct a policy as weak as its military power.

These sentiments, though they could, of course, have been more tactfully worded, might have come straight out of the British Government's own White Paper in July 1971, which set out its reasons for recommending British membership of the European Economic Community. Indeed, the main thrust of Acheson's speech was his enthusiastic endorsement of the Macmillan Government's original application to join the Common Market in 1961. He warmly applauded this move and hailed it as 'a decisive turning point' for modern Europe. In the subsequent furore, the British Ambassador in Washington, Sir David Ormsby-Gore (now Lord Harlech), was at first reported as wondering what all the fuss was about. Acheson's chief conclusion was very much in line with British Government policy. But it soon became clear that, by speaking out so boldly, he had touched on a very sensitive nerve. The Macmillan Government was seeking to enter the European Community in an attempt to establish a new power base. But Britain still clung to the image of itself as a major power of the front rank. Not a great superpower, comparable to the United States and the Soviet Union, perhaps; but nevertheless a nuclear power, a great trading nation whose currency was used in financial transactions throughout the world and therefore formed an integral part of the international monetary system, one of the Big Four with special responsibilities for keeping the peace in Europe and in Asia, a permanent member of the United Nations Security Council, assured of a place at the top table in any international conference called to discuss momentous world issues.

Whatever private doubts they may have had about Britain's limited capacities, neither Harold Macmillan nor Harold Wilson after him smiled publicly on critics who warned that Britain's independent role on the world stage was 'about played out' and then proceeded to counsel contraction. Macmillan's immediate reaction to the Acheson strictures was splenetic. The British press soon published one of the most curious documents of the decade, the text of a letter from the Prime Minister to a former Cabinet colleague, Lord Chandos, in the latter's capacity as President of the Institute of Directors. In it, Macmillan accused Acheson of appearing to denigrate the resolution and will of the British people. He went on to link him with Philip of Spain, Louis XIV, Napoleon, the Kaiser and Hitler, other ignorant foreigners who had made a similar error in the past. Re-read today, the letter affords a much better insight into the workings of Macmillan's mind than it does into Acheson's.

The curse of British foreign policy in the 1960s was that it was, for the most part, committed to worthy, well-meaning, but unrealistic goals. In an era of frequent, debilitating economic crises, when erstwhile friends and neighbours began to point to Britain as the 'sick man of Europe' and take careful precautions lest they too catch the dreaded 'English disease', many British politicians continued to think and act as though nothing had fundamentally changed – as though the successive upheavals were merely temporary aberrations and, given only a rapid change of government, the country would soon be restored to its former influence and glory. The age of the Pax Britannica was clearly over. But no one could accuse British policy-makers of excessive introspection. Although conscription had been abolished, Britain continued to maintain large military contingents in South East Asia and the Middle East, as well as in Western Europe. In the 1964 General Election, few commentators thought it absurd that Sir Alec

Douglas-Home should devote so much time and energy to speeches about the continuing need for an independent British nuclear deterrent. The Conservative Party manifesto talked proudly of keeping Britain 'in her rightful place at the centre of international affairs' and scorned Opposition policies of nuclear abdication which would 'relegate Britain to the sidelines'.

There were moments in the sixties when the sidelines appeared, in some eyes, more attractive than the field of play and therefore the best place for Britain to be. Various protest movements on the Left, like the Campaign for Nuclear Disarmament, contained a strong neutralist streak. There was a growing desire to opt out of international power politics and adopt an aloof, moralising, Nehru-like posture. But after Hugh Gaitskell had withstood the onslaught from the C.N.D. forces in 1960-1, this was shown to be a minority feeling even inside the Labour Party. British foreign policy under both parties was still dominated by Churchill's famous vision of Britain at the heart of three concentric circles. The first represented the Commonwealth and Empire. The second embraced Western Europe, of which Britain was geographically and historically a part. The third symbolised the United States and the cherished 'special relationship'. Even the most ardent advocates of Britain's entry into the Common Market were loth to see any contradictions and strains. Like Macmillan himself, they seemed to think that Britain could successfully apply for membership of the E.E.C. and maintain its traditional outside links with only minor adjustments. But times were changing. As the years went by, the concentric circles failed to remain static. Indeed, they began to develop alarming, centrifugal tendencies. Britain was too weak to prevent them from pulling apart. But it was determined to make the effort, if only to avoid making a deliberate, conscious choice about the direction in which it should itself move. The result, inevitably, was a bad case of schizophrenia, an indentity crisis which has yet to be fully resolved.

Britain's basic political and military weakness had become increasingly obvious during the course of the 1950s. It was most glaringly exposed by the events in the Suez affair in the second half of 1956. The first sense of overwhelming frustration and bitter disillusionment at the imbalance in the special relationship with the United States stems from that date. But, with Macmillan in 10 Downing Street and President Eisenhower in the White House, the nostalgic ties of wartime partnership lingered on. Despite his resentment at the way he thought Britain had been let down over Suez by its closest and most powerful ally, Macmillan moved swiftly and expertly to repair the breach in the transatlantic alliance. He was determined to secure American help in the task of maintaining Britain as a leading nuclear power, automatically assured of a seat at the Summit. Moreover, at first, he was astonishingly successful. He persuaded the Americans to amend the McMahon Act – the United States atomic energy law which prohibited the sharing of vital nuclear information with foreign powers – and bent it in Britain's favour, thereby ensuring that his Government had access to certain atomic secrets made available to no other nation.

He also persuaded Washington to supply Britain with some of the most sophisticated and modern weapon systems with which to deliver British-owned nuclear warheads. When the Blue Streak missile – the last genuine attempt to produce a wholly independent British nuclear deterrent – was shown to be already obsolescent and vulnerable to Soviet attack early in 1960, Macmillan was faced with an embarrassing defence problem. But he quickly switched to the American-designed and American-made Skybolt. When the Skybolt programme too ended in fiasco as development costs escalated and the United States defence chief, Robert McNamara, decided to end the project, the Prime Minister hurried off to Nassau to meet President Kennedy in December 1962 and averted a serious domestic political crisis by pulling off his greatest diplomatic coup. Acting in haste and against the better judgement of some of his closest advisers, Kennedy agreed to supply Britain with America's own latest pride and joy, the most formidable weapon in its armoury, the submarine-launched Polaris.

Unfortunately for Macmillan, his biggest triumphs also contained the seeds of his greatest tragedies. The Bermuda Agreement in 1957, which led to the amendment of the McMahon Act, laid the groundwork for the future nuclear quarrel with France. And the Nassau Agreement provided President de Gaulle with just the public excuse that he wanted in order to sustain his veto of Britain's Common Market application. The British decision to switch from Skybolt to Polaris, itself the consequence of a decision already taken in Washington, emphasised the fragile nature of Britain's independence from the United States. Although not reduced to the status of puppet or satellite, Britain was shown to have many of the attributes of a client-state. With one party to the 'special relationship' in such a subordinate posture, the sense of partnership was wearing thin.

Judged on military terms alone, the Polaris deal turned out to be a fairly good bargain. It provided Britain with an extremely potent nuclear striking force at a comparatively cheap price, without the burden of having to pay for ruinously expensive development costs. At the same time, it enhanced Britain's status and enabled it to play a continuing role in nuclear diplomacy – notably in the Nuclear Planning Group of NATO, a committee which has done valuable work in laying down nuclear guide-lines for the Alliance. Significantly, once in office, the Labour Party quietly forgot its previous promises to renegotiate or de-negotiate the Nassau Pact. The debate about nuclear weapons, which had raged so fiercely at the beginning of the sixties, was curiously muted at the end of the decade. The 1963 Nuclear Test Ban Treaty, for which Macmillan himself worked so hard, had taken much of the heat out of the situation. However, the crucial problem of strategic arms limitation was being discussed in the cloistered secrecy of the SALT talks between the United States and the Soviet Union in Vienna and Helsinki – negotiations to which Britain was not invited and in which it had no direct, participating voice.

It is often said of Macmillan that he gave assurances of continuity and fostered delusions of grandeur, while making deep and fundamental changes in policy; that he realised Britain's growing weakness, but declined to inform the British public of the simple facts of life. A politician who seemed for a time to be endowed with an infallible magic touch, Macmillan occasionally demonstrated an astonishing sleight of hand. But he appears to have made the mistake of falling for his own tricks, eventually believing his own SuperMac propaganda. Though he may have deceived others, his most serious fault was that of self-deception.

Such a failing is not unusual amongst politicians. Harold Wilson's Labour Government was in power for more than three years before the overwhelming pressure of events forced it to face up to the logic of its own thinking on the subject of foreign affairs and defence. Despite facing tremendous economic difficulties from the very outset, it was just as eager as its Conservative predecessor to assert Britain's world role. Wilson made it plain that he had no intention of being corralled in Europe. And there were, of course, many excellent reasons for resisting demands for a precipitate withdrawal from East of Suez.

Britain has important business and commercial interests in South East Asia and the Persian Gulf. It therefore also has an interest in the preser-vation of political stability in these areas. Labour Ministers rightly felt that they could not simply pull out, leaving behind a dangerous power vacuum, which might be filled by a hostile force or, alternatively, give way to anarchy and chaos. The arguments for a substantial, long-term British presence put forward by their fellow Socialist, Lee Kuan Yew, the Prime Minister of Singapore, were especially persuasive. So the potentially explosive commitment to defend Malaysia from Indonesian intrusion, in the form of President Sukarno's 'confrontation' campaign, was faithfully carried out. And left-wing motions, calling for savage cuts in military spending overseas, were valiantly warded off.

Once again, a British Government succumbed to temptation and over-reached itself. By the mid-1960s, a thorough reexamination of Britain's overseas commitments, together with a revision of its basic defence philosophy, was long overdue. The country had been battered and bewildered by a series of chronic balance of payments crises. One of the most blatant causes of these had been the rapid increase in Government spending abroad, which had risen from just over £50 m. in 1952 to more than £400 m. in 1964. Defence items accounted for roughly two-thirds of the bill. And yet Britain's economic power in relation to its chief trading competitors had been steadily waning. By the late sixties, its Gross National Product was estimated at $109 billion – well behind West Germany ($150 billion), France ($140 billion) and Japan ($167 billion). However, Japan devoted less than one per cent (0·9 per cent) of its G.N.P. to expenditure on defence, while West Germany spent only 4·3 per cent. The figure for Britain was a whopping 5·7 per cent – a proportion exceeded among West European nations only by Portugal, which had serious colonial problems in Angola and Mozambique on its plate. The size of Britain's armed forces had been slashed from a level of almost 700,000 in 1957, when Duncan Sandys announced the end of National Service, to less than 400,000 ten years later. But Britain's obligations to render military aid to its partners and allies overseas had not been cut back accordingly.

The initial defence review carried out by the Labour Government acknowledged that the steady expansion in military spending at home and abroad had to be checked. The Labour Cabinet set itself the target of restricting the defence budget to an annual ceiling of £2000 m. calculated at 1964 prices. Working within this framework, Labour's Defence Minister, Denis Healey, displayed remarkable skill in making economies and persuading the service chiefs to acquiesce in them. Ambitious aircraft projects, like the strike-reconnaissance T.S.R.-2, were cancelled. So too were plans for an additional aircraft carrier for the Navy. But for the first three years of Labour rule, the knife cut neither fast nor deep enough.

The Government as a whole did not realise that expensive overseas commitments could only be kept so long as the nation could afford to pay the necessary bills. It allowed itself to be persuaded that it would retain influence in Washington, where the major decisions were actually made, only if it continued to keep the United States company in a wide-ranging peace-keeping role, acting as a resolute and reliable policeman in parts of the world where a purely American presence might be unwelcome or resented. Meanwhile, the Prime Minister personally showed every sign of revelling in the role of world statesman and global strategist. His instinct for self-preservation enabled him to wriggle out of arm-twisting gestures from the White House, intended to persuade him to send a token British battalion to support the American action in Vietnam. But he seemed to believe that Britain could and should play a crucial mediating role in Asia and the Pacific.

Addressing a meeting of the Parliamentary Labour Party, called to discuss the East of Suez situation in June 1966, Wilson talked of the terrifying dangers in the situation if Britain were to withdraw from the Far East altogether, leaving the United States and Communist China to glare at each other in an eyeball-to-eyeball confrontation. What more certain prescription could there be, he asked, for a nuclear holocaust? It was a carefully composed speech, appealing to a wide range of prejudices inside the Labour Party – pro-Americans and anti-Americans alike – and it carried the day. But there was nothing synthetic about Wilson's enthusiasm for the East of Suez cause. His sincerity on this point at least was genuine. He was not the victim of brutal blackmail by Lyndon Johnson.

It took the shock of the devaluation of the pound in November 1967 to bring home to the Labour Government the full extent of Britain's declining power. The decision to speed up the pull-out from East of Suez was announced early the following year. It was agreed that, with one or two exceptions such as Hong Kong, all British forces should be withdrawn from the Far and Middle East by the end of 1971. These arrangements have been slightly modified by Edward Heath, but not fundamentally revised. We are unlikely to see British forces deployed on a large scale outside Europe and the Mediterranean in the foreseeable future. The retreat from Empire, which gathered pace in the last two years of Labour rule, is not the kind of trend that can easily be reversed, even if the desire exists.

The withdrawal from East of Suez would probably have come sooner, and with much less agonising, had it not been for the fact that the Labour Government started out with a strong emotional bias in favour of the Commonwealth and an optimistic belief in the future development of United Nations peace-keeping missions. This naïve faith in the effectiveness of the U.N. as a guardian of the peace was first eroded by its unwillingness to act in Vietnam and finally destroyed by its failure to prevent the outbreak of hostilities in the Middle East in June 1967, even though it had troops on the spot. The British Cabinet had its own bold plans for breaking the threatened Arab blockade of Israeli shipping through the Gulf of Aqaba, one of the moves which helped to spark off the conflict. But George Brown, then Foreign Secretary, was unable to mobilise international support for his proposals and they soon collapsed. Many Labour Ministers were surprised at Britain's obvious impotence when the crunch came. They were appalled by U Thant's apparent lethargy and indifference in the days leading up to the first shots in the Six Day War. After the fighting which followed, the Arab defeat and the subsequent rapid Soviet arms build-up in the Middle East, it was hard to summon up enthusiasm for the world organisation as a peace-maker or to believe that Britain could make a meaningful contribution to an international peace force under U.N. supervision. When economic sanctions against Rhodesia were repeatedly breached by member nations and it became painfully evident that Ian Smith's rebel régime could not be brought to its knees by such means, the United Nations' prestige sagged even further.

Scepticism about the value of the Commonwealth as a unifying institution, a forum for debate and a springboard for action, developed over a longer period and was nurtured by a variety of factors. Because of the Attlee Government's action in granting independence to India, Pakistan and Burma, Labour supporters were inclined to look upon the modern Commonwealth as their Party's very own creation. They were suspicious of Conservatives, whom they accused of hankering for the bad old imperial past. They were inclined to forget Macmillan's celebrated 'Wind of Change' speech to the South African Parliament in Cape Town in 1960. They overlooked the achievements of Conservative Colonial Secretaries – especially those of Iain Macleod – in granting independence to Ghana, Malaysia, Cyprus, Nigeria, Sierra Leone, Tanzania, Jamaica, Trinidad and Tobago, Uganda, Kenya, Malawi, Malta and Zambia. Confronted with the inescapable fact that the white settler-dominated Central African Federation was also a Labour creation, they argued that a Labour Government would have acknowledged the mistake earlier and dismantled it faster when the wind of change really began to blow. Pro-Commonwealth feelings played a large part in Hugh Gaitskell's decision to tip the Labour Party against the Macmillan Government's Common Market negotiations in 1962 and Harold Wilson's speeches in the early sixties were full of pious exhortations about the need to expand Commonwealth trade and advice to stop worrying about the marginal advantages to be derived from selling washing machines in Dusseldorf. Dean Acheson's low opinion of the Commonwealth was not widely shared in the Mother Country at the time of his West Point speech. Macmillan in his letter to Lord Chandos testily accused Acheson of misunderstanding its purpose. Critics on the Left, ever wary of American motives, suspected that the United States wanted to get Britain out in order to get U.S. business interests in.

The Commonwealth still had a profound appeal. It was possible to imagine Britain presiding benevolently over an expanding family of nations, an organisation of 800 million people of various creeds, colours, cultures and languages, bound together by historical traditions, economic ties and a common regard for the sanctity of democratic institutions. What this strange conglomerate would do, what positive function it would fulfil, was not always made plain. But it was the kind of vision that stirred the imagination.

The idea of Commonwealth harmony and partnership lost its impetus very slowly. As the club grew larger, so it became more unwieldy. In 1960, there were only ten full members of the Commonwealth. It was dominated by nations of common European ancestry, retaining the atmosphere of a cosy, intimate club. Conversations could be kept confidential, differences discreetly and privately resolved. By the end of 1970, the club had expanded to take in no fewer than thirty-one members and the shape and size of Commonwealth Prime Ministers' meetings had altered. As the pace of decolonisation increased – two or three African, Asian or Caribbean nations becoming independent every year – so the old mystique began to fade. The sense of cohesion vanished. The Commonwealth found itself bedevilled by problems of poverty and race. Prime Ministers' meetings ceased to be the occasion for relaxed exchanges and instead often deteriorated into angry, vituperative debates – with the gory details instantly leaked to the press. There were arguments about South African membership, Britain's bid to join the Common Market and to control immigration, Wilson's failure to deal swiftly and conclusively with Rhodesia's Unilateral Declaration of Independence and Heath's plans to sell arms to South Africa under the Simonstown Agreement.

As criticism of Britain's behaviour grew more strident, so British public opinion was progressively alienated from the Afro-Asian bloc. Observers in Britain had been shocked by the first reports of corruption in Dr Nkrumah's Ghana. They were unhappy at the establishment of authoritarian one-party régimes in newly-independent Commonwealth states. Sir Alec Douglas-Home and the Conservative right wing were furious at what they considered to be the exercise of hypocritical double standards by African and Asian Commonwealth members in casting important pro-Communist, anti-Western votes at the U.N. And they were naturally reluctant to support a campaign of punitive sanctions against Rhodesia or South Africa, which would cost the majority of its Afro-Asian sponsors hardly anything, but might inflict considerable damage on the British economy. All these factors gave rise to doubts about the meaning and value of the Commonwealth.

These misgivings were compounded by the war between India and Pakistan in 1965, when Britain's peace-making efforts were spurned and the two Commonwealth nations turned to an outsider to mediate – the Soviet Union through the person of Prime Minister Kosygin eventually bringing the adversaries together in a peace settlement at Tashkent. Then there were the terrible civil wars in Nigeria and Pakistan – conflicts which stirred consciences and aroused humanitarian feelings in Britain while placing the British Government in a hideously embarrassing situation. One of the main suppliers of arms to Nigeria and of economic aid to Pakistan, it was conspicuously unable to moderate the bloodshed or bring about a quick end to the killing in either tragedy.

The changing pattern of Commonwealth relations and Commonwealth trade played some part in persuading Macmillan to launch Britain's first application to join the E.E.C. in August 1961. But in that year British exports to the Commonwealth (£1302 m.) were still worth almost twice as much as those to the six nations of the European Community (£714 m.). Exports to the Commonwealth were slightly higher than sales to Western Europe as a whole. In the next ten years the underlying trend became much clearer as the tendency to switch markets accelerated: Commonwealth trade increased very sluggishly, while dealings with Europe surged ahead. By the end of 1970, exports to the E.E.C. alone exceeded those to the Commonwealth and the total to Western Europe was almost twice as high. Chastened by the hard experience of actually trying to run the British economy in a hotly competitive world, Wilson began to take a much more favourable view of the marginal advantages and profitability to be gained from the sale of washing machines and other consumer durables in Dusseldorf. Accompanied by George Brown, he completed a tour of Common Market capitals which convinced him that the time for a second application was ripe. In May 1967 the House of Commons approved the decision to apply again by a vote of 488 to 62. But President de Gaulle was unconvinced of Britain's willingness to divest itself of all non-European ties and his second veto was just as brutal, but much swifter, than the first.

The years 1967 and 1968 marked a low point in Britain's fortunes. All the deflationary measures administered by the Government and rescue operations mounted by international bankers were insufficient to prevent devaluation. And yet sterling continued to have a feeble, sickly look about it. With the international monetary system shaken and the pound suffering badly from the rush to buy gold, there were rumours of another big crisis to come. The way into the Common Market was closed – at least so long as de Gaulle was in power. The Suez Canal too was blocked and there was little or no prospect of that being soon reopened. Wilson journeyed hopefully to Moscow, but his talks there made no progress on the main issues. Summitry and Macmillan-style fur-hat diplomacy had gone out of fashion. The idea that Britain could somehow act as a broker between the United States and the Soviet Union – the aspiration so scathingly derided by Dean Acheson – seemed absurd. After his inability to get Vietnam peace talks going during Kosygin's visit to London in February 1967, Wilson must have known in his heart of hearts that he was not about to bring off the 'diplomatic coup of the century' he so coveted. Formerly the most ingenious of super-optimists, he gave up trying to send personal emissaries to Hanoi or patch together special Commonwealth peace missions.

Meanwhile, the Rhodesian rebels were showing unexpected stubbornness and economic sanctions against them were slow to bite. U.D.I. had not turned out to be the nine-day wonder Ian Smith had said it would be. But Wilson's prediction to the Commonwealth Premiers' meeting in Lagos in January 1966 that the rebellion would be ended in weeks rather than months was equally wide of the mark and politically much more embarrassing. The Cabinet was split by a nasty squabble over the rights and wrongs of resuming arms sales to South Africa. Colonel Ojukwu led the breakaway state of Biafra out of the Nigerian Federation and fired the first shots in a civil war which disrupted Nigeria's oil supplies and caused further balance-of-payments headaches for Britain. A Gallup Poll, taken in November 1967, indicated that as many as forty-one per cent of those questioned would like to leave Britain and settle in another country, if only they were free to do so. The proportion of would-be emigrants amongst those aged under thirty-five was particularly striking.

The sixties ended with the nation's morale at a low ebb. Britain had lost its former self-confidence and self-esteem. And yet, in the aftermath of Empire, several outstanding problems demanded urgent attention. One of these was to find an honourable and efficient escape-route from the looming racial conflict in Southern Africa. It was not easy to see a miraculous formula by which Britain could reconcile the insistent demand of white liberals and African Nationalists for unimpeded progress towards majority rule in Rhodesia with the Smith régime's natural desire to hold on to the reins of power and preserve the familiar way of life of a white-dominated society. There was also the dilemma of what to do about South Africa and apartheid. Could Britain go on trading indefinitely with South Africa – its sixth best customer – add to its vast investments there, even sell arms to Prime Minister Vorster and still maintain excellent relations with the rest of black Africa, acting as the host to a multi-racial Common-wealth? When the expected racial explosion in Southern Africa finally came, could Britain contrive to escape unscathed?

In Europe too there were awkward questions waiting to be answered. The Americans were betraying ominous signs of wanting to go home. The Vietnam war had been a traumatic experience. It had undermined the fundamental principles on which the post-war foreign policy of the United States had been based. Now Washington was in a querulous, introspective mood. There was talk of neo-isolationism. President Nixon had tried to counter this by introducing his Vietnamisation policy and by promulgating the Nixon Doctrine. In future, he said, the United States did not intend to get bogged down in costly wars in far-off countries. It would stand by the Atlantic Alliance and honour its commitments to NATO, but it would only help those African and Asian nations that were prepared to help themselves. Nixon's critics were not appeased and soon there were irritable murmurings. If the United States could withdraw from South East Asia, why not begin to pull out from Europe as well? If the defence of Vietnam could be left to the poverty-stricken South Vietnamese, why should the affluent West Europeans not look after Europe? Backing for Senator Mansfield's resolution, calling for substantial troop cuts in Europe, grew appreciably stronger. It began to dawn on many people that the 300,000 Americans would not be kept there indefinitely. Moreover, the general drift of American policy cast grave doubts on the credibility of the United States deterrent, the nuclear umbrella under which Britain and the other NATO nations had sheltered for more than twenty years. Gaullists on both sides of the Channel insisted that the General had been right on this point all along.

Since there was no obvious, short-term remedy for a large-scale Ameri-can withdrawal from Europe, most British policy-makers tended to close their eyes and hope that it would not happen. Occasionally, there was speculation about an Anglo-French nuclear entente, a pooling of resources designed to form the basis for a European deterrent, which would be controlled by Britain and France but held in trust for West Germany and the others until the process of political unity in Europe was complete.

The idea was popular on the Conservative Right and by no means confined to the armchair strategists of the Monday Club. In Opposition, Heath himself flirted with it, but then cautiously drew back. In office, he seemed sceptical. For the lessons contained in the classic speech of the American Defence Secretary, Robert McNamara, at Ann Arbor, Michigan, in June 1962 were as valid as ever. Limited nuclear capabilities – such as those possessed by Britain and France – if operated independently, are 'dangerous, expensive, prone to obsolescence and lacking in credibility'. That, after all, had been the lesson of Blue Streak. In a world of advanced nuclear technology – incredibly complex offensive and defensive missiles such as M.I.R.V.s and A.B.M.s – the nations of Western Europe are far from the superpower league. Britain's forty-eight Polaris missiles and France's force of Mirage bombers is pitifully small when placed alongside the nuclear striking power of the United States and the Soviet Union, which can amass more than 1000 land-based I.C.B.M.s each and almost 900 submarine-launched S.L.B.M.s between them. As far as the European members of NATO are concerned, there can be no quick or easy substitute for the American deterrent.

The 1960s opened with Labour Party propagandists drawing up elaborate international league tables to prove that Britain was slipping behind its nearest industrial rivals in economic growth and increased living standards. The decade ended with the Conservatives publishing updated versions of those same tables to buttress the case for British entry into the E.E.C., a move which was branded by critics as a gesture of despair. But it would be wrong to write off the sixties as a period of unparalleled gloom or unrelieved decline. The picture was not entirely bleak. There were gains as well as losses and not all the losses were to be regretted. Genuine adjustments were made, attitudes altered, illusions abandoned. The process of disengagement from old historical commitments was uncomfortable and ungainly. But it could have been much more exhausting and involved many more disasters than it did. Compared with the disintegration of previous empires and the experience of some of their closest friends and neighbours – the French in Algeria, the Belgians in the Congo, the Americans in Vietnam – the British had things nice and easy. The final break-up of the Central African Federation, inevitably a messy business, was handled with consummate skill by the wily Rab Butler. The military operations against President Sukarno's confrontation campaign in Malaysia were conducted with a rare combination of efficiency and restraint which minimised the dangers of escalation. British troops moved swiftly to protect Kuwait from Iraqi threats and to prevent the governments of the newly-independent East African states from being over-thrown by army mutinies. And they were withdrawn from Aden just in time to save Britain from getting involved in a bloody conflict in a distant land which it could not expect to win.

Although still a member of SEATO and CENTO, organisations for regional security in South East Asia and the Near East, Britain was at last concentrating its military strength much nearer home. In the final years of the Wilson Government, the Prime Minister's closest confidants, when carried away by fits of chauvinistic glory, dropped their former boast that Britain's frontiers were on the Himalayas. Instead, they emphasised the shrinking size of the defence budget – down to only 5·1 per cent of Britain's G.N.P. at the end of Labour's last full year in office. For the first time in the nation's history, a Government was spending more on education than on armaments and defence. And Healey was able to announce with pride that a full twelve months had passed without a single British soldier having been killed on active service overseas as the result of a shot fired in anger – though that was, of course, before the British army became seriously embroiled in Ulster.

The second British application for membership of the E.E.C., submitted by Wilson's Government and carried through by Heath's, differed in one important respect from the original Macmillan initiative in that it had a more pronounced political emphasis. It represented much more than a despairing last-gasp effort to discover the secrets of growth by merging into a wider trading market. The Churchillian concept of the three concentric circles had finally been discarded. The British Government was steeling itself to make the choice that Macmillan had hoped he could avoid. But the process of conversion was not complete. Even the most ardent of the pro-Marketeers could not make up their minds about the nature of the community they expected to join – whether it would be a loosely co-ordinated confederation of states or a closely integrated, nascent superpower. In addition, the great mass of the British electorate had not been conclusively won over.

Throughout the sixties, public opinion had oscillated wildly in its enthusiasm for the Common Market. Its faith in Europe had burned brightest when actual membership of the E.E.C. seemed least attainable – in March 1965, when the formidable figure of de Gaulle barred the way, 57 per cent of those questioned by the Gallup Poll were reported to be in favour, but in January 1971, when the road was almost clear, only 22 per cent approved. In the meantime, the British Government had made many of the changes demanded by the General. It had made them either voluntarily or through the pressure of events – in spite of, rather then because of, de Gaulle's arguments. But the nation as a whole was not emotionally committed to Europe. It did not feel comfortably European or share its leader's own shining vision of its future inside an expanded European community. Many of the old barriers to closer unity with the Continent remained. Britain's long standing identity crisis had moved nearer a solution. But it was not yet over.

4 Industry and Technology

VICTOR KEEGAN

The Labour Party's sudden discovery of technology, forged in the white heat of Harold Wilson's speech to the 1963 Party Conference at Scarborough, had a double significance for the politics of the sixties. Not only did it set Labour on the path back to power; it also heralded a style of Government interventionism quite new in British politics.

Almost overnight, the speech injected a new sense of purpose into a Labour Party all too willing to seize on such an uncontroversial issue after the internecine struggles over the H-bomb and whether to drop the dogmatic Clause Four approach to nationalisation from its Constitution.

The inspired rhetoric of the speech captured the headlines and seduced the nation. Here, it seemed, was an ideal which rose above the trivia of political slogans.

Wilson had managed to satisfy the passions of the diehard nationalisers and the pragmatic ideals of those, nurtured on the political philosophies of Anthony Crosland, who were content for a future Labour Government to control but not necessarily own the 'commanding heights' of the economy.

An unashamed admirer of the way Harold Macmillan had led the Conservative Party away from the philosophy of the Suez invasion while waving the Suez banner, Wilson was doing something similar himself. The party could now march under the banner of technological intervention as the memories of Clause Four, which at one point nearly wrecked the party, receded more and more into distant memory.

Wilson told a mesmerised audience scientific horror stories of computers doing calculations in three millionths of a second, but already superseded by machines 1000 times as fast. If there had never been a case for Socialism before, automation would have created it, he said, and added:

It is a choice between the blind imposition of technological advance, with all that means in terms of unemployment, and the conscious, planned purposive use of scientific progress to provide undreamed of living standards and the possibility of leisure ultimately on an unbelievable scale.

If, in retrospect, the Scarborough speech is seen to be a clear case of 'oversell', there is no doubt that it marked the start of a new era of intervention in politics and gave Harold Wilson the claim to have been the first British Prime Minister to harness technology to the winning of an election.

In Labour's plan, public ownership, either by itself or in partnership with private industry, was to be used to develop science-based industries to reduce imports and, in Wilson's words to avoid 'a mass sell-out to foreign concerns'.

However, despite the popular impression, the return to power of a Labour Government in 1964 did not mark a sharp change from 'laissez faire' to increased Government intervention in the technology industries. Although Government involvement in industry undoubtedly increased under Labour, Wilson's 'planned, purposive use of scientific progress' was not a new discovery: it reflected what was beginning to happen already as a result of a changed public attitude to planning.

In other sectors of the economy this was apparent in the creation by the Conservatives of such bodies as the National Economic Development Council, an initiative of Selwyn Lloyd, and the National Incomes Commission. In science and technology the new approach could be seen in a more critical attitude to research and development spending. This involved a drift away from 'matching grants', a system in which the Government matched spending made by industry, but had little control over the industries which took advantage of the service, to more discriminatory ways of handing out public funds.

As Lewis Gunn has pointed out [in *The Impact of Technology*, edited by J. N. Wolfe (London, 1971)], matching grants were unrelated to national needs and were thinly spread over too wide a front. They tended to increase the gap between innovative industries and the rest, yet made it impossible to discriminate in favour of particular industries which contributed to the balance of payments or which helped applied rather than basic research.

Under Lord Hailsham, the first Minister for Science, the last years of Conservative Government saw a pronounced increase in Government intervention to control the direction of funds channelled into companies for the benefit of technology. Research associations were promised a shake-up to bring their research closer to the needs of industry (this was a constant if unsuccessful theme throughout the sixties) and the Government started handing out 'earmarked' grants and contracts, enabling it to concentrate resources on selected industries and objectives.

Even Government action on the four 'bridgehead' industries (machine tools, computers, telecommunications and electronics) which were singled out for special development by Labour can be traced back to the previous Government.

The first big discriminatory contracts for financing research (in 1961; for computers and machine tools) were hailed by Lord Hailsham as 'a major breakthrough in the relationships between Government and industry in the encouragement of science'.

Labour, in opposition, promised a speeding-up of this process, and in his Scarborough speech in 1963 Wilson looked to the day when contract research might lead to 'some new breakthrough in marine propulsion, in aircraft guidance, in transport, in electronics, in agriculture or textile machinery'.

Perhaps the most extraordinary feature of policies on technology in the sixties was the contrast between the wide agreement among political parties and commentators on what was wrong, and their inability to translate this into effective action.

Most people agreed that Britain needed to concentrate her research and development effort – which was thinly spread over the entire range of technological development – into selected fields with a proven potential. Yet the obviousness of the problem did not make a solution any less difficult to find.

Secondly, there was general agreement that research in Government laboratories must be brought nearer the market place – as had happened in the United States – in order to make it more cost-effective and less geared to prestige projects with no more commercial potential than a back room in the Science Museum.

As early as 1959, a Select Committee of the House of Commons urged that industry be brought into closer contact with the work of the Atomic Energy Authority and in 1966 Professor Patrick Blackett, Scientific Adviser to the Labour Government, warned that Britain had made a strategic mistake after the war when (largely through mistrust of the ability of industrial management) it placed the main emphasis of research policies on Government laboratories, instead of adopting the American approach of contracting research to industries.

Britain's reluctance throughout the decade to give up her painful effort to compete in every major area of advanced technology may best be explained perhaps as a psychological need by the British people to maintain a technological empire at a time when her colonies were disappearing and her traditional diplomatic influence in the world was in decline. But, whatever the reason, Britain entered the sixties as a technological conglomerate maintaining, or trying to maintain, a total capability in everything from aerospace and nuclear power to computers and electronics, not to mention the enormous resources devoted to defence. By contrast, Japan was purposively selecting a few industries known for their growth potential, like electronics, motor vehicles and steel, pouring funds into them through a partnership of industrial and governmental interests and not losing any sleep over the fact that the basic knowhow was purchased from abroad and not home-grown.

Christopher Layton has noted [*European Advanced Technology* (P.E.P., 1969) p. 53] that if in the nine years to 1964 all the defence projects entered into by the British Government had proceeded, they would have absorbed double the R and D (research and development) funds actually available.

The result of this clash between proud ends and limited means was a predictable series of cancellations. The history of the first half of the sixties is littered with jettisoned projects ranging from Blue Streak (at a cost of £84 m.) and the Skybolt air-to-surface missile (£27 m.) to the T.S.R.-2, killed by Labour in 1965 after £195 m. had been spent.

Outside the defence field, the decade appeared full of promise for British technology. In 1959, although the Russians photographed the far side of the moon, Britain's effort still looked enviable: in that year the world's most advanced fast breeder reactor at Dounreay, went critical; a new British invention, the Hovercraft, was tested for the first time; Alastair Pilkington invented the revolutionary 'float glass' technique; the Rolls-Royce 'Flying Bedstead', out of which vertical take-off planes sprang, was demonstrated at Farnborough; Dr Barnes Wallis was toying with the idea of variable geometry aircraft; and the proposed supersonic aircraft was beginning to look more than a π in the sky.

Of these, only the float glass principle has proved an outstanding commercial success so far. It was also incidentally the only case where the research and development was done very close to the 'market'.

Also, at the beginning of the decade, Britain had – according to research by the National Economic Development Office – a not unfavourable 'product profile': that is to say, she had strength in sectors, like chemicals and advanced engineering, in which world trade was growing fastest. But as the decade progressed she developed weaknesses in just these important areas where world trade was accelerating. If recent trends were to continue, the N.E.D.O. paper added, Britain would by the mid-seventies have one of the worst product profiles of any industrialised country.

Britain's problems in the sixties cannot be divorced from a European context. A report by the Organisation for Economic Co-operation and

Development in 1967 showed that the United States spent six times as much as the E.E.C. on research and development and three times as much as Western Europe. What is more, it found that the U.S. got better value for money by devoting it to definite ends while European countries spread their effort too thinly and lost far too much of it in stillborn projects like the T.S.R.-2 and a number of joint projects which became too expensive to maintain.

The report supported the view that the technological gap between Europe and the U.S. was most pronounced in those industries – space, aviation, computers etc. – where R and D effort was much greater in the States, Where R and D spending was more comparable, as in steel, textiles and machine tools, there was no such equivalent gap. But such gaps as there were seemed all the more alarming because they were concentrated in the growth industries.

What made the situation tragic, from a European point of view, was the number of different countries which were duplicating each others' work, yet whose individual contributions were woefully inadequate. The whole of Europe was spending less than a third as much as the U.S. on R and D yet this feeble effort was squandered among eighteen competing administrations.

Consider. In computers, the fastest-growing sector of science-based industries – which is dominated by the American giant I.B.M., with over 70 per cent of the world market – Britain, France, Holland and Germany were each pushing ahead with their own nationalistic efforts. In the development of fast breeder reactors, a rare area in which Britain and Europe can claim a technological lead, the story is similar. While the American Atomic Energy Commission was systematically building up a capability to be ready for large-scale development, Europe was dissipating its resources through an unnecessary triplication of effort as Britain, France and Germany tried to steal a marginal lead on one another. In 1962, during the first Common Market talks, Britain, while offering Dounreay as a common research centre for Europe, chauvinistically insisted that construction of a fast breeder prototype must remain an independent commercial matter. By the end of the decade Britain was still proceeding alone with the development of the fast breeder and, for the record, had not sold a single conventional nuclear power station abroad during the whole of the ten years.

This is not to say, of course, that co-operation with Europe was the only means of salvation. Far from it. But in so far as Britain's problem during the sixties was recognised to be a choice between 'going it alone' in a few selected fields or maintaining a full capability in partnership with others, Europe offered the nearest reservoir of duplicated resources.

The Labour Party certainly came to power with ideas of developing specific areas where Government spending on technology should be concentrated. In a speech in January 1964 Wilson promised that any Labour Government would work out in detail 'all those imports which rise sharply when production increases. The next job would be to discuss with industry, providing research and development contracts where necessary, the prospects of developing home-produced substitutes.

All this was seen as part of a grandiose National Plan in which the mandarins of Whitehall would set each industry a target and tell it what help it could expect from the Government. The National Plan, of course, was stillborn and quietly buried. But what success did the Government have in its attempts to help industry?

Curiously, in the early years, there was little difference in the number of discriminatory grants given to industry. Writing in the journal *Minerva* at the end of 1967, Lewis Gunn noted that spending on earmarked grants and development contracts did not show a marked increase over the early sixties and hardly constituted the promised 'major breakthrough in the relationships between government and industry'. However, this partly reflected the lack of power which the newly-created Ministry of Technology had in the Cabinet against the Treasury (the balance was to alter in later years) and also the fact that other vehicles for Government help were found.

In fact, as the years progressed, the promised intervention materialised on a massive scale. Whether acting directly through Ministries (using funds provided by the Industrial Expansion Act) or at arm's length through the Industrial Reorganisation Corporation, the Government left no industry unturned in its Wilsonian quest to 'drag firms kicking and screaming into the twentieth century'.

It is difficult to assess the success of 'import substitution' policies as such because, in a sense, any strengthening of Britain's efficiency removes the scope for imports – so any successful policy could be regarded as replacing imports. Also, progress in identifying those sectors where there was a high propensity to import was held up by the need to introduce special legislation to obtain the information from customs sheets – which the Board of Trade regarded as confidential. Nevertheless, certain projects stand out. These include an I.R.C. loan to establish a de-inking plant so that waste paper could be 're-cycled' instead of buying expensive Scandinavian pulp; an attempt by Skefko, the Swedish ball bearing group, to spread its wings was thwarted by a controversial move by the I.R.C. to establish a stronger British capability by merging the remaining British companies. A similar move established a stronger British unit in compressed air technology. Half a dozen similar examples could be quoted.

Import substitution undoubtedly reached its zenith with the successful implementation of an idea thrown up by Wilson at the 1967 Labour Party Conference for the construction of three aluminium smelters in development areas in Britain which were expected to save £50 m. for the balance of payments. Construction of these smelters depended on the availability of 40 per cent investment grants and long-term contracts for cheap electricity.

It was freely admitted by the companies later that they would never have been built under the Conservative administration once investment grants had been abolished. Rival companies claimed that the smelters worsened the glut in the world aluminium market. Other important areas of import substitution were the encouragement of natural gas and oil exploration in the North Sea and the help given to mineral explorers, which turned Britain into one of the most attractive places in the world (from the point of view of financial inducements) for mining, with considerable promise for the future. The balance of payments advantages of these moves was left for a Conservative Government to reap.

The four 'bridgehead' industries were left in a stronger position in 1970 than they had been in six years before, as a result of Government intervention. But there remained serious reservations. The micro-electronics industry was given £5 m. in a research grant (repayable out of future sales), yet there was little sign that the three British companies involved would link up into stronger units in the face of intense American competition. Steps were taken to break the cartel of telecommunications manufacturers by introducing more competition, but limited success in encouraging new methods and organisation in machine tools did not prevent that industry from going through a serious crisis in 1971–2.

The outstanding success in terms of Government intervention – at least in the short term – was the computer industry. It was the most complete example of the Government selecting a growth area and pumping in funds (over £20 m.) to make it viable. People will long argue over whether the methods chosen were right, but few will deny that the present shape, indeed the very existence of a big computer industry in the shape of International Computers was a direct consequence of purposive intervention: I.C.L. was Wilson's White Heat incarnate.

On Labour's accession Britain's three remaining computer companies, led by I.C.T., were struggling for control of the British market, growing then at the rate of 25 per cent a year, in what appeared to be the last stand of independent companies against the Divine Right of the Americans to make these machines. On three separate occasions, the Government helped to save I.C.T. from collapse. In the spring of 1965, £4 m. was given by Mintech through the National Research Development Corporation, which committed the Government to a British solution of the problem of U.S. dominance of the industry. In contrast, the previous Conservative administration had given not one penny to the company. The Government helped to resolve a second crisis in the middle of 1967 when loans of £50 m. were raised in the City to finance the upsurge in demand for leasing I.C.T.'s computers.

Finally, in 1968, the Government persuaded I.C.T. to take over the computer interests of English Electric (which by now included Elliott Automation as a result of a separate I.R.C. initiative). The Labour Government must stand praised or blamed for whatever happens in future to I.C.L. (as the new group was called), since the final solution was entirely its own. It included giving £17 m. of public money to I.C.L. in 1968, partly in the form of an unrepayable grant and partly in exchange for 10 per cent of its shares. The Government also persuaded Plessey not to bid for the company.

By the middle of 1971, I.C.L. had annual sales of £130 m. with a small but improving profit record. A question mark hung over its future since it depends on whether it can forge a new generation of machines out of the basically incompatible technologies of the English Electric and I.C.T. ranges of computers. Until that is resolved no final judgement can be made. In the meantime it can be said that the company, with 40 per cent of the British market, has been given the confidence of survival and a healthy export order book. Britain still remains the only country in the world where the American giants, led by I.B.M., have not swept all before them. I.C.L.'s biggest achievement, admittedly helped by Government procurement contracts, is that it is still here at all with a fighting chance of success for the future. It was the Labour Government's most overtly successful intervention and Government support was maintained by the Conservatives, though in a less obvious manner.

In other areas of technological development, the Government was also active. Steel was ritualistically nationalised. The I.R.C. sanctioned the take-over by the well-managed G.E.C. electrical engineering complex firstly of A.E.I., which had run into difficulties, and then of English Electric (except its computer interests). Considerable rationalisation then took place, and the new group, by far the biggest of its kind in Britain, is almost certainly stronger than the sum of its constituent parts would have been in the absence of the mergers. The new British Leyland company, formed on Government initiative from B.M.C. and Leyland, is also stronger than it would be otherwise from the point of view of its contribution to the balance of payments though there remain serious problems to be overcome.

In nuclear power, the number of consortia was reduced from three to two, with the Atomic Energy Authority having a closer industrial involvement. This, broadly speaking, had the support of the industry and the Central Electricity Generating Board and would probably have happened in much the same way under a Conservative administration.

By the end of the decade the British nuclear industry, which had tied up some of the most brilliant manpower resources in the country (the A.E.A. employed 40,000 employees against 6000 in its, admittedly somewhat different, American equivalent) had not fulfilled the hopes of the early sixties. The big breakthrough into an undisputed commercial advantage over oil-fired power stations had proved as elusive as selling any more nuclear stations abroad.

As the Ministry of Technology, under its effervescent Minister, Anthony Wedgwood Benn, acquired sponsorship for more and more industries, including engineering, motor vehicles and fuel and power, its influence in the Cabinet grew, though some would say that by the end of Labour's term its portfolio of industries had grown to unmanageable proportions.

Besides its considerable role in restructuring industry, Mintech was also developing new strengths in other directions. It began a process of 'interrogating' international companies over their power to influence Britain's balance of payments by adroit changes in the price at which their subsidiaries sold components to each other. At the same time the Ministry was experimenting with new techniques of costing high-risk projects. It was freely admitted that application of such techniques would have killed the Concorde at birth.

Mintech could also claim success in moving resources away from defence and aerospace towards bread-and-butter export industries and in shifting research nearer to industry. Figures prepared by the Ministry show that whereas in 1966 the amount of civil research done on Government account ('intra-mural') at £75 m. was roughly equal to that done extra-murally, by 1969 extra-mural research had shot ahead to nearly £125 m., while intra-mural research had hardly increased over the 1966 level.

Over the same period, Mintech spending on R and D for defence was reduced from about £235 m. to less than £200 m. while expenditure on civil R and D rose from £150 m. to £200 m., overtaking defence spending.

The aircraft industry also achieved substantial reorientation with the proportion of output going to the military reduced from 76 per cent in 1964 to 57 per cent in 1968 on an increased turnover. Exports increased from 17 per cent to 31 per cent of output.

Part of the credit for this change of policy must go to Mintech; but it was also partly dictated by the imperatives of the situation. The reduction in defence spending was partly enforced by circumstances – too many projects chasing too little money with the result that many of them more or less cancelled themselves. A reduction in military orders naturally sent the aircraft industry scampering after export orders – with a considerable degree of success.

Plans were afoot, when the election intervened, to forge closer links with industry by allowing all R and D for industry to be carried out under contract to organisations or firms which could make use of the results for the benefit of the country. A Green Paper proposing the merging of some of the Atomic Energy Authority establishments and the National Research Development Corporation into an industrial R and D corporation which would develop closer working relationships with industry was published in 1970. The new body, to be called British Research and Development Corporation, was the implementation of an idea popularised by the Fulton Report, which the Conservatives were to take up with great gusto – 'hiving off'.

Yet for all this, progress towards solving the two major problems – moving research closer to industry, and concentrating the national technological effort in selected areas with a proven 'payoff' – was still surprisingly slow. The fact that three different official reports at the end of the decade – those of the Central Advisory Council for Science and Technology (1968) and the Science Research Council (1970), and the proposal for the B.R.D.C. itself (1970) – should emphasise these points shows how difficult the problem was to resolve, in spite of the wide agreement on a diagnosis of what was wrong.

Labour can certainly point to the substantial progress made in shifting resources away from aircraft and into areas like computers. But equally surely it must admit that the basic problem inherited in 1964 remained unsolved.

Britain was too small to support such a vast array of advanced projects by herself. Something had to give, as the subsequent collapse of Rolls-

Royce – for financial rather than technological reasons – in 1971 proved only too well.

Towards the end of Labour's period of office, it was possible to detect signs of disengagement, or at the very least a swing away from the thoroughgoing interventionism of the first five years. Mintech was less active, whether burdened down by the weight of all its new departmental responsibilities or simply running out of steam and ideas, it is not clear. The Ministry was perhaps also affected by a reaction in the public mood against the 'merger mania' of the previous few years. Both in America and in Britain, there was increasing questioning of the benefits of certain kinds of mergers and growing scepticism among academics about the supposed benefits of economies of scale. An iconoclastic book by Gerald Newbould of Liverpool University, *Management and Merger Activity*, demonstrated, on the basis of evidence gleaned from questionnaires sent to companies, that surprisingly few took the right action to rationalise their activities after mergers which all too often were entered into without sufficient thought and for defensive reasons. The point was not lost in Whitehall.

By this time the Industrial Reorganisation Corporation had already shifted the emphasis away from mergers towards lending money for investment projects where there was good scope for productivity improvements or balance of payment gains. In 1970 its chairman, Charles Villiers, had bluntly told the annual dinner of the Machine Tool Trades Association that they had merged enough and that the future lay in product rationalisation. In this context the proposed British Research and Development Corporation also involved a measure of disengagement from the management of research projects.

At the same time the Conservatives, who had moved sharply away from the pragmatic planning of the Macmillan administration, were pursuing new policies, proclaiming a more radical disengagement of Government from industry and especially from nationalised industries.

It was thus both surprising and ironical that, in its first year of office, while loudly proclaiming ideals of disengagement, the Conservative Government achieved a degree of intervention which was the envy of the Socialist Opposition. In less than twelve months they had nationalised Rolls-Royce without compensation (which no Labour Government would have dared to do), taken over management charge of Harland and Wolff, the troubled Belfast shipyard, effectively increased the Government shareholding in Upper Clyde Shipbuilders (which later went bankrupt) to 75 per cent through a scheme involving increased dividend entitlement, sacked the chairman of the Post Office, intervened to keep prices and wages down in the public sector and virtually taken charge of the management of the British Steel Corporation for several months.

In May 1972, they astonished even their own supporters by introducing the Industry Bill, which gave the Secretary of State for Trade and Industry discretionary power to spend up to £550 m. to help companies in difficulties. The Government had clearly come a long way from the 'let lame ducks die' approach of its early days.

To Conservatives, this marked an unavoidable bout of interventionism to correct the mistakes of the last administration before disengagement proper. However, cynics on both the Right and the Left, believing that industrial policies are as much determined by the imperative of events as the small print of party manifestos, could be forgiven for thinking, at least in 1971: 'Plus ça change, plus c'est la même chose'.

FURTHER READING

1. Christopher Layton, *European Advanced Technology* (P.E.P., 1969).
2. Lewis Gunn, in 'Impact of Technology', ed. J. N. Wolfe.
3. Gerald Newbould, *Management and Merger Activity* (Liverpool: Guthstead Ltd).
4. Anthony Crosland, *The Future of Socialism* (1956).
5. Paul Foot, *The Politics of Harold Wilson* (Penguin).

5 Social Welfare and Housing

ANNE LAPPING

Britain has never quite achieved its welfare state. A fair amount of foundation-laying and construction work was done by the 1945 Labour Government, but little further progress was made in the 1950s. During the sixties the half-built edifice became the victim of persistent sniping although no major frontal attack was mounted against the social services.

In fact, at the beginning of the sixties the Conservatives appeared to be trying to make amends for previous neglect. It was generally accepted that a modern industrial society had, among its other duties, an obligation to provide for the young, the sick, the old and the poor. This view was thought to be so widely held that few people bothered to say it any more. Indeed, such principled statements were thoroughly out of fashion. And even those who wanted on moral grounds to expand the welfare state used the language of profit-maximising economists to avoid the charge of soft-centredness. One did not say: 'Local authorities ought to be able to give cash to families if it will prevent the misery of separating children from their parents . . .'; but instead: 'It's cheaper to help the family now than to take the children into care at $£x$ a week later'. Towards the end of the decade, the moral argument was raised anew, and in a more compelling form. Whereas the old and slightly embarrassing (and therefore disused) line had been 'We have a duty to do this for them', the new moral argument stated: 'The disadvantaged have claims against the community'. And what was more, the poor began to say this for themselves.

During the decade, spending on the social services grew at a faster rate than the economy. In 1960, current spending on the social services was 7·4[1] per cent of gross national product; by 1968, it had risen to 9·2 per cent and was still going up. In addition capital spending on social services (including public housing) rose from 1·9 per cent to 3·5 per cent of Gross National Product over the period. (These figures include spending on education, which is dealt with in more detail in Brian MacArthur's essay.)

In face of the pressures for expansion these figures can be understood only as a minimum response.

Behind the sniping was the feeling that the welfare state represented an alarmingly open-ended commitment. There was evidence of this to be garnered from the history of existing services. Lord Beveridge's assumption that national assistance would be a tide-over phenomenon till his social security scheme got off the ground, and Aneurin Bevan's confident pronouncement about the levelling out and probable decline in costs of the health service had become sick jokes. And it was easy to see, in just two of the measures introduced early in the sixties by the Conservatives, that the pattern of rising costs was to be repeated. In 1959, the Mental Health Act, with its emphasis on voluntary rather than compulsory admissions to hospital and on 'community care' rather than incarceration in ancient, isolated mental institutions, led to a reduction in the number of long-stay patients, an increase in the number of patients returning to hospital for short periods and to more outpatient treatment. These people all now needed help outside hospital. But a benign policy of 'community care' became for some an individual or family burden because, by the end of the sixties, there were still not as many staff as had been thought necessary to do the job when the Act was passed. Similarly, the Children and Young Persons Act 1963, which obliged local authorities to try to prevent the break-up of families, was not used as constructively as it might have been because of lack of funds. Both these services could have been money-gobblers.

While each progressive piece of welfare legislation opened the way for a series of hungry demands, the ratio of dependents to workers had been increasing for decades (and is likely to continue to do so in the seventies). In 1941, the number of children and retired people per 1,000 workers had been 488; by 1969 the figure was 655.[2] In short, the number of people using social services grew faster than the number financing and manning them. At the same time people expected more of their social services. They wanted to be healthier. The number of patients treated in hospital rose faster than the population. Greater numbers were staying on for education beyond the legal minimum. There was a demand for more housing as couples married younger and bachelors and spinsters wanted individual nests. And professionals working in the labour-intensive health and social work services wanted more equipment and handmaidens to satisfy their clients' and their own legitimate aspirations. They were also beginning to question whether the fragmented administrative structures in which they worked would ever enable them to provide comprehensive services. The structure of the health service was the result of a forced compromise. And the social work services had all grown up like caricatures of only children; isolated, self-conscious, and co-operating with difficulty.

The major trends in social services in the sixties were responses to these pressures.

Towards selectivity
The move away from Lord Beveridge's proposals and the drift towards selectivity in social security and income maintenance programmes shows how far wrong even a great and cautious planner can go. The task of a social security system is to provide an acceptable standard of living for individuals or households whose earnings have been interrupted or are inadequate. The wage-earner who is sick or unemployed or retired relies on the social security system. So does the widowed, single, divorced or abandoned mother; and the family whose income does not match its size. William Beveridge, on whose report the British welfare state was based, proposed a scheme for dealing with these eventualities. The essence of the plan was that the state should provide flat-rate subsistence-level benefits for those who had paid flat-rate contributions. Separate insurance schemes against unemployment and sickness, old age and widowhood were replaced by a unified, and, with a few exceptions, compulsory scheme. Anyone who wanted to ensure himself more than a subsistence income in times of misfortune had to make his own arrangements. Beveridge thought that, with a government committed to full employment, a comprehensive social security system, a national health service and an allowance for all but the first child (everyone was thought to be able to afford one child without help) poverty might be eradicated in post-war Britain. There was an additional safety net. For what he hoped would be an interim period, Beveridge recommended setting up a National Assistance Board to make cash payments on a means test to people who had somehow or other slipped through the main system. By 1948, all these proposals were in force (though some of the benefits were not paid at as high a rate as Beveridge had intended).

What went wrong at once has remained wrong ever since. And in trying to solve the difficulties one by one, successive Governments moved further and further away from Beveridge's original conception. The post-war Labour Government planned a once-and-for-all rise in pension rates. But by the time it was introduced, national assistance had already gone up, and a pension income remained lower than a national assistance income. As national assistance was supposed to be the ultimate safeguard, and as it was geared to what the Government considered to be the minimum required to live on, it was clear that old people who relied solely on their pensions were living below the poverty line. The same was true of others receiving flat-rate benefits.

The assistance board, it might have been said, rather than national insurance, had become the support of the old. But that was not true either, for a large proportion of pensioners have always failed to claim assistance. The 1964–70 Labour government tried to get round this by standing Beveridge on his head. Instead of abolishing the National Assistance Board, they tried to write national assistance into the conventional social security system. This followed an official inquiry in 1965[3] which showed that over 700,000 pensioner households who were eligible for assistance were not applying for it. In 1966, the Government transmogrified the National Assistance Board into the Supplementary Benefits Commission and merged it with the Ministry of Pensions to form the new Ministry of Social Security. And in the Act they referred to people's *entitlement* to the new benefit. At first it looked as though the move was successful. In 1969, the total numbers claiming supplementary benefit were up by 30 per cent. Unfortunately it has since been shown that between a half and two-thirds of this increase can be accounted for by increases in rates at the time (higher rates meant that more people were poor enough to be eligible). Three-quarters of the 700,000 formerly not claiming their benefit probably continued not to claim.[4]

It was during the fifties that Beveridge's pension scheme ran itself into difficulties. The proportion of old people was growing, and while Beveridge had envisaged that after twenty years or so the Exchequer would be paying half the cost of pensions, no Government wanted to impose this on taxpayers. They thought contributions ought to cover what was, after all, an insurance scheme. It also became politically necessary to increase pensions in line with the rising incomes of people at work; but this was made difficult by the need to keep down the flat-rate contributions at a level the lower paid could afford. Any new pensions proposal had to provide for the low-paid a retirement income sufficient without recourse to assistance. And in order to stop pensioners falling back into relative poverty pensions had to be linked to rises in earnings.

In 1957 the Labour Party published a scheme, *National Superannuation*, which was later partly pirated by the Conservatives, and then largely abandoned by Labour itself in office. Labour proposed that the existing flat-rate national insurance contribution should be the foundation for a larger wage-related pension, the two portions adding up to roughly half pay on retirement to the average wage earner, and a lower proportion to those with above average earnings. The scheme, financed by wage-related contributions, would provide pensioners with a standard of living related to that of their working lives. The new principle was introduced of considering pensions as deferred wages, thus legitimising maintaining differences in income after retirement (though the scheme involved some redistribution).

The 1957 Labour scheme was designed to supplant many of the private occupational pensions schemes that had grown up. Yet one of the main aims of the Conservative graduated pension scheme, in April 1961, was to encourage the private sector (see p. 155). The Conservatives' first object in introducing graduated contributions was to raise more money for the increasingly hard-up national insurance fund. Without going into details, one did not have to be an actuary to see that the Conservative pensions scheme gave less value to its contributors than Labour's. But the theoretical breakthrough – abandoning Beveridge's flat-rate contribution and relating the size of the state pension to former earnings – was important.

In 1966, Labour followed up the Conservatives' graduated pensions scheme with earnings-related benefits for unemployment, sickness, industrial injuries and widowhood. And in 1968, flat-rate family allowances too were replaced by an earnings-related scheme. In the summer of 1966, the Ministry of Social Security had carried out a survey which showed that out of seven million families with children in Great Britain, half a million, with about 1¼ million children, had incomes below the new supplementary benefits rates which were to be introduced later that year.[5] Roughly 160,000 of the poorest of this group, with half a million children, could not be brought up to supplementary benefit level. The fathers were either in full-time, low-paid work – which meant they were ineligible for supplementary benefit – or they were out of work but not able to receive the full supplementary benefit because of the 'wage stop' regulation (which ensures that no one will be better off unemployed than he is at work). It was clear that the only way these families could be helped was by a substantial increase in family allowances, for which the newly formed Child Poverty Action Group had been pressuring since 1965. But an increase in family allowances for all would have been impossibly expensive. So the Group devised a new gambit for the Government called 'clawback'. For the second and each subsequent child the allowance was raised by 10s, but at the same time all families paying tax at the standard rate paid back the 10s in tax (with graduated payments for those earning not quite enough to pay the full tax rate). The benefit was dished out on a universal basis, but the 'clawback' ensured that it benefited, selectively, only those who needed it most.

It is clear that the basic social security structure had never succeeded in supporting most poor people. These were (and still are for that matter) the long-term unemployed (whose earnings-related benefits cease after six months), the chronic sick and disabled, fatherless families, the elderly and low-paid wage earners and their families. During the sixties it was argued that we should be more selective in the help we gave, concentrating on the poor. And in fact before and during the intellectual debates on the subject in the sixties means tests were becoming more important and means-tested benefits, as a proportion of social security payments, were going up. In 1968 there were either 1386 or 1733 different means tests, depending on the strictness of your definition.[6] Among the most recently added were differential rent schemes run by local authorities, rate rebates, and means-tested schemes for the supply of contraceptives under the Family Planning Act; and the reintroduction of prescription charges in January 1968 brought with it a means test in the shape of exemptions for some categories of patients. So it looks as though the selectivists had won. But there are a number of difficulties connected with these selective benefits (in contrast with the selective clawback system for family allowances) that undermine their stated aim. Many people who are entitled to collect means-tested benefits fail to do so for a variety of reasons (ignorance, shame, the benefit not being worth the form-filling). This failure to reach all who are eligible is a gain if means tests are thought of cynically as a money-saving. But if the objective is to help those in need it is a symptom of inefficiency. Another drawback of the means test is the difficulty of telling whether you have reached all those eligible – assuming you want to. And, finally the multiplicity of schemes, their differing standards of eligibility and the lack of relationship between them, can mean that a small rise in a family's earnings will lead to a disproportionate fall in the benefits it receives.

Peter Kaim-Caudle, in the Fabian booklet *Social Services for all?* (September 1968), gives this example:

According to the Rent Rebate scheme advocated in the Ministry of Housing and Local Government circular 46/7, a married couple with three children living in a house which has a standard rent of 55s per week and a minimum rent of 15s would lose 3s 4d rent rebate for each £1 by which their income rises between £11 and £16, and 5s for every £1 of income between £16 and £20. The same man, if his local rates come to £30 15s for six months, would lose 5s rates rebate for each £1 by which his income rises between £14 10s and £18 10s. When his earnings exceed about £15 10s his children will lose their free school meals. If they continue to take them, which is most unlikely, this will increase his expenditure by 15s a week. On top of all this, he will have to pay 11½d in the £ graduated pension contribution for each £ earned between £9 and £18. To sum up, this man, if his earnings increase from £15 to £18 will lose 15s worth of school meals, 13s 4d in rent rebate, 15s in rate rebate, and will have to pay an additional 2s 10d in graduated contributions, a total of 46s 2d in 60s, say 15s 4d in the pound.

And some wage-earners, if they could work it out, might realise that they have no financial reason to carry on working.

Proponents of the most comprehensive form of selectivity – negative income tax – exercised great ingenuity in trying to get round this 'disincentive problem' as it is called. The nub of the negative income tax proposal is the amalgamation of income tax and social security so that people with low incomes can draw money out, just as people with incomes above the specified level pay over a proportion of their earnings in taxes of various kinds. The variations[7] on this theme are numerous. But as well as the question of tapering allowances in such a way as not to discourage people from working, there are other problems. How can the system be made flexible enough to respond to short-term fluctuations in income – a notorious characteristic of those living in poverty – without frequently subjecting them to those same means tests which it is the object of the operation to get rid of? In the sixties the Treasury and the Inland Revenue settled the argument. They said negative income tax was impracticable – for one thing most of the poor were not in the tax system anyway. But the notion lingers on. And it is certainly true that such a comprehensive system would do away with the many little bureaucracies against which the welfare rights groups of the sixties were trying their strength – with some success.

Encouraging the private sector
Perhaps the most noticeable sniping against the welfare state in the 1960s came from enthusiasts for the market economy. Why, they asked, shouldn't people pay directly for their own pensions, housing, medical treatment and so on? The 1961 graduated pensions scheme was tailored to encourage private occupational pensions. And it succeeded. Over 900,000 employees were covered for the first time in the year following the Act, many in schemes newly planned to make use of the Act's provisions for

contracting out.[8] Over the period the numbers covered by occupational schemes rose from eight million in 1956 to over twelve million in 1967. By the time the Labour Government came to publish its long gestated National Superannuation Plan in January 1969[9] it, too, had developed an amiable attitude towards the private sector, despite the fact that occupational pension schemes showed no signs of being able to provide what the national scheme had to offer. They did not offer transferability or protection against inflation; they could not guarantee real pension increases after retirement; they gave no hope of a better deal for the lower-paid worker.

Nonetheless, the Government bent over backwards to encourage occupational pensions schemes because of the economic importance of the investment finance which they provided. In the event, the pensions Bill reached the end of its committee stage in parliament on the day the 1970 General Election was announced. So that was that for wage-related, inflation-proof pensions, a better deal for women, the low-paid and so on. The long progress of the measure was blocked by the 1966 economic crisis, Ministers who did not understand it, wrangles with the Treasury and protracted negotiations with the private sector. But what the thankless process showed was that, in the sixties, the position of the private market in pensions was entrenched.

Encouraging the private sector was one of two complementary trends in housing policy. (The other was part of a general social policy swing towards concentrating resources on geographically defined areas of need.) Changes in the pattern of tenure over the period 1960–9 show that developers of houses for sale and owner-occupiers responded to official encouragement; but those landlords who supplied rented accommodation to the poor were not offered large enough incentives to continue in their scapegoat role. Of all dwellings, the proportion in owner occupation rose from 42 per cent in 1960 to 49 per cent in 1969. Homes rented from private owners fell from 25·7 per cent to 15·8 per cent. (The stock of council-built homes rose over the same period from 26·6 per cent to 30 per cent.[10]) It was during the fifties that the Conservatives removed the building industry's wartime shackles. And from then on, politicians had vied with each other as to who would 'build' the most houses – though most of them were actually built by private industry. Labour's target was that half should be built for local authorities. As it turned out, the best year for new private dwellings came in 1968 under Labour.

Owner-occupiers did well throughout the period being, as always, the most highly subsidised group of householders because of the tax relief they obtain on mortgage interest payments. They also made good use of the improvement grants that had been introduced primarily to persuade landlords to repair and improve property they were letting. The urge to owner-occupation being stronger, it seemed sensible of the Labour Government to try and extend this source of private housing finance down the market. In 1968 the Government introduced the Option Mortgage. An insurance guarantee was offered to building societies to encourage them to lend to people they otherwise would not have thought safe and the buyer was subsidised by a lower interest rate. The scheme was not as popular as had first been expected because buyers had to choose between the option mortgage and the usual tax allowance. For those earning over £1200 the latter was preferable, and most prospective home-owners were – presumably – optimistic about future earnings.

In 1964, the Conservatives tried tapping another source of private finance. They established the Housing Corporation to advise and lend to cost rent and co-ownership housing societies. But though this was meant to help the less well-off, the Corporation had trouble finding low-cost schemes to fund. The Corporation was, quite fairly, exploited by the middle classes until in 1968 a ceiling was put on the cost of dwellings it could finance. In Britain, housing co-ownership and co-operatives failed to catch the public imagination.

Landlords were even more unresponsive to Government prodding. The 1957 Rent Act, progressively removing rent controls, was designed to increase the supply of privately rented accommodation. And in 1959 improvement grants were increased to induce landlords to repair and improve what were often pretty low standard dwellings. But despite these two measures, private landlords, as we have seen, began to opt out. Take-up of improvement grants went down year by year and between 1960 and 1968 only 22 per cent of the grants that were claimed went to landlords.[11] In 1965, following the Rachman scandals and the subsequent Milner Holland report on housing in London, the Labour Government brought back a modified form of rent control. The Government showed that they realised the Conservative carrot was not juicy enough, but they offered no direct substitute policy to increase the supply of rented accommodation, which was under so much pressure, especially in the city centres where the poor – newcomers, large families, the unemployable – congregated. The feasibility of housing allowances for this, the poorest group of tenants, was discussed within the civil service. The idea was to subsidise those people who needed it, rather than attaching subsidy to the buildings under the established scheme. But it was left to one city, Birmingham, to introduce in 1968 a unique Parliamentary Bill authorising rent rebates for private tenants.

Despite these policy failures, over half Britain's new housing was being financed through private funds in the sixties. If the proponents of private health insurance could have achieved a similar position they would have been delighted. On the face of it, the case to be made for getting more money, by any method, for health was overwhelming. Despite the fact that, by most conventional indicators, we were getting healthier (though diseases of affluence like coronary thrombosis were increasing), a crisis loomed over the health service throughout the decade. It was partly produced by the familiar chain – technical improvements, leading to higher but more expensive standards, higher patient and professional expectations, leading to more technical improvements. But in the end, although in 1969 the Chief Medical Officer of the Department of Health was complaining[12] that 'the resources available fall short of what is required even to make full use of the trained manpower available', the public was most affected by the shortage of man and woman power and its poor quality in some cases. This was thrown into relief by the particular plight of the long-stay mental and geriatric institutions.

The inadequacies of capital equipment, the shortage of staff, restricted spending on running costs, and the effect of these factors on the exploitation of technical breakthroughs in medicine led to detailed propaganda for private insurance. Such hopes as the national economy, with its disappointing level of growth could not fulfil, private insurance would. The fact of the matter was that in 1969 about 1·5 m. people were privately insured for hospital care (50,000 being covered for general practice treatment as well). But a vociferous pressure group, the Institute of Economic Affairs, and a section of the British Medical Association hoped to improve on this. In 1967 the B.M.A. commissioned a report, *Health Services Financing*,[13] in the preparation of which they involved several I.E.A. economists, and the plan was produced in 1970. The report advocates a three-lane financial approach to medical care: general taxation as well as compulsory and voluntary insurance. The hospital costs of the chronic sick, the old, the long-term mentally ill and subnormal and babies needing special treatment are defined as suitable cases for general taxation. So are the training of the medical professions, research, central administration and the bulk of capital expenditure on hospitals. The (proportionately small) remainder of medical services (apart from expensive or experimental in-patient procedures) ought, according to the report, to be financed out of insurance. And a minimum insurance premium would be compulsory in either a state or private scheme. The report made no impact. This reaction shows that the commitment to the health service as much more than a dumping ground or safety net was so well established in the sixties that, though the problems were admitted, and the principle of 'free service at the time of need' was increasingly violated, solutions other than 'going private' were to be sought.

Rationalising the Health Service

It was the Conservative Government under Harold Macmillan which ended the neglect of the health service dating from Churchill's last premiership. In 1962, Enoch Powell, then Minister of Health, launched his Hospital Plan,[14] shortly to be followed by a plan for community health and welfare.

With these promises the Government had begun making up for lost time; and what it promised, the succeeding Labour Government began to fulfil. Although a large proportion of the hospitals taken over in 1948 were obsolete, more than half having been built before 1891, only £16 m. was spent on new hospitals between 1948 and 1961. Then capital expenditure on the hospital sector increased from £42 m. in 1961–2 to £128 m. in 1969–70. Over the same period expenditure on local authority health and welfare capital projects, like hostels and geriatric day centres, more than doubled. And for general practitioners serious investment in health centres, in which groups of doctors could share modern facilities, began. In 1961 there were 25 health centres; in 1966, 44; and in 1969, 163. Even so, developments fell far short of meeting needs. To take just one example, there are still some areas which have no hostel accommodation for ex-mental patients. But the fact that neither hospital expenditure nor finance for health centres suffered in the cuts of January 1968 shows that these programmes were given some priority. Local authority spending, on the other hand, was cut. This was particularly unfortunate, as one of the major changes in policy emphasis, both in mental health and in treatment of old people, was towards treatment or support in the community (that is, on the local authority's budget) rather than in hospital.

In 1957, a terrible mistake was made in manpower planning: a Ministry of Health Committee under the chairmanship of Sir Henry Willink[15] advised a 10 per cent reduction in the intake of medical schools to avoid the risk of a surplus of doctors. The effects of this mistake were profoundly felt in the sixties, and in 1968 the Royal Commission on Medical Education came to the conclusion that we were still facing a crisis. Nearly half our junior hospital staff came from the Commonwealth, and still hospitals

were understaffed. In 1959, there were just over 25,000 general practitioners. By 1969, there were a thousand fewer, with a consequent rise in
the average number of patients looked after by each family doctor.
Between 1961 and 1967 the proportion of the population living in what the
Ministry of Health considered to be 'under-doctored' areas rose from 17
per cent to 34 per cent. The effects on professional morale were serious.
Junior hospital doctors were not getting the training to which their posts
entitled them. General practitioners complained of not having the time
to do a proper job. Emigration of doctors was considered a clear reflection
of dissatisfaction (with pay as well as conditions of work). In nursing the
story differs in detail but comes to the same conclusion.

And while long waiting lists for less urgent treatment were common,
often followed by further waiting in outpatient departments and harried
treatment by overworked medical staff, it was in the mental and sub-
normality hospitals, isolated and unpopular with staff, that the major
breakdowns in the health service occurred. In 1967 a book, *Sans Everything*,[16] was published by an association called Aid for the Elderly in
Government Institutions (AEGIS), about the treatment of old people in
seven mental hospitals. Subsequently committees set up by the hospitals
themselves to investigate the charges presented a horrifying picture, even
though they refuted some of the specific charges. One patient was, in the
words of the official report, 'dragged from his bed by a charge nurse and
shaken like a rabbit, while he dangled about a foot from the ground,
before being thrown with great force on the floor'. Another hospital
was referred to by the Committee of Inquiry as a 'dumping ground'. And
nearly all the hospitals suffered from overcrowding and shortage of
medical, nursing, and domestic staff, while such staff as they had were often
inadequately trained. In March 1969, an official report on Ely Hospital,
Cardiff,[17] disclosed another picture of cruelty and mismanagement in a
hospital housing mentally ill and subnormal patients. Again the hospital
had too few staff, many of whom were not trained for the job.

These reports illustrated the same tragedy, but the way they were
handled showed two different political styles. The first report was put to
Kenneth Robinson, then Minister of Health, who tried, even after the
committees had reported, to make light of the disclosures. The second
was a private report prepared for the Department of Health and Social
Security when Richard Crossman was Secretary of State. He decided,
against the advice of the civil service, to publish. He then got regional
hospital boards to divert £2 m. to their long-stay institutions and set up
the Hospital Advisory Service both as part of a strategy for dealing with

the problems of long-stay hospitals, and as a way of increasing Government authority over them.

Of course scandals like these and the other inadequacies of the health service can be prevented only by changes in organisation and administration as well as by greater expenditure. All these issues were discussed at length, notably in the two Green Papers[18,19] which were the sum of the Labour Government's achievements in health service reorganisation. There was clearly a need for a body responsible for the health requirements of a whole area. With hospital costs rising by about 10 per cent a year, it was important not to keep patients in expensive beds longer than necessary. (Anyway the general assumption is that people prefer to be at home.) Getting people out of hospital early, especially mentally-ill patients, makes demands on general practitioners (organised under their own executive councils), and home nurses and social workers (separately organised by local authorities). Though it was not achieved, the case for integrated management for health was firmly made in the sixties.

In improving management within the most expensive sector of the service – hospitals – progress was somewhat more impressive. Belatedly, the Department of Health, which had been notorious for its passivity towards the detailed development of the service (in contrast with the Department of Education's relationship with its local authorities), began to push for improvements – but still in a gentlemanly rather than a business-like manner. In 1966, a report recommended the reorganisation of the nursing hierarchy[20] to give nurses scope to work on the lines of management in industry. And the Department issued reports on how to organise medical work in hospitals[21] and on the responsibilities of consultants[22] which, if nothing else, made the higher echelons think. By the end of the decade hospital productivity was going up. With a 4 per cent decrease in the number of beds between 1959 and 1969 there was a 30 per cent increase in inpatients and outpatients treated.

By the end of the sixties, the health service was still too much under the sway of the medical professions, whose interests might well differ from those of administrators and the community they were to serve. But there were signs in the activities of the Department, and in the increasing morale and improved calibre of hospital administrators, that the balance of power was starting to shift.

One Social Work Service

Social workers were in a different situation from the medicine men, under whom many of them worked and whose vocabulary they had perhaps too easily adopted. They wanted to establish themselves as a homogeneous profession. What the various groups of social workers had in common was their predominantly casework technique, which involved forming relationships, analogous to that between psychoanalyst and patient, to help clients deal with their problems. The social workers felt that an almost universal method of working should unite them. If they worked together problems of co-ordination, of several workers dealing with the same family unit, of clients falling between the responsibilities of several local authority departments (health, housing, welfare, children) would disappear. As one profession in one department, they would be in a stronger position to press for a bigger slice of the cake; and by the same token, career opportunities in social work would broaden. In 1962, child care officers, family caseworkers, psychiatric and medical social workers, mental and moral welfare workers and even probation officers joined in the Standing Conference of Organisations of Social Workers. The conference's brief was to work for a single association. By 1970 they had found out enough about each other to come together in the British Association of Social Workers.

Amazingly the Government had worked faster than the pressure group and by 1970 the Local Authority Social Services Act (creating a single social work department in each local authority as recommended by the Seebohm Committee) was on the statute book.

Positive Discrimination

If 'selectivity' was a woe word to the Left of the sixties, 'positive discrimination' was a progressive phrase. Not just because of its overtones of American radicalism but also because it tended to mean pouring money and other kinds of help into a small geographical area, rather than invidiously singling out individuals. Area discrimination made sense in housing too. Since the middle of the fifties it was becoming clear that housing problems could not be dealt with simply by building new houses. While shiny new suburbs sprawled out, central areas rotted. What was needed was concentration on decaying areas. The process began in 1956 with the replacement of general housing subsidies by subsidies directed to particular problems, one being slum clearance. And under the 1969 Housing Act, local authorities were given the duty of working out what to do about 'unsatisfactory areas'. They could declare 'general improvement areas' in which they would be able to buy up houses and land, and spend environmental improvement grants.

On the same basis, taking geographical areas of need, a package was developed that resembled a miniature poverty programme. In July 1967 the Government decided to inject money into what the Plowden Committee on primary education (see page 175) had defined as educational priority areas. In 1968 the Urban Programme was launched to provide money for schools, centres for the elderly, community and family advice centres and so on; central Government paid 75 per cent of the costs of these schemes, nominated by local authorities in areas of 'acute social need'. And then, in January 1969, the Government began to talk tactfully to local authorities about its even more specifically directed community development project.[23] The theory behind the project ran as follows: people who need social services and are not getting them tend to live in impoverished areas; directing more resources into such localities helps, but not enough; you can keep pouring money in through the traditional structure but if residents do not take advantage of the facilities it will all be a waste; if they know about them, more people will use the existing social services but social workers are not good enough at peddling their wares; 'community development' may get round these difficulties and bring out leaders from among local people. So community development areas of about 3000 inhabitants (experimental, like educational priority areas) were allotted teams of about a dozen people – two or three full-time social workers, and a collection of part-timers like teachers or youth employment officers, to assess the needs of the area, set up an advice centre, tenants' associations, playgroups, etc. The aims of the project were what might loosely be called social work aims. But the method of attack was new, and appealed to politically minded social workers.

Signs for the Seventies

In 1965 a man called Stan Daniels revolted against Kent County Council. Not a world-shattering event; but a sign of the sixties. His wife and family were living in King Hill hostel for the homeless, where husbands were not allowed. And the council defined the statutory term 'temporary accommodation' which they were obliged to provide, as three months. After this period, women and children were turned out. And if, as was often the case, they had nowhere to go, the children were compulsorily taken into care. Stan Daniels moved into the hostel with his family and they barricaded themselves in. The King Hill campaign continued with the help of a group of outsiders, including Jim Radford and Ron Bailey, who moved on to other hostels and later led organised squatting in the London boroughs. This was direct action – of which the main consequence was to force discussion in legal terms about the rights of the homeless under the 1948 National Assistance Act.

At about the same time, claimants' unions were developing gradually to help people in their dealings with the National Assistance Board (or Supplementary Benefits Commission as it later became). And the Child Poverty Action Group began encouraging social workers to help their clients appeal to Social Security tribunals if they thought they were not getting the full benefits to which they were entitled. The Group also pressed for the publication of the 'A Code', a book of instructions issued by the Supplementary Benefits Commission to its local officers. A few lawyers began worrying publicly about the restricted access of poor people to the law. Community action groups were in the news, typically led by middle-class liberals – notably in the Notting Hill area of London. The publicity gained by most of these groups was probably disproportionate both to the actual numbers of people involved and to their long-term influence.

The actions of Stan Daniels did not cause a revolution in the way homeless people were treated. But they did cause local authorities to attend more closely to their responsibilities. Neither claimants' unions nor the Child Poverty Action Group, nor socially conscious lawyers, nor local protesters have overturned or much modified the institutions supposedly helping poor people. But this wave of activities raised an issue which will have to be resolved in the seventies. The recipients of social services began to want more say in their management. Indirect control through central and local elections was no longer thought to be enough. The poor, to whom the social services could be crucial, were most affected by the vague way in which accountability worked in practice; but the whole community was aware of the growing power of the social service sector, usually benevolent, sometimes negligent. People asked questions about exactly how priority points for council house waiting lists were apportioned. They began to wonder why old people were not on the committees governing the homes they lived in. And they also began to look at the composition and functions of such lay boards as do exist running schools, hospitals and so on. The Seebohm Report dealt in a few pages with what it called 'citizen participation' in the new social service departments. But a lot of detailed work remains to be done on the way non-professionals and clients can both participate in the running of social services and call for explanations of the technical decisions which they cannot themselves make. The second consultative document on the health service gave a nod in this direction by recommending local, though powerless, committees for the catchment areas of district general hospitals. Similarly the Home Office documents setting the scene for the community development projects contained little on client participation – though arousing local leadership was said to be a prime aim.

The social services become a political battleground when the country is, or feels itself to be, economically vulnerable.[24] The 1930s were ridden with scare stories about scroungers; Ramsay MacDonald is said to have been haunted by visions of ladies in fur coats driving up to collect unemployment benefit. Public opinion in the sixties seemed to echo the middle-class nervousness of the 1930s, the distasteful anxiety of the better-off that the poor or unemployed might do too well out of schemes designed to prevent them from starving. But in the end, such attitudes are irrelevant to the development of the social services. The seventies will see the tensions of the welfare state take a different political turn. The important questions remain: how to make massive services more responsive to individual needs; and how to increase the flow of resources to the welfare sector without increasing the divisions between different classes of consumer.

NOTES

1. *Social Trends No. 1* (H.M.S.O., 1970).
2. Ibid.
3. *The Financial and Other Circumstances of Retirement Pensioners* (H.M.S.O., June 1966). Another official report, *Report of the Committee of Inquiry into the Impact of Rates* (Cmnd. 2582, H.M.S.O., February 1965) had already indicated that about 500,000 retired householders were apparently eligible for assistance but not getting it.
4. A. B. Atkinson, *Poverty in Britain and the Reform of Social Security* (Cambridge, 1969).
5. *Circumstances of Families* (H.M.S.O., 1967).
6. M. Reddin, 'Local Authority Means Tested Services', in *Social Services for All* (London, 1968).
7. Brandon Rhys Williams, *The New Social Contract* (Conservative Political Centre, August 1967); Barney Hayhoe, *Must the Children Suffer?* (Conservative Political Centre, March 1968); Dennis Lees, 'Poor Families and Fiscal Reform' (*Lloyds Bank Review*, 1967); *Policy for Poverty* (Institute of Economic Affairs, January 1970).
8. Tony Lynes, *Pension Rights and Wrongs* (Fabian Tract no. 396).

9. *National Superannuation and Social Insurance* (Cmnd. 3883, H.M.S.O., January 1969).

10. *Social Trends No. 1* (H.M.S.O., 1970).

11. *Old Houses into New Homes* (Cmnd. 3602, H.M.S.O., April 1968).

12. *On the State of the Public Health* (Annual Report, Department of Health and Social Security, H.M.S.O., 1969).

13. *Health Services Financing* (British Medical Association, 1970). Apart from the main argument, this contains much useful historical data and some interesting contemporary research papers.

14. *A Hospital Plan for England and Wales* (H.M.S.O., 1962).

15. *Report of the Committee to consider Future Numbers of Medical Practitioners and the Appropriate Intake of Medical Schools* (H.M.S.O., 1957).

16. *Sans Everything*, presented by Barbara Robb (London, 1967).

17. *Report of the Committee of Inquiry into Allegations of Ill-Treatment of Patients and other irregularities at the Ely Hospital, Cardiff* (Cmnd. 3975, H.M.S.O., 1969).

18. *The National Health Service: The Administrative Structure of the Medical and Related Services in England and Wales* (H.M.S.O., 1968).

19. *The National Health Service: The Future Structure of the National Health Service* (H.M.S.O., 1970).

20. *Report of the Committee on Senior Nursing Staff Structure* (H.M.S.O., 1966).

21. *Report of the Joint Working Party on the Organisation of Medical Work in Hospitals* (H.M.S.O., 1967).

22. *Report of the Working Party on the Responsibilities of the Consultant Grade* (H.M.S.O., 1969).

23. *Community Action*, edited by Anne Lapping (Fabian Tract no. 400, 1970).

24. R. Skidelsky, *Politicians and the Slump* (London, 1967).

6 The Education Debate

BRIAN MacARTHUR

The sixties were aptly marked for education by the reigns of Sir Edward Boyle and Anthony Crosland, who ruled at the newly-created Department of Education and Science under different administrations for most of the decade. Although Crosland was explicit where, for political reasons, the policy of Sir Edward was implicit, it was the era of the consensus – a consensus which was to be swiftly broken by the arrival after the 1970 General Election of Margaret Thatcher armed to smash it, and the departure of Sir Edward to the Vice-Chancellorship of Leeds University.

Students revolted, and the Right shouted 'More means worse'; a start was made towards the abolition of the 11-plus and the introduction of a universal system of comprehensive schools; and there were new universities with 'new' maps of learning and the 'new' primary schools using the methods advocated in the Hadow reports of the 1920s. It was the decade when the sons and daughters of the new middle class created in the forties and fifties by the 1944 Education Act either became student rebels and sat in, or graduate parents of the first generation who clamoured loudly for better nursery and primary schools and stronger links between schools and homes.

The gloss is not so fanciful as it will seem to some at first sight. There is no doubt that education *is* the seedcorn of any society, whether in Britain or Tanzania or China, nor that the achievements of one generation are reflected by rising educational demand in the next. Satisfy the demand for universal secondary education, as Britain did in the sixties, and you have created the demand for universal higher education, which is the prospect for the seventies.

Although educationists (a profession which boomed in the sixties) always look to the debits rather than the credits, there is no doubt that the sixties were a decade of real achievement. Nearly 150,000 of the 600,000 school-leavers in 1967 got five or more G.C.E. Ordinary level passes, compared with 98,000 out of 700,000 in 1962. At Advanced level, almost twelve per cent had two or more passes, compared with six per cent in 1962. Successes in the Certificate of Secondary Education, a new examination for secondary schools controlled by teachers, were booming. Standards of literacy improved: in 1964, children of eleven were on average reaching the standards reached in 1948 by pupils seventeen months older. English primary schools, with their emphasis on learning by discovery instead of by rote, were the envy of the world. The school building programme stood at nearly £200 m. a year, and spending on education rose during the decade to more than £2200 m. a year, at last surpassing the defence budget and consuming about six per cent of the gross national product.

There were other achievements, too. Student numbers in universities, polytechnics and colleges of education doubled, and it was confidently predicted that they would go up to more than 800,000, another doubling within a decade, by the early eighties. A start at least had been made on helping schools in educational priority areas, the twilight areas of Britain's big cities. Thirty new polytechnics were being established as new comprehensive centres of higher education. The 11-plus examination, a spectre which had haunted the nation's children since 1945, was slowly on the way out (though it lived on in other, less obvious terms, as it must). School teachers were trained for three years – and had a new degree, the Bachelor of Education course. Student participation in university government had started to become meaningful – if only the students would grasp their opportunity.

On all these counts, the sixties were undoubtedly the era when education moved decisively into the arena of popular debate and controversy. At all stages of its development, however, the swelling demands of the education service have run up against a national budget which was not rising sufficiently rapidly to meet the full needs of each new generation, and its greater expectations. At each stage, therefore, the job for Government has been to select its priorities, or to advance slowly on every front, the policy that was largely adopted between 1966 and 1970, when it was broken by Margaret Thatcher with her declaration of an overriding priority for primary schools.

A look back at the issues that were dominating the debate in the first few months of 1960 illuminates the gap between aims and achievement.

The report of the Crowther Council, which recommended the raising of the school-leaving age to sixteen, had just been published: the school-leaving age is to be raised to sixteen in 1972–3.

Sir David Eccles, then Minister of Education, proclaimed that smaller classes were the first priority and that all oversize classes would be eliminated by 1970: up to three million children were still in oversize classes in 1970.

The Association of University Teachers was telling the University Grants Committee that 170,000 places would be needed in universities by 1970: there were, in fact, more than 200,000.

The London County Council, familiarly, was protesting about cuts in its education budget; the University of Cambridge was discussing the introduction of sociology (still a lively issue in 1969); schools were suggesting that Latin should no longer be a compulsory university entry requirement; and, at least in the pages of *The Times*, there seemed to be only two universities, Oxford and Cambridge, although such ancient cities as York, Lancaster, Canterbury, and Colchester were preparing for the new universities that shortly were to arrive on their doorsteps, whilst the civic universities, as usual, were preparing to take the brunt of the decade's expansion.

Nor, at the end of the decade, had the undoubted progress eliminated the problem areas of education service. Nursery education was still almost non-existent, especially in the deprived areas where it was most needed; and selection at eleven was still the rule. According to J. W. B. Douglas, 30,000 students of university potential were leaving school each year at the age of fifteen. Only about a quarter of all secondary schoolchildren were still in school at sixteen, and only 15 per cent went on to universities, colleges of education or polytechnics, compared with 25 to 35 per cent in the U.S. Young teachers were still earning a net starting salary of about £13 a week. A surplus of teachers was not expected at the earliest until 1978. The problems of schools in the twilight areas still remained largely untouched.

The education system, moreover, remained riddled with caste distinctions. Students in grammar schools and universities had a monopoly of the best buildings and the better-qualified teachers (to say nothing of a unique system of maintenance grants for universities) compared with their contemporaries in secondary modern schools, technical colleges and even polytechnics. Spending per pupil in 1966–7 was £150 in grammar schools, £132 in comprehensives and £114 in secondary moderns. Similarly, it was £1054 on a university student, compared with £812 on a college of education student and £319 in advanced further education. The concept of equal opportunity remained a mockery for too many.

So the problems in 1970 were still as great as ever. Yet just as some of the tasks set by the generation of R. H. Tawney and Sir Henry Hadow in the twenties and thirties were still being tackled in the 1960s, so the educationists of the 1960s were setting out the agenda for succeeding generations;

and it may be that the sixties in education will be chiefly remembered for the magnificent progression of reports which appeared under Lord Crowther, Sir John Newsom, Lord Robbins, Lady Plowden, Newsom again, and Professor David Donnison, successively dealing with the fifteen to eighteen age group, the secondary modern schools, higher education, primary education and the public and direct grant schools. All through the sixties, although it was still a mockery for many, the concept of equality of opportunity was clarified and refined. Each major report in turn argued the case, whether for the slow or the quick, so that cumulatively the great achievement of the sixties was to draw up the agenda for the next twenty-five years.

Set up to consider the education of boys and girls between fifteen and eighteen, the Crowther Council showed that only twelve per cent of the twenty-year-old age-group were still in full-time education. It criticised the waste of potential that the country was tolerating, and recommended the raising of the school-leaving age to sixteen between 1966 and 1968 and the introduction of County Colleges early in the 1970s. It also advocated a twenty-year programme to ensure that by 1980 half the boys and girls in the country should be in full-time education until eighteen. Using the new evidence from sociological studies, it suggested that early leaving was a social rather than an academic phenomenon, and demonstrated that many pupils failed to fulfil their academic potential because of the social limitations of their family backgrounds. Its philosophy, which was to be restated and refined in all the succeeding reports, was expressed early in its pages:

This report is about the education of English boys and girls aged from 15 to 18. Most of them are not being educated. But they are all at a highly impressionable age, with their characters still being formed, and, except in rare instances, with their minds still capable of considerable development. It seems to us clear that it is both necessary and practicable greatly to extend in the next few years the provision made for boys and girls in their later teens . . . We could not as a nation enjoy the standard of living we have today on the education we gave our children a hundred or even 50 years ago. If we are to build a higher standard of living, and – what is more important – if we are to have higher standards of life, we shall need a firmer educational base than we have today. Materially and morally, we are compelled to go forward.

Using a survey of Army and R.A.F. recruits, the report showed just how significantly social background determined whether children left school at 15. Among families of manual workers, it was still the exception for a child to stay at school after fifteen. The report added that among national servicemen entering the army 42 per cent of those who were among the top ten per cent in ability had left by sixteen.

Another characteristic of students who stayed at school beyond fifteen, it said, was that the great majority were the first generation in their families to attend grammar schools. The report went on:

> The Social Survey brought out the fact that both parents of two thirds of the boys and girls who attended selective schools themselves left school at 14 . . . only 12 per cent of the boys and girls came from homes where both parents had had a larger education than the legal minimum. This is a measure both of the task that confronts English schools at the present, and of the promise that lies ahead.

After Crowther, the Newsom report considered the education between thirteen and sixteen of pupils of average or less than average ability. It reported in 1963 and followed Crowther in recommending the raising of the school-leaving age to sixteen. It showed that four out of five schools for 'Newsom children' (as they came to be known) were seriously deficient. Schools for Newsom children, moreover, got less than their fair share of resources and more than their fair share of the least well qualified teachers. It also followed Crowther in suggesting that many children were being held back more by social than genetic factors, although school standards were rising sharply. Another recommendation, which was to be expanded in the Plowden Report, was that a joint working party should be set up to look at social services in slum areas. It also called for accelerated action to remedy the 'functional deficiencies' of the schools.

Above all, however, the report pleaded for a change of heart towards the pupils whose education it was considering. 'Our concern', it said,

> is lest the relatively unspectacular needs of the boys and girls with whom we are concerned should be overlooked. They have had far more than their share of thoroughly unsatisfactory buildings and desperately unsettling changes of staff. Given the opportunities, we have no doubt that they will rise to the challenge which a rapidly developing economy offers no less to them than to their abler brothers and sisters. But there is no time to waste. Half our future is in their hands. We must see that it is in good hands.

Apart from its own recommendations, however, the Newsom Report was the occasion for a momentous breakthrough in official thinking and in the definition of equality of opportunity. It was heralded in the fore-word to the report, signed by Sir Edward Boyle, Minister of Education. One of the most significant movements of the past twenty-five years, according to Sir Ronald Gould, General Secretary of the National Union of Teachers for more than twenty years, was the swing in educational philosophy from its belief in predestination, or that all children are born with fixed abilities, to a belief in salvation, or that nurture is as crucial as nature. The first official breakthrough for the nurture theorists arrived when Sir Edward, writing of the Newsom children, said:

> Their potentialities are no less real, and of no less importance, because they do not readily lend themselves to measurement by the conventional criteria of academic achievement. The essential point is that all children should have an equal opportunity of *acquiring* intelligence and of developing their talents and abilities to the full.

Attention then turned to the group which achieved the greatest extra concentration of resources throughout the sixties: students and higher education, particularly the universities. Again, as in the Crowther and Newsom reports, the Robbins Committee pointed to social rather than genetic factors as determinants of the flow of students to higher education. It recommended that by 1980 the percentage of the age group going into higher education should be raised from 8 to 17 per cent and that the student population, 216,000 in 1962–3, should expand to 390,000 by 1973 and to 560,000 by 1980 (all of which targets were to be substantially exceeded). Another major recommendation was that responsibility for the colleges of education should be transferred to the universities. It also mooted the idea of the Bachelor of Education degree which was eventually adopted (although the colleges themselves stayed outside the universities).

The axiom of the committee was that higher education should be available for all who were qualified by ability and attainment to pursue it, a significant refinement of the concept of equality of opportunity. Anticipating any challenge, the report also offered a vindication of its recommendations, a vindication which foreshadowed the development of the theme of Secondary Education for All into the theme for the second century of state education of Higher Education for All. It said:

> Conceiving education as a means, we do not believe that modern

societies can achieve their aims of economic growth and higher cultural standards without making the most of the talents of their citizens ... To realise the aspirations of a modern community as regards both wealth and culture, a fully educated population is necessary. But beyond that, education ministers to ultimate ends, in developing man's capacity to understand, to contemplate and to create, and it is characteristic of the aspirations of this age to feel that, where there is a capacity to pursue such activities, there that capacity should be fostered. The good society desires equality of opportunity for its citizens to become not merely good producers but also good men and women.

Again emphasising the arguments of earlier reports, Robbins pointed out that the provision of higher education in the United States, the Soviet Union and some Commonwealth countries greatly exceeded our own, and that the British system was well down the list judged on opportunity offered for entry. A much greater effort was needed, it declared. 'Our investigations have suggested the existence of large reservoirs of untapped ability in the population, especially among girls.'

There was immediate action on the report. Within a day of publication, the Macmillan Government accepted the targets until 1973, and announced that funds had been made available for meeting them, including £650 m. for university building. The seven new universities – Sussex, York, Lancaster, Essex, East Anglia, Kent and Warwick – were already under way. Now, in the wake of Robbins and on its recommendation, the Colleges of Advanced Technology were upgraded to university status as technological universities, and the number of universities doubled in the space of a few years, as did student numbers. As the statistical team that worked for Robbins put it: 'Apart from electronics and natural gas, higher education grew faster than any other major national enterprise in the 1960s.'

Was it this expansion which caused the sudden student uprisings that started in 1967 and which continued to erupt on many campuses for the next two years? Was this just a brief interlude in university history, since by 1971 student revolt had simmered down? Only time can answer the question. Students, however, certainly jolted the system, at first violently by sit-ins, demonstrations and strikes, particularly at Essex, the London School of Economics and Warwick University – and for a mixture of motives ranging from Vietnam to Rhodesia and germ warfare to the influence of big business on universities, confused, at the same time, with an often incoherent academic critique of syllabuses and courses, and a demand for participation and representation on university governing bodies.

After initial uncertainty and vain attempts at authoritarianism the universities slowly gave way, and each, in turn, announced a measure of student participation or representation on academic boards, senates, and councils. Yet it may be that what was most significant about student revolt in the sixties was the transformation of attitudes among a new generation, all born after 1945 and with different expectations of the morality of British society, shared and led by their contemporaries in American and Europe. It was summed up superbly and percipiently by Professor Richard Hoggart in *Higher Education, Demand and Response* (Tavistock). Throughout the decade, he argued, universities had been the proving ground for immense changes of attitudes among young people generally. They were acting out a phase in what could be one of the most important secular changes in attitudes of the last two or three hundred years: the beginning of the end of the Protestant ethic in its two main terms of expression, its attitudes to competitive work and to the sexual life.

At provincial universities only about five years ago there would be a shocked response if it were discovered that (say) the campus hairdresser was selling contraceptive sheaths; at such places today the Pill is likely to be available, if not exactly on demand then certainly without stringent conditions. Over the last few years, in most universities, there has been a steady loosening of the rules in halls of residence, of the conditions on which students may go into flats, and so on. Most members of staff know that a great many students live together.

Or one may get a hint of these changes through the difference in students' attitudes when they discuss with a member of staff a problem which involves sexual behaviour. As, for example, when an unmarried girl asks for two or three weeks off so as to have a baby. Up to seven or eight years ago such a girl was likely to be at least slightly embarrassed. Latterly, this doesn't seem so. A girl may be upset about the mess she has got into or composed because she has sorted out the difficulties. But she does not feel, in my recent experience, that she is telling you something in which you are morally concerned. In case anyone has mis-understood me, I am not saying that students today are promiscuous. I am suggesting that in their attitudes towards sex – in so far as one can tell from the sort of meetings a university teacher is likely to have – they seem to have made two important changes; they do not give the moral weight we were taught to give to the idea of premarital virginity, or, if that is broached, of confining sexual relations to one member of the opposite sex, the one you eventually marry; second, and this follows from the first, they do not think we have a role as moral mentors in matters such as these.

It would be wrong to put the main stress on changes in attitudes towards sexual life. More important and trickier to describe is what looks like a change in attitude towards ambition and competitiveness. Many intelligent students today are deeply suspicious of internecine strife, of 'getting on'. They have decided to be unpushing. I have known them to settle for a Second Class degree rather than a First, not so as to 'have a good time' in the old way but, as they argued, so as to stay with their group – because that is more 'real' than the kind of ladder-climbing isolation the degree structure invites. The stress is on the small-scale, particular, personal, non-materialistic. Or think of the student case against examinations; it is not at bottom a reformist case – that examination methods need to be improved. It is a revolutionary case – that they must be done away with. This is part of the wider rejection of quantitative competitiveness, the insistence on the importance of communality and on the superior reality of the personal and particular. The ideal is of a world much more fluid than ours, much less pyramidal.

It was, nevertheless, the Plowden Report on 'Children and their Primary Schools' which most significantly shifted the public mood at the end of the sixties. It appeared at the end of a period when most of the attention had been concentrated on secondary schools and university expansion; and when public interest, stimulated by a new generation of young parents who were showing an unprecedented interest in state education, was starting to turn towards the primary schools. It was now twenty-three years since the last major Education Act, and a new Act was being mooted. Above all, there was the cumulative impact of four major reports in eight years. After the stately succession of Crowther, Newsom, Robbins, and Plowden, the next leap forward was irresistible.

Once again, the Plowden Report, published in 1967, argued the case for equality of opportunity; and its most important recommendation concerned the impact of social disadvantage on children at primary schools. It was the most eloquent of the reports and enunciated a new principle that was adopted by the Government, and which continues now. The principle was that 'positive discrimination' should be exercised throughout the education system to combat the adverse effects of a poor environment.

It went on to suggest the establishment of educational priority areas (by 1970, firmly a part of the education scene), and suggested a formula by which the areas of greatest need could be detected and defined. Apart from this, it advocated an expansion of nursery education and devoted a great deal of attention to relations between schools and homes, to the participation of parents in school activities, to heredity and environment, and to a critical assessment of the practice of 'streaming' pupils into separate classes, according to their ability – judged, albeit, at the tender age of seven.

The concept of the educational priority area aroused the public imagination and Anthony Crosland, Secretary of State for Education, was able to announce a £16 m. programme for them shortly afterwards. The Plowden Report was the final refinement of the philosophic discussion of the decade and its plea for the priority areas was at the heart of its argument. 'Some of these neighbourhoods', it said,

have for generations been starved of new schools, new houses and new investment of every kind. Everyone knows this; but for year after year priority has been given to the new towns and new suburbs, because if new schools do not keep pace with the new houses some children will be unable to go to school at all. The continually rising proportion of children staying on at school beyond the minimum age has led some authorities to build secondary schools and postpone the rebuilding of older primary schools. Not surprisingly, many teachers are unwilling to work in a neighbourhood where the schools are old, where housing of the sort they want is unobtainable, and where education does not attain the standards they expect for their own children. From some neighbourhoods, urban and rural, there has been a continuing outflow of the more successful young people. The loss of their enterprise and skill makes things worse for those left behind. Thus the vicious circle may turn from generation to generation and the schools play a central part in the process, both causing and suffering cumulative deprivation.

The many teachers who do so well in face of adversity cannot manage without cost to themselves. They carry the burdens of parents, probation officers and welfare officers on top of their classroom duties. It is time the nation came to their aid. The principle, already accepted, that special need calls for special help, should be given a new cutting edge. We ask for 'positive discrimination' in favour of such schools and the children in them, going well beyond an attempt to equalize resources. Schools in deprived areas should be given priority in many respects. The first step must be to raise the schools with low standards to the national average; the second, quite deliberately to make them better. The justification is that the homes and neighbourhoods from which many of their children come provide little support and stimulus for learning. The schools must supply a compensating environment. The attempts so far made within the educational system to do this have not been sufficiently generous or sustained, because the handicaps imposed by the environment have not been explicitly and sufficiently allowed for. They should be. . . .

At last, after Plowden, the principle of 'positive discrimination', of defining a problem and tackling it with determination, was enshrined by Government in social policy, and was eventually extended to other social services.

As the stately progression of reports was published, however, one issue was dominating the *action* of the decade. It was secondary education, surrounded and often confused by the issues of selection, streaming, the nature of intelligence, social divisiveness and the public schools.

It is a fair judgement that by 1970 selection for secondary education by means of the 11-plus examination was universally discredited, in spite of its success. This, perhaps, is an ironic statement: but there were many idealists of the forties and fifties who spent their lives trying to extend opportunity to the working class through the means of selection by examination – and not by wealth – for entry to the grammar school. And the grammar school in its time (and it still flourishes) was undoubtedly a highly successful institution, whatever the merits or demerits of the 11-plus examination.

One strand of the debate, as we have seen from the Newsom Report, rested on a challenge to the belief that intelligence tests could detect and measure inborn ability. It was conclusively shown, however, that heredity and environment were too closely entangled to be clearly identified, so that children from literate homes had an inbuilt advantage over those from social backgrounds which were culturally deprived.

A lot of effort was made to modify the examination and to offer second chances. Yet as Professor Robin Pedley put it, the result of all this honest effort was that out of every twenty children selected for grammar school, six or seven were unsuited for it, whilst another six or seven who were allocated to secondary modern schools were suited, in fact, to grammar school. Success breeds success, moreover, and failure breeds failure, so that some children who went to secondary modern schools might have succeeded in the atmosphere of a grammar school. At the same time, other studies were demonstrating that the grammar school remained a predominantly middle-class institution; and the two arguments formed the nub of the case for the universal comprehensive school.

State comprehensive education had existed in England and Wales since after the war. Only in the late sixties, however, did the groundswell gather an irresistible momentum, although many had been built under Conservative governments before 1964 without any noticeable fuss. The fuss, predictably, started only when Anthony Crosland and the newly elected Labour Government carried the logic of the argument all the way and threatened the grammar schools. All too often until then, comprehensive schools had been a synonym for secondary modern schools. 'Comprehensive' education had coexisted with selection, a contradiction in terms.

Circular 10/65, to be repealed by the new Conservative Minister of Education, Margaret Thatcher, in Circular 10/70, five years later, requested education authorities to submit plans for the reorganisation of secondary schools with the object of eliminating selection into separate and different types of school at 11-plus. The declared objective of the Government, it stated, was to eliminate separation in secondary education; although almost simultaneously Crosland was instituting it in higher education with his famous binary policy, separating autonomous universities from the polytechnics and colleges of education, which were to remain under the direction of the state and education authorities.

The Labour Government also appointed a Commission on the Public Schools, under Sir John Newsom, to advise on the best way of integrating the public schools with the state system of education. The Commission, and its successor under Professor Donnison on the direct grants schools, was interpreted by some as a means of appearing to tackle an awkward problem without being forced to *do* anything about it. A blueprint for integration exists, but the issue disappeared in 1970 with the election of a Conservative Government.

Both Commissions outlined schemes for integration which may one day be serviceable. Once again, however – and it is a useful decennial exercise – the Newsom Report demonstrated the still very secure, though slowly diminishing success of the public schools in securing 'success' for their pupils. (See Tables I and II, pages 180–1.) So, at the end of the decade, the case for extending equality of opportunity had been successively made and refined. Most attention – and money – was still devoted to the ablest and brightest – and, therefore, to the middle classes; but a small start had been made in shifting the emphasis of policy towards new areas of concern. Under the Labour Government, special grants were made for the education priority areas and Mrs Thatcher, the Conservative Secretary of State in 1970, had started a vigorous policy to redeem her pledge to get rid of the oldest and most dilapidated primary schools.

Yet were the sixties the decade of illusion – or of disillusion; of optimism, or creeping pessimism? The optimists certainly dominated the debate – and won it, as the staggering rise in spending on education demonstrated. Spending on schools, colleges and universities rose through the sixties at an annual rate of six to seven per cent a year. Yet in 1970 the crucial question was whether that rate of growth could be maintained in the seventies, and one omen was that it had already been cut back to about four per cent. The prospect, moreover, was daunting. The school population was expected to grow from more than eight million to ten million by 1980 and the number of pupils gaining two A-levels was expected to double to 200,000 a year by 1990. Student numbers in higher education were expected to double to 825,000 by 1980 and the best estimates were that, *simply to stand still and maintain present policies*, spending on education would need to rise to £5000 m., or eight per cent of the gross national product, by 1980. As Mrs Shirley Williams put it, in a crucial statement about spending on higher education: 'It is difficult to see it being sustained for the next ten years at a rate of growth so great that it exceeds the capacity of the growth in the G.N.P. to match it.'

There lay the rub for education at the end of the sixties; and at least in the view of this writer, it was unrealistic for educationists to expect to maintain the momentum of the sixties through the seventies, unless there was a sudden transformation of the British economy. There could only be choices: expansion of nursery education at the expense of higher education; or, if higher education was to expand, it would have to expand more cheaply than before. And so arrived the creation of the Open University (originally conceived by Harold Wilson as the University of the Air – a national university teaching mainly through the medium of radio, television and correspondence courses), the talk of introducing student loans, and the first cuts in school milk and meals provisions.

Social engineering was the rallying cry of educationists in the sixties, but it looked as though the arguments of Crowther, Newsom and Plowden could be implemented only by determined, specific Government action, coupled with a new realism by educationists themselves. At the end of the decade, moreover, the movement against 'permissiveness' in British society in general, exemplified by Mrs Mary Whitehouse (secretary of the National

Viewers' and Listeners' Association) was also being reflected in a still small but growing volume of criticism of 'permissiveness' in education. Spurred on by student demonstrations, but against all objective evidence, there were cries that more had meant worse in universities and there was also a proposal to start a private, independent university, among whose advocates was Sir Sydney Caine, the former director of the London School of Economics. Sir Edward Boyle was under growing pressure from rank and file Conservatives in the constituencies, although ironically more and more Tory M.P.s were coming to recognise the value of his policy, since the children of Conservative parents also fail the 11-plus. Among the critics, there was also – perhaps with some justification – a concern about the lack of solid drill in the three Rs in primary schools; some justification because a few teachers may have been over-enthusiastic in applying the principles of learning by discovery instilled in them at their colleges of education. All this was ventilated in three 'Black Papers' on education, in which such critics as Professor Brian Cox, Robert Conquest, Angus Maude, M.P., and Kingsley Amis figured predominantly.

Yet the achievements easily outweighed the disadvantages of over-enthusiasm, and whatever may have been the worries of the economists of education, educationists are optimists and their lobby is persuasive. If the past teaches any lessons, it is that expansion in education is irresistible and that somehow, however late, it is usually achieved.

Table I Civil Service/Diplomatic Service Recruitment

	Ratio of successes to competitors Administrative Class (1963–1967)	Ratio of successes (1963–1967) to school leavers entering university in 1962
Public schools	1:4·6 ⎫	
Other independent schools	1:7·8 ⎭	1:99
Direct grant grammar schools	1:4·4	1:171
Maintained schools	1:7·5	1:483
	Diplomatic Service	
Public schools	1:9·3 ⎫	
Other independent schools	1:23·3 ⎭	1:287
Direct grant grammar schools	1:10·8	1:1106
Maintained schools	1:20·6	1:2970

Source: Civil Service Commission evidence to the Newsom Commission. Department of Education and Science Statistics 1962, Part III.

Table II Educational background of leading citizens

Percentage (taken of the total for whom details are known)

0 10 20 30 40 50 60 70 80 90 100

14 year olds (1967)(England and Wales)

17 year olds (1967)(England and Wales)

School leavers (England and Wales) going to all universities (1965–66)

School leavers (England and Wales) going to Oxford and Cambridge (1965–66)

Vice Chancellors. Heads of colleges and professors of all English and Welsh universities (1967)

Heads of colleges and professors of Oxford and Cambridge (1967)

Labour cabinet (1967)

Conservative cabinet (1963)

M.P.s Labour (1966)

M.P.s Conservative (1966)

Admirals, Generals and Air Chief Marshals (1967)

Physicans and Surgeons at London teaching hospitals and on the General Medical Council (1967)

Directors of prominent firms (1967)

Church of England Bishops (1967)

Judges and Q.C.s (1967)

Fellows of the Royal Society elected between 1962 and 1966

Governor and Directors of the Bank of England (1967)

0 10 20 30 40 50 60 70 80 90 100

Charterhouse, Eton, Harrow, Marlborough, Rugby, Winchester

Other public schools

Other independent schools recognised as efficient

Direct grant schools

Source: Newsom Commission report.

7 Immigration

ROY HATTERSLEY

In the early fifties it was easy to be enlightened about immigration – easy both for the progressive middle class, who have always judged immigration policy with the objectivity that comes from rarely seeing a black face and never living next to a black neighbour, and for the industrial workers of Bradford and Birmingham into whose streets the West Indians and Pakistanis came during the second half of the decade. For until 1955 immigration was barely an issue. Immigrants already here exerted little or no pressure on scarce hospital beds and scarcer municipal housing. The magnet of British prosperity had not begun to pull in Karachi and Kingston. The few Commonwealth citizens who had already landed were either accepted or tolerated. The politicians could afford to stand on principle.

As late as 1955, the Conservative Government was officially 'totally opposed to immigration control'. It was the dawn of the Macmillan dream of a new multi-racial Commonwealth. The idea of preventing its citizens from returning to the motherland was out of keeping with his paladian paternalism. But by the middle of the decade, others were beginning to see immigration in a more prosaic light. In 1954, John Hynd – Labour Member of Parliament and a Minister in the Attlee Government – had raised the issue of immigration control for the first time. His was virtually a single voice. But by 1956 the influx had grown large enough to be described by Patricia Hornsby-Smith, Parliamentary Under-Secretary at the Home Office, as a 'headache'. As the pain increased during the following year, attempts were made to negotiate bilateral controls with the Governments of India and Pakistan: they failed.

By 1959, the idea of the 'immigrant problem' was firmly implanted in the public mind. A handful of Tory M.P.s – notable amongst them Cyril Osborne and Norman Pannell – saw it as their duty to draw the nation's attention to the 'danger'. At first they received little encouragement. But by the end of 1958 their big breakthrough came. In Vancouver, Lord Home – then Commonwealth Secretary – announced that, sooner or later, restrictions would have to be placed on the entry of West Indians into Britain.

But the Labour Party at least remained firm in its commitment to the open door and from its Left wing Fenner Brockway (in April 1958) and John Baird (in July) made unsuccessful attempts to introduce Bills that would outlaw discrimination in public places, in housing and in employment.

Despite the Vancouver speech of their Commonwealth Secretary, the Conservative Government moved gradually – and at least in the case of Harold Macmillan and Iain Macleod reluctantly – towards immigration control. Public opinion probably moved rather more quickly. The Notting Hill 'race riots' of 1958 were reported in some newspapers as if signalling the beginning of continual communal strife and there is no doubt of the fear the idea provoked. In the General Election of 1959, Oswald Mosley in North Kensington and William Webster in St Pancras North campaigned on an overtly anti-immigrant policy. That year, the number of West Indians who settled in Britain was almost twice as large as the year before and even the pretence that India and Pakistan were parties to effective bilateral agreements to limit emigration to Britain could no longer be sustained.

By 1960 it was only a matter of time before controls were imposed. But in the opening months of the decade, Harold Macmillan made the speech which at least put the problems of international racial tension in their historical perspective. At Cape Town on 3 February 1960 the British Prime Minister told the South African Parliament of 'the wind of change' which was blowing across their continent. But even whilst that statement of the new reality was still echoing around the Commonwealth, members of Macmillan's own party were campaigning for stricter immigration laws in Britain. In Birmingham three Conservative M.P.s – Harold Gurden, Leslie Seymour and Leonard Cleaver – proposed a total ban on immigration for five years. During the following year, the pressure for control built up. So did the number of new immigrants.

In 1959, the net inflow of Commonwealth immigrants was 21,600. In 1950 it was 57,700. By 1961 it stood at 136,400.* It can be argued that the threat of legislation and the talk of imminent control was the real cause of the explosion – that families who had planned to travel in the mid- or late sixties brought their plans forward to beat the ban. Perhaps the pressure

* *Immigration from the Commonwealth*, Government White Paper, August 1965. The figures are measured by deducting the number of those who left the country from those who entered.

for legislation increased the numbers. Certainly the increased numbers – the 'cancer' as it was called by Sir Cyril Osborne – made controls inevitable. But as late as April 1961 Iain Macleod was still able to insist that his Government had no plans for immigration controls.

In 1961 Iain Macleod left the Colonial Office to become Leader of the House of Commons. Perhaps more important that year, forty resolutions calling for immigration control appeared on the agenda for the Conservative Party's autumn Conference. R. A. Butler's reply to the Conference debate was characteristically delphic. There was no promise of controls, but little doubt that controls would come.

The Commonwealth Immigration Bill was presented to the House of Commons on 1 November 1961. Its contents were simple. Part I specified that Commonwealth citizens could only enter Britain if they possessed a voucher issued by the Ministry of Labour or if they were married to or the dependent children of an immigrant who was legally entitled to enter and live in Britain. There were three classes of voucher: A for immigrants who had a specific job awaiting them in Britain; B for immigrants with special skills and C for the rest. But the Bill did not specify the number of vouchers to be issued each year. That decision was taken by the Government who could therefore regulate the flow according to their judgement of how many new workers industry needed and how many families society could absorb. In theory the number could be changed in either direction. In fact, each change has been a reduction.

To critics of the Bill, its power to control new immigration was not its only objectionable feature. In the fifties, there had been much exaggerated talk of the disease that immigrants brought to Britain. When the Bill became law, prospective entrants could be rejected – despite the possession of a voucher – if they failed a health test. The idea of 'exclusion on medical grounds' was attacked as pandering to the crudest prejudice, as were the provisions for deportation of criminals that appeared in Part II of the Bill.

Labour's opposition was predictable, determined and almost unanimous. A dozen Labour M.P.s – amongst them Gerry Reynolds and Christopher Mayhew – had doubts about the wisdom of a commitment to total repeal. But the official Opposition spokesmen, Patrick Gordon Walker and Denis Healey, and above all the Party Leader, Hugh Gaitskell, reflected the view that they shared with an overwhelming majority of their colleagues. The Labour Party believed that the Bill was in practice unnecessary and in reality a sop to racial prejudice. A future Labour Administration might ask Commonwealth Governments to restrict the number of their citizens who left for Britain. But that was as near as the Government (with a few liberal rebels) and the Opposition (with a handful of 'realist critics') actually got.

The Commons debate was long, bad-tempered and inevitably limited by a Parliamentary guillotine. Some amendments were made on the insistence of the Opposition. The Irish – excluded from the necessity to obtain vouchers before their entry to Britain on the doubtful grounds that such regulations could not be enforced – were at least included in the deportation provisions of Part II. More important, Part I was made subject to the Expiring Laws Continuance provision. Thus it became not wholly permanent law but required annual renewal procedure by annual debate.

The Bill became law in July 1962. In the previous six months 86,700 immigrants entered Britain. In the following six months the figure was 8,290.

Under Hugh Gaitskell's leadership, the Labour Party's unswerving opposition to immigration control was assured. His successor, Harold Wilson, had, since 1962, taken specific interest in integration and chaired a special committee created by the Labour Party to consider help to immigrants already here. His first major speech as Leader of the Opposition dealt extensively with the need to outlaw discrimination. But between that speech and the November debate on renewal of Part II of the Bill, a split developed in the Parliamentary Labour Party. Some members – amongst them Frank Soskice, Chris Mayhew, Anthony Crosland and Patrick Gordon Walker – joined the ranks of those who argued cautious opposition. George Brown, Herbert Bowden and Michael Stewart pressed for forthright condemnation. The outcome was a typical compromise. The Bill was attacked – during the debate on its renewal – as racialist and discriminatory. But the Opposition did 'not contest the need for the control of Commonwealth immigration into this country'. Control had become the policy of both major parties. Labour still nailed its colours to the shaking mast of bilateral agreements. But even so, whilst such agreements were negotiated, a Labour Government would continue the 1962 Act.

And the idea of a Labour Government was in everybody's mind – particularly the corporate mind of the Labour Party. Only two or three obstacles stood between them and victory. One was the 'white backlash' against immigration and against Labour, the Party which had opposed its control.

For the British public was growing increasingly anxious about immigration. There were deep anxieties in the areas into which the immigrants had already moved, and even deeper apprehension in the areas where their arrival was expected daily. The 1962 Act had dispelled some fears, but by focusing attention on the 'problem' it had erected others.

Henry Brooke, the Home Secretary, made escalating claims about the success of his policy. In November 1963 he said that 300,000 immigrants *might* have entered Britain but for the Immigration Act. In July he was categoric that they *would* have come. Tension mounted in areas where, it was whispered, the tidal wave would flow if a Labour Government opened the floodgates.

Most strident of all the prophets of racial doom was Peter Griffiths, the Conservative candidate for Smethwick. He had an immigrant programme of his own. It included a total ban on immigration for five years, summary deportation of Commonwealth citizens convicted of felony or permanently unemployed and the splitting of schools into white and coloured classes.

Griffiths's election victory – a defeat for Labour's shadow Foreign Secretary and a swing to the Conservatives of seven per cent at a time when Britain was swinging to Labour – caught the headlines. But in other places, immigration had a direct effect on the campaign. In 1964 there was virtually no immigrant vote to compensate Labour for the votes it lost because of its supposedly pro-immigrant position. Few Pakistani or West Indian names appeared on the Electoral Register – often because the immigrant householder had no idea how to go through the complicated process of registration, sometimes because landlords of overcrowded property were reluctant to reveal how many tenants were crushed into their houses. The few immigrants who were qualified to vote were often apathetic or uncertain of their rights. Labour, no longer the Party of the open door, was still thought to be the party which supported immigration. But it got little support from the immigrants themselves.

Anti-immigrant feeling was a crucial factor in at least two other seats. In the Perry Barr constituency of Birmingham, the Conservative Party delivered a last-minute leaflet warning of the immigrant invasion that would follow a Labour victory. Dr Wyndham Davies, the Tory candidate, defeated the sitting Labour Member by 327 votes, whilst other Conservatives who refused to use the leaflet lost their seats in the nationwide swing to Labour. At Eton and Slough, Fenner Brockway – the most vocal supporter of the immigrants' cause – lost by eleven votes. For him, the anti-immigrant vote must have made all the difference.

Indeed, the anti-immigrant vote changed more than the lives of three Labour Members of Parliament. The Government of 1964 survived on a majority of five and administrations which hold to life by such a slender thread live from day to day. They have neither the will nor the power to make long-term plans or to make initially unpopular decisions. In 1964 the economy needed both. With three extra victories – and but for the immigration issue there might well have been more – Labour's majority would have been barely less than that on which the Conservatives survived from 1951 to 1955. Earlier economic remedies would have been possible. After earlier remedies, the Labour Government might well have survived in 1970.

On the opening day of the 1964 Parliament, Harold Wilson made his now famous attack on Peter Griffiths. According to the Prime Minister, if the Tory Party were to remain true to their protestations of belief in racial equality, the new Member for Smethwick would pass his days as a 'Parliamentary leper'. The language was violent. But the new Government's policy was cautious. In February 1965 Frank Soskice, Labour's Home Secretary, announced that 'we have always been in favour of control' as he tightened the regulations governing the entry of dependent relatives and sought powers to repatriate illegal immigrants.

Officially, Labour still hoped for a solution based on the old panaceas of bilateral controls agreed with individual Commonwealth Governments and applied in the country of the immigrants' origin. A committee under the leadership of Earl Mountbatten visited Commonwealth capitals. It returned to report failure.

From then on, Labour's race relations policy had two distinct and separate strands. The control of entry – so bitterly opposed in 1962 – was continued and intensified. But the Government also asserted the rights of Britain's coloured citizens and took the initiative in promoting their integration into the community.

Integration policy has many forms. Its positive aspects range from prosaic English language classes to lofty campaigns designed to remind new citizens of their civic duties and legal rights. But there is another essential element in the programme. In the Britain of the early sixties some basic rights were denied to the immigrant population. In housing, in employment and in the provision of credit facilities, there was undoubted discrimination. There were publicans who would not serve coloured customers. Like the estate agents and the mortgage brokers, they could discriminate with legal impunity.

Fenner Brockway had promoted six Race Relations Bills. None of them had reached the statute book. In 1965, the Government approached the Opposition to see if a similar Bill would be acceptable to them. Peter Thorneycroft – who had replaced Edward Boyle as shadow Home Secretary, much to the concern of the race relations lobby – agreed on one consideration. Offenders should not be subject to immediate criminal prosecution. Attempts should first be made to conciliate – to bring the sinners to willing repentance.

The Government agreed. The Bill that they commended to Parliament applied to only two aspects of discrimination. It prohibited any restriction on the transfer of tenancies imposed because of the race of the prospective tenant and it outlawed discrimination on grounds of race (though not on grounds of religion) in public places. As a bonus to the disappointed devotees of legally-backed integration, it extended the old Public Order Act so as to increase the penalities for incitement to racial hatred.

The Race Relations Board – whose principal powers derived from the Act – was charged with the management of the 'conciliation process'. Its local Conciliation Committees accepted complaints of discrimination. Where it could settle the dispute amicably, it was its duty to do so. Where discrimination was proved but could not be ended, the case was referred to the Attorney-General, who alone had the power to prosecute.

To the militants amongst the immigrant community – and their political associates – the Act was an inadequate pretence at protection that never really existed. Certainly its scope was so limited that much blatant discrimination continued unchecked. But it was a beginning. The Government and Parliament had at least set a tone. Prejudice was publicly and unanimously condemned – at least in theory.

In August 1965 the Government published a White Paper setting out new policy for immigration and race relations. One section of the White Paper – Part III – dealt extensively with the positive aspects of race relations – classes were to be established for non-English speaking immigrants, schools were told to limit the number of non-English speaking children in any one class to a third, new initiatives were promised for housing in the areas of high immigrant concentration. The National Committee for Commonwealth Immigrants was to be given new standing and extra responsibilities.

Part I of the White Paper contained the statistics of immigration – the number of voucher holders entering the country and the number of disappointed applicants. (About 400 vouchers were issued each week; not all of them were taken up.) Virtually all the vouchers which had been issued had gone to skilled workers in categories A and B. Three hundred thousand unskilled applicants for C vouchers still awaited admission.

From these figures, Part II of the White Paper concluded that further reductions were needed. The definition of 'eligible dependant' was altered – the qualifying age of children was reduced from eighteen to sixteen,

Category C vouchers were abolished. The total number of new vouchers to be issued each year was reduced from 10,000 to 8500. The powers of the Home Office to repatriate were extended and new immigrants were warned that they might be required to keep in touch with their local police.

There was immediate uproar in the Labour Party and beyond. The *Spectator* – edited by Iain Macleod – carried a defence of the White Paper by a regular contributor, but dissociated the magazine from the article's general conclusions in a front-page editorial. Because of the pressure in the Parliamentary Party, the White Paper was never debated. Part II, which caused so much offence, could however be implemented without House of Commons approval, as long as the Expiring Laws Continuance Bill was passed. All that was really lost was the opportunity to begin a real campaign for integration. Repulsion over Part II blinded many Labour M.P.s to the value of Part III.

Before the General Election of 1966, two important changes took place in the administration of immigration policy. Frank Soskice retired from the Home Office and was replaced by Roy Jenkins. Knowing that he must face the odium of administering control, the new Home Secretary insisted that the more positive aspects of race relations policy should also be run from his Department. Maurice Foley – who had started his Ministerial career as an Under-Secretary in George Brown's D.E.A. – had been asked to add immigration to his other responsibilities. In the D.E.A. it had been virtually a spare-time occupation, but the task had been discharged with obvious success. In December 1965 he moved to the Home Office and concentrated his entire efforts on immigrants and immigration.

Race relations was not an issue in the 1966 General Election. Donald Finney, a former Conservative Councillor from Smethwick, offered to assist any candidate who ran against Maurice Foley on a ticket similar to that on which Peter Griffiths had won the election in Smethwick two years earlier. Edward Heath issued an immediate rebuke. Immigration was no longer an issue big enough to win and lose elections.

But in some areas it was still an issue that raised passions – though not quite the same passions as were roused in 1964. When immigration was discussed amongst the British electorate, Labour was still thought of as the pro-immigrant party – though the antagonism that created was swamped by the great pro-Labour tide that was running that year. The immigrants themselves felt less certain of the affection which Labour was supposed to feel for West Indians and Pakistanis. In parts of the country – notably the West Midlands – immigrants urged their compatriots to abstain in protest at the White Paper. There was even talk of immigrants running against Labour in marginal seats where the Black vote could be crucial.

With Labour's overwhelming victory and the self-confidence that comes with a large majority, the Government began to consider an extension to the limited Race Relations Act. Roy Jenkins – still Home Secretary – had already established his enthusiasm for the development of a positive policy for what came to be called 'community relations'. At a meeting of the National Committee for Commonwealth Immigrants he gave the classic definition of integration as not 'a flattening process of assimilation, but equal opportunity, accompanied by cultural diversity in an atmosphere of mutual tolerance'. The N.C.C.I. and the other organisation working to achieve that aim left the Home Secretary in no doubt about what was needed to bring it about. Their arguments were soon reinforced by powerful evidence.

Professor Harry Street – working for P.E.P. on a survey commissioned by the Institute of Race Relations – produced a report on discrimination in employment. What he found could not be refuted – even by the sentimentalists of the T.U.C. and Ministry of Labour who refused to believe that either British employers or employees would discriminate against coloured workers. The Street Report found that they did – that a whole range of jobs were denied to immigrants, that their promotion prospects (especially to supervisory jobs) were severely limited and that much of the discrimination came not from the boardroom but from the man at the factory gate.

The extended Race Relations Bill was not presented to Parliament until after the devaluation of November 1967 which brought with it the resignation of James Callaghan from the Treasury and his exchange of portfolios with Roy Jenkins. But other things moved more quickly. The illegal immigrant story became fashionable in popular newspapers and the accounts of pathetic groups of bewildered Pakistanis picked up by the police whilst wandering on South East beaches became increasingly common. In August of that year, the Wilson Committee – set up under the chairmanship of Sir Roy Wilson to enquire into the desirability of providing appeal machinery for immigrants excluded from this country – presented its report.

The report was detailed and specific. Immigrants should be provided with the right of appeal against exclusion at the ports, refusal of an entry certificate or a proposal for deportation. There was a piece of wise as well as humanitarian advice to the Government. Everything possible should be done to encourage Commonwealth citizens to apply for entry visas before they left for the United Kingdom.

But in early 1968 the country was growing increasingly unsympathetic to proposals designed to safeguard immigrants' interests. The issue of new work permits had been pegged at so low a level that it was no longer possible to argue that new voucher holders were flooding into London Airport. The argument, therefore, changed its ground. The 'danger', it was said, now stemmed from the dependants of workers already here – dependants entitled to join the heads of their households. A second new 'risk' was discovered, the birth rate of the immigrant families.

The problems that might stem from the black birth rate were a generation away and, in any case, were discredited by the publication of official statistics showing that young immigrants produced no more children than other families of child bearing age. But another issue had to be faced at once. In late 1967, the Kenyan Government had enacted legislation that made aliens in that country work there and live there 'on a temporary basis'. The intention of the legislation was clear. Asians – who dominated Kenyan commerce – were to be driven out of the country. Even before the legislation had become law, the Kenyan Asians began to leave for Britain. Most of them carried British passports, for at the time of Kenyan independence they had accepted the offer of the British Government and opted for what they believed to be British nationality.

In November 1967, 1334 Kenyan Asians entered Britain. In January 1968 the figure was 2294. In the face of such figures the Government felt that it must act. Malcolm MacDonald – the 'troubleshooter' for Africa of successive British Governments and son of the old Labour Leader – visited Kenya in the hope that Kenyatta could be persuaded to change his mind and end the harassment of the Asians. He could not.

A Bill was already in draft to correct a number of small anomalies in the Immigration Act of 1962. In February 1968, the Government decided to add to it specific measures to restrict the entry of residents living in ex-colonial territories who held British passports. Clause I of the new Bill altered the 1962 Act to extend the definition of prospective immigrants who could be excluded from Great Britain. Entry – irrespective of legal status or the nature of passport – was only automatic for applicants who could demonstrate that one parent or grandparent had been born in the United Kingdom, or naturalised as a U.K. citizen or a citizen of Great Britain under the provisions of the 1948 and 1962 Nationality Acts.

The Act also enabled the Home Office to impose a variety of entry conditions and prescribed penalties for ships' captains who knowingly smuggled illegal immigrants into Britain. But those were the original intentions of the draft Bill. The important part was added later. Its simple intention was to keep the Kenyan Asians out.

With the prospect of planeloads of immigrants trying to beat the ban, the Bill was rushed through the Commons in three days. Not a single member of the Labour Government resigned, but thirty-five Labour M.P.s voted against the Bill. So did fifteen Conservatives, despite the tacit support the Opposition Front Bench gave to the Bill, and the entire Parliamentary Liberal Party.

As a result of the Bill's passage, 150,000 Kenyan Asians were made virtually stateless. They had – as Iain Macleod reminded him in an open letter – been made a specific offer of British citizenship by Duncan Sandys, once Colonial Secretary, but by 1968 one of the most determined supporters of restricted entry. The Bill was a retrospective withdrawal of the offer that Sandys had made and an abandonment of the promise it implied. The Kenyans who had taken the British Government at their word could boast a passport embellished with the British coat-of-arms, but in terms of status and protection it was worthless.

In defence of the Bill, James Callaghan and his new Under-Secretary, David Ennals, argued the pragmatic necessity of not allowing the entry of more immigrants than the nation was willing and able to assimilate. Privately there is no doubt that they hoped for a change of heart in Nairobi. If Britain would not let the Asians in, surely Kenyatta would not drive them out. In part, the bluff certainly worked, but there is no doubt that the principle on which the Bill was based dealt a crucial blow to the morale of the Labour Party. To many of the Party's members the Bill – more even than the previous Immigration Act – seemed based on a willingness, if not desire, to discriminate on grounds of colour. The 'grandfather clause' looked ominously like a determination to allow Commonwealth immigrants with white faces to enter Britain – despite the ban on immigrants in general. The Labour Party needs to believe in its moral purpose and idealistic intent. After the Bill, there were a lot of *New Statesman* readers in suburban Britain who felt less willing to write the Ward minutes.

In the early sixties it was often said that 'integration without limitation was impossible whilst limitation without integration was indefensible'. The theory behind that slogan was simple. Unless the people in the areas into which the immigrants had come were promised an end to pressure on their scarce resources they would not co-operate in the provision of a full and free life for Britain's new citizens. But in the middle and late sixties a new psychological truth became clear. The Race Relations Act had given the official stamp of approval to racial tolerance. It was hoped that the people would follow suit. The panic caused by the influx of Kenyan Asians and the Government's immediate response also had an effect. It seemed to some to give a new respectability to the bar-room theories that the country might easily be overrun. Within days of the Bill's passing into law Enoch Powell voiced the basic fears. At Birmingham on 20 April he made the first of his 'immigration speeches':

> We must be mad, literally mad, as a nation to be permitting the annual flow of some 50,000 dependants, who are in the most part, the material for the future growth of the immigrant descended population. . . . It can be no part of any policy that existing families should be divided: but there are two directions in which families can be re-united . . . In short, suspension of immigration and encouragement of re-immigration hang together.

The idea of repatriation, soon to be developed by Powell, had been floated for the first time. But it was not that aspect of the speech which caught the headlines. There was a story of an old woman (unnamed and undiscovered by investigating newspapers) who was 'afraid to go out' and found 'excreta pushed through the letterbox'. When she went out, Powell announced, 'she is followed by children, charming wide-grinning piccaninnies . . . one word they know: "Racialist" they chant. When the new Race Relations Bill is passed, this woman is convinced she will go to prison. And is she so wrong? I begin to wonder.'

That was the general argument against the new Bill – the idea that the Englishman in, or immediately outside, his own castle should be allowed to say what he liked about immigrants and choose to whom he sold his house, or give employment by whatever standards he preferred. Three days after that speech, the Bill was presented to the House of Commons. It fulfilled Roy Jenkins's promise to prohibit racial discrimination in housing, all commercial services and employment. It was employment around which much of the argument raged.

The employment clauses of the Bill were unpopular with the T.U.C., the C.B.I. and the Ministry of Labour – particularly so with Ray Gunter who left the Ministry as the Bill was being prepared. Most trade union leaders, like the representatives of the employers, preferred to rely on what they regarded as 'the good sense and decency of ordinary people'. But experience suggested that such reliance was not enough. Experience also suggested that there were pitfalls in the administration of the proposed Act into which managers of local Employment Exchanges would fall.

It would be their duty to supervise the working of the employment provisions. If they acted rigidly, they would lose the confidence of many employers. If they interpreted the rules too loosely, they would risk complaints to the Race Relations Board. This, they claimed, was a serious problem, unlike some of the fears that the Act provoked – notably the awful terror that Chinese restaurants would be prohibited from advertising for Chinese waiters.

To meet this special problem the idea of 'racial balance' was born and built into the Act. The idea was bitterly attacked, but its intention was honourable. There were dozens of employers in the Midlands, London and Yorkshire whose attitude towards the employment of coloured workers was beyond reproach. Twenty or thirty per cent of their work force were born in the Commonwealth – indeed there was a danger that assimilation was being held back by the creation of 'black factories' and 'black jobs'. Yet should such a firm decide to limit its coloured work force it might, under the original provisions in the Bill, be acting illegally by keeping its immigrant employees down to four hundred out of a total work force of a thousand. Meanwhile a firm with no coloured employees would escape if it accepted the occasional immigrant who applied for a job.

It was eventually agreed that a firm with a high proportion of immigrants already on its staff could reject new applicants in the interest of 'racial balance'. To many critics it seemed the Bill's second retreat from principle. The first was the removal from the formal provisions of the Bill of all those companies which could set up 'joint conciliation committees' with constitutions approved by the Ministry of Labour. These committees, partly composed of trade unionists, partly of employers' representatives, considered complaints of discrimination within their own factories. Only if they remained dissatisfied was the issue passed on to the Race Relations Board. The machinery appeared admirable as a device for keeping the discrimination issue off the boil. It seemed less likely to set right genuine grievances.

The Bill could hardly be described as revolutionary. Yet the official Opposition were unable to support it. During the Second Reading debate a 'reasoned amendment' was moved by Quintin Hogg reaffirming the Tory Party's abhorrence of discrimination, but declining to give approval to a Bill which aimed at taking one teetering step towards its abolition. In the vain hope of securing all-Party agreement, James Callaghan offered to set up a Select Committee of the House, to watch over the workings of the Race Relations Act. The Tories still voted against the Bill.

For the Tory Leadership was under pressure. Enoch Powell had caught the imagination of the provincial Conservatives by his support for a number of high Tory issues – not least the prohibition of all future immigration and the repatriation of immigrants already here. As a result of his Birmingham speech, he had been dismissed from the Shadow Cabinet, but at Eastbourne on 16 November he returned to the same theme and commented on the first speech's reception.

> The reaction to that speech revealed a deep and dangerous gulf in the nation . . . I mean the gulf between the overwhelming majority of the people . . . and . . . a tiny minority with almost a monopoly hold on the channels of communication. . . . The resettlement of a substantial proportion of the Commonwealth immigrants in Britain is not beyond the resources and abilities of this country. . . . It ought to be and could be organised now.

In face of the straight populist appeal, Edward Heath's seven-point plan for immigration set out in a speech on 2 September 1968 seemed pretty pallid. It was in fact a shift to the Right: intention to bring dependants should be registered before arrival; unconditional residential rights only to be conceded after a year of satisfactory citizenship. It did little to prise Powell from the hearts of the Conservative constituency workers. There he was to remain until the General Election of 1970.

But before the election there were two further steps forward. The Immigration Appeals Act (implementing the recommendations of the Wilson Committee) became law in 1969 and in the following year the Alien (Appeals) Order gave similar rights to foreign nationals. Between the two there was the usual crop of Parliamentary initiatives aimed at limiting immigration still further.

In the election of 1970 immigration played a vicarious role. If Enoch Powell won votes for the Tory Party he won them, in part, because of the notoriety he had obtained by his speeches on immigration. But there were few votes to win or lose as a direct result of the immigration issue. The British people, told by a senior Conservative politician of the 'rivers of blood' that he saw in prospect for the British nation, remained calm. A few immigrants – notably Marilyn Neufville, who broke the 400 metres world record in the Commonwealth Games, found the barrage of continual rejection too much to bear; but most West Indians and Pakistanis stood stoically calm. For in the back streets of Bradford and Birmingham it was increasingly clear that they were increasingly accepted. Their

children, English-speaking from the start, were obviously like other
children – black but British. Their habits were occasionally quaint, sometimes alien, but basically the same as their neighbours. They shared, with
the other people in their streets, the deprivations of bad houses, old schools
and the fear of unemployment. They became part of the decaying roads
and back-to-back houses. Which is much to their credit – and much to the
credit of the native population who, without knowing it, behaved better
(and with less self-interest) than most of the politicians who sought to
govern them.

8 The Quality of Life

DAVID McKIE

'Your middle class man', wrote Matthew Arnold in 1871, 'thinks it is the highest pitch of development and civilisation when his letters are carried twelve times a day from Islington to Camberwell, and from Camberwell to Islington, and if railway trains run to and fro between them every quarter of an hour. He thinks it nothing that the trains only carry him from an illiberal, dismal life at Camberwell to an illiberal, dismal life at Islington . . .'

A century later he could have quoted journeys much more ambitious in conveyances of much greater technological magic. But Arnold's misgivings about the unquestioned belief in progress, regardless of anything beyond material considerations, were being echoed more and more as the sixties ended.

After all, it was increasingly said – most of all by middle-class men – there must surely be more to life than the relentless pursuit of a greater and more glorious gross national product. Maybe those conjoined benefits of modern technology, the motorway and the motor car, could, if ordered, contrive to get you from Camberwell to Islington in no longer than it had taken Matthew Arnold to compose his disapproving sentence. But if life in Camberwell was dull and illiberal, if the peace of your Camberwell garden was then to be utterly spoiled by the howling noise and the nauseating fumes of the very motorway which carried you there – then was the growth and the progress really worth the statistically uncounted cost?

Such things had been predicted. In *The Future of Socialism* (1956) Anthony Crosland foresaw a time, perhaps a decade away, when, having eliminated poverty, assured a continuing high level of unemployment, and set ourselves on a steady Social Democratic course, we would be able to lift our eyes to another kind of political issue: the freedom of the individual, the appearance of town and countryside, the health of cultural institutions.

The confident predictions of a serene economic future, like a good many optimistic assumptions in that book, were to be proved bitterly misplaced:

but social and cultural preoccupations began to force their way into the politics of the middle and late sixties even so. Many of the reforms for which Crosland was arguing at this time – liberalisation of the laws on divorce, homosexuality and abortion, the freeing of authors and play-wrights from the censor's hampering hand – were in fact achieved in the lifetime of the Labour Governments of which he was a member. In July 1967, homosexual acts between consenting men over twenty-one ceased to be an offence. Three months later, the Abortion Act allowed a woman to have an abortion if she could satisfy two doctors that this was justified on specified medical, social and psychological grounds. In October 1969, the divorce law was radically amended: the old doctrine of the matrimonial offence was replaced and divorces were now to be granted when it could be shown that a marriage had irretrievably broken down – after two years if both partners agreed to it, and after five on the unilateral demand of one.

Already, back in 1959, the Obscene Publications Act had attempted to rescue works of genuine artistic merit from being prosecuted as porno-graphy. The measure was piloted through the House by Roy Jenkins, and the lessons learned from that campaign were to help other liberalising legislation later on. In this case, in fact, the reform misfired a little. Finding that juries were impressed, as in the trial of *Lady Chatterley's Lover*, by a parade of expert witnesses testifying that this was literature not filth, the police began bringing prosecutions through magistrates' courts instead, where experts were less readily venerated. 'Stand up straight and take your hands out of your pockets', a London magistrate ordered a university lecturer pleading the case of *Fanny Hill*, which was then not unexpectedly condemned. An attempt by Jenkins, during the passing of the Conservative Obscene Publications Act of 1964, to stop this evasion of the intention of the 1959 Act was unsuccessful. But, in 1968, the Theatres Bill ended the long reign of the Lord Chamberlain – a hereditary official, which made his operations seem all the more irrational – over the London stage.

And in December 1969, the death penalty, which had been suspended for five years in 1964, was finally swept away. Hanging is not, like other issues considered here, in any strict sense an issue of individual liberty, but it was habitually classed as one of those on which M.P.s should obey their consciences rather than the Party Whips. The abolition of hanging was seen by its supporters as an integral part of the campaign to civilise Britain, by its detractors as an equally integral part of the nation's steady descent into permissiveness.

Other issues listed by Crosland and also by Jenkins in his Penguin Special, *Why Labour?*, in 1959, still remained to be tackled when Labour lost power in 1970. Repeated attempts to change the Sunday Observance laws all foundered, and the licensing laws remained unmoved, though pubs in some Welsh counties did begin to open on Sundays. But these were lower priorities: if they had commanded the same attention among the bulk of M.P.s as divorce and abortion law reform, they too would have got through.

Why, after these reforms had, in many cases, been fruitlessly canvassed for years, was so much done in such a rush in the late sixties? Chiefly because Labour was now in a majority, and Labour M.P.s had always been friendlier to reform than the Conservatives. The liberal tradition was far stronger on the Labour side than the Conservative, and the Party was in any case more philosophically disposed to change than one whose political outlook makes much of the need to consolidate and conserve. The conviction that no man is beyond redemption is also stronger on the Left than the Right. The introduction of Life Peers had made the Lords less of a graveyard for liberal reform (they were actually ahead of the Commons in voting for reform of the law on abortion and homosexuality).

Two circumstances finally guaranteed that the liberals would succeed. The first was the character of the new Labour intakes of 1964 and 1966. At the start of the 1966 Parliament, they filled more than 150 seats and made up some 40 per cent of the Parliamentary Party. Predominantly, they were young, middle-class, well educated and sceptical. They came largely from a generation which had not been accustomed to take the wisdom of its elders unquestioned: faced with a moral prohibition, their response was likely to be: 'Prove it'.[1] Above all – to use a word which, in the sixties, was one of the highest tributes a man could pay to himself – they were *rational*. This was the time of the management consultant, the preferred solution, the costed alternative. Issues of public morality must be subjected to rational scrutiny like the rest of them, not treated as some unfathomable mystery, like the sacraments of the Church or the evolution of the Leader of the Conservative Party. The other essential signal for reform was the arrival at the Home Office in December 1965 of that most rational and civilised of politicians, Roy Jenkins.

And it was easy, in every case, to show that existing laws were anomalous, archaic, irrational – either, as in the case of abortion and homosexuality, because they suffered from regional variations, had different effects on rich and poor, and were nowhere clearly defined; or, in the case of hanging, because the Conservative Government of 1957, ignoring the unequivocal warning of its own Royal Commission, had tried to divide murder up into hangable and unhangable varieties.

Two symbolic events helped to spread dissatisfaction to a wider public. The case of the thalidomide children, born grievously deformed because of a drug their mothers had taken in pregnancy, increased public support for easier abortion; while the case of Timothy Evans, in which the State had to admit that it had hanged a man for a crime he did not commit, made the morality of hanging even more suspect. Even so, while the reformers could show increasing public support for changes in the law on homosexuality, abortion and divorce, as measured by the public opinion polls, there continued to be huge majority against the abolition of the death penalty.

The text for the reformers might well have been taken from the Wolfenden Report, which had recommended a change in the law on homosexual offences in 1957: 'We do not think it proper for the law to concern itself with what a man does in private unless it can be shown to be so contrary to the public good that the law ought to intervene in its function as guardian of the public good.' There were, indeed, some recent Conservative precedents: the Street Offences Act of 1959, implementing the other half of the Wolfenden Report, cleared the streets of prostitutes, and the Betting and Gaming Act 1960 cleared them of bookies' runners.

In marked contrast to some older Labour members, the intake of 1964 and 1966 did not take the view that this kind of social reform stood on the periphery of politics. To them, it was at least as urgent a political commitment as the nationalisation of steel, or even more so. At one stage in a debate on divorce, Simon Mahon – one of two Liverpool Catholic brothers who made interminable speeches against reform on homosexuality, abortion and divorce – began to complain that this kind of measure was not what had inspired him, and his father before him, to work so many years for the Labour Party. 'I hope', said Donald Dewar, the new young Labour M.P. for Aberdeen South, 'that my honourable friend will accept that there are many Members on the Labour benches who feel very strongly that we are in the Labour Party partly because we want to see progressive and humane social change.'

Against all this, older Conservative Members, and some Labour ones too, protested at the irrevocable damage which reforms might do both in themselves and in the wider context of that indefinable phenomenon, the social fabric. But for all the impact this kind of argument had on the reformers, they might have been reading from the Old Testament, and in the original Hebrew at that. It is striking how often the solemnest passages in an anti-reformer's speech were brought to a halt by laughter from the other side. One man's declaration of sacred principle, in this House of

Commons, could often be another's roll in the aisles.

'I believe', said Ian Percival, a Conservative lawyer who represented Southport, 'that there are in this life some things which we cannot understand or put into words although we believe just as sincerely that they matter.' He was talking on the sanctity of marriage, but it had a wider application. Do not tamper, warned Conservative voices, with what you do not understand. The death penalty, for instance, was not just a penalty for murder: it was the 'cornerstone' of law and order: remove it, and the whole fabric might be fissured. In the same way, the divorce law was represented as a cornerstone of the institution of marriage, and abortion law as a cornerstone of our respect for human life.

Next to cornerstones, floodgates were the metaphorical machinery most often brought into use. The divorce Bill, said Victor Goodhew, Conservative M.P. for St Albans, was 'part of a pattern of gradual erosion of the standards of Christian upbringing, which are being forced upon the country by a small minority, the Humanists among them . . . a gradual erosion of the standards by which most of us have been brought up, by a minority in the country, and, strangely enough, forced through by the votes of a minority in this House. Once they open the floodgates [by making it easier to end a marriage] the numbers will be much larger than they ever imagined.'

The 1960 Betting and Gaming Act, which for all its good intentions, had led to a gambling boom, breeding new social problems no one had foreseen, was constantly invoked. 'I grow rather mistrustful', said the Conservative M.P. for Ashford, W. F. Deedes, in a debate on abortion, 'of the view that the right cure for social abuse is to legalise it with suitable restraints. We tried that once with gambling, and that experience does not encourage me to apply that doctrine in this far more difficult subject.' Homosexual law reform, declared Edward Taylor, the young Tory M.P. for Glasgow Cathcart, might lead to the spread of 'queer clubs' – the same kind of unintended effect we had seen from the Betting and Gaming Act.

Abortion was seen as a first step along the road to euthanasia. 'Once we accept that it is lawful to kill a human being because it inconveniences us, where do we end?', asked one of the Bill's most persistent critics, Jill Knight, Conservative M.P. for Edgbaston. Denouncing the Bill as 'utterly evil', Lord Longford, Labour Minister and a prominent Catholic layman, told the Lords: 'I am horrified, indeed terrified, by what might lie behind it. If we pass these measures, we are driving in the thin end of a wedge whose final limit may well be foreseen by the promoters of this Bill, but I would guess by few others, perhaps by hardly anyone in this

House . . . the execution time of old people may not be so very far off.'
Simon Mahon saw divorce reform as part of an attack which could lead
on to the destruction of church schools and the introduction of euthanasia.

The Bill to abolish capital punishment (though not the later move to
make abolition permanent), the reform of the law on abortion, homosexuality and divorce, were all the work of private Members. Even so,
they were to a large extent Labour measures, and they would not have
got through without Government favour.[2] Redeeming a pledge given by
Harold Wilson at the 1964 election, the Government was generous with
time and drafting assistance. It intervened in the 1964 hanging Bill, and
again over abortion and homosexuality, to rescue the Bills by extra allo-
cations of time when they would otherwise have foundered. Without
such help, said Richard Crossman, then Leader of the House, at a meeting
of the Parliamentary Labour Party, no controversial private measure could
hope to survive the opposition of a determined minority.

Each of these reforms had the support of a predominant number of
Labour members: and on each, the great bulk of opposition came from
Conservatives. 'Only on homosexuality', concludes Peter Richards, in
his study of this legislation, *Parliament and Conscience*, 'was the balance of
Conservative opinion other than overwhelmingly conservative.'

Not all Labour members liked the look of these reforms – the Clydeside
and Merseyside members were particularly disturbed by them. And they
were undoubtedly more of a favourite cause among the new young
Labour M.P.s than they were in the working men's clubs of Consett and
Ashton-under-Lyne. But they were certainly not forced by the younger
Labour M.P.s on their unwilling seniors. The sense among older Members
that reform was more urgent, more desirable, or simply more inevitable
was as important to the result as the reforming zeal of the newcomers of
1964–6.[3]

Much of what happened later made opponents of reform even surer
that they were right. The crime rate, with crimes of violence setting the
pace, continued to rise: Quintin Hogg, the Conservative shadow Home
Secretary, tried at the 1970 election to blame this on Labour, but it was
pointed out in return that crime had grown fastest of all in the Conservative mid-fifties. The rates of illegitimacy and venereal disease continued
their uncontrollable upward sweep. But to say that the dark side of the
permissive society was increasingly in evidence by the end of the sixties
is not to say that the equation of liberty with licence by conservatives had
been right. The reform legislation of the sixties was a symptom, not a
cause, of deep social, cultural and psychological changes, on a scale which

was bound to produce ill-effects as well as good.

Meanwhile, progress had also been made towards another of the targets set by Crosland and Jenkins in the late fifties: to make Britain a brighter and more culturally satisfying, as well as a more liberal and tolerant, place. Public spending on the arts, which in the fifties had been notoriously stingy by any standards, increased sharply, especially (despite the generally depressing economic climate in which the Government was working) when Wilson made Jennie Lee Minister for the Arts. The Arts Council, the principal distributor of this largesse, was given more than a million pounds to spend, for the first time ever, in 1958–9. In 1964–5, the allocation was £3,205,000. In 1970–1, it was over £9 m. Government spending on the arts, which, apart from the Arts Council, went mainly to the museums and galleries and to the British Film Institute, passed the £20 m. mark in 1970–1: it had more than doubled in five years.

New theatres added lustre to the lives of provincial cities, even though some of the old commercial ones, groaning miserably under the imposition of Selective Employment Tax, shut their doors. If B.B.C. Radio 1, aping the forbidden pirate stations without their spontaneity and conviction, operated on a level of un-Reithian banality matched only by Radio 2, Radio 3 broadcast more good classical music in a month than Matthew Arnold could have heard in his lifetime. The British cinema, long sunk in uninventive Rank starletry, arose and impressed the world. And if the local Roxy had long ago gone over to Bingo, at least there was much more likelihood at the end of the decade that a specialist film theatre would be somewhere around, offering a repertoire the Roxy never dreamed of.

Meanwhile, with some of the old restraints on individual liberty swept away, the air was rich with the sound of alarmed voices, anxiously proclaiming new ones. Civil liberties, a relatively unfamiliar term in the late fifties, took on by the end of the sixties the appearance of a light industry with formidable prospects of growth.[4] In 1962, the Conservatives rejected the demand for an ombudsman, an official to take up people's grievances against the Government machine. In 1966, Harold Wilson, redeeming an election pledge, announced that one was to be appointed: he would be known as the Parliamentary Commissioner and could only be approached through an M.P. His promise that a further tribe of ombudsmen might be engaged to watch over local authorities remained unredeemed.

While the Right lamented the appalling growth of crime, the Left, especially the demonstrating Left, grew more preoccupied with the alleged threat to law and order of the forces of law and order. (In 1971, one police chief, presumably despairing of interesting intellectuals in the increasingly troubled state of our streets, shrewdly suggested that crime ought to be regarded as a branch of that increasingly fashionable phenomenon, pollution.) The public outcry which broke out in 1959 over the Thurso Boy case, in which a fifteen-year-old boy was said to have been roughed up by two policemen in a dark alley, is a useful indication of how things have changed since then. The boy's father, getting no satisfaction in the courts, got the case taken up by his M.P. An official tribunal was appointed, which reported, at the length of 8000 words (and a cost to the taxpayer of £1 a word) that, under provocation, one policeman had struck the boy once and had then been rebuked by the other. By 1970, a public which read the papers and watched TV programmes like the *Z Cars* series, designed to show the police as human beings under strain who sometimes went further than they should, would hardly have given the Thurso case a second thought.

Growing distrust of the police, though sharpened by a number of well-publicised cases of abuse, was part of a bigger phenomenon: an increasing fear of the State as Big Brother. Towards the end of the sixties, there was mounting alarm over the operations of computers and the creation of data banks. The assembling of large amounts of personal information in a centralised location could, it was argued, give the State a formidable dossier on every citizen. Private industry, too, with its increasing use of computerised research, was stacking up information about people's lives which could be used against them without their even knowing.

The computer, indeed, became more and more the target of fear, suspicion and abuse as the sixties advanced. And in this, it was typical of the new political preoccupations of the time. The computer was seen as one example among many of the way in which technology, that great new engine of prosperity and growth, was operating against the interests of the private citizen.

By the end of the decade, this revulsion against the blind pursuit of growth had acquired a vivid demonology and its own morose and mystical prophet in Ezra Mishan, an economist with no taste for the world we were creating for ourselves, and least taste of all for the power of the motor car.[5] It was a curious and ironic reversal. For at the start of the decade, in Labour policy statements and above all in the driving speeches of Harold Wilson in 1963 and 1964, technology had been convincingly sold as the people's friend, the key to a better life at home and at work; the dependable generator of wealth to pay for new hospitals, homes and houses, to buy a richer life at home and dispense greater assistance to less fortunate folk overseas.

In his Scarborough speech in October 1963, Wilson conjured up a vision of pent-up ingenuity and innovation, ready and able to build new science-based industries which would carry us forward to a prosperous future, but held back by the blinkered, irrational, amateur and unscientific political leadership of the Tories, under which privilege and nepotism took pride of place over native ability and talent.

It was a wonderfully shrewd appeal. The new science-based industries were to be the substitute for those old forms of state enterprise to which many in the Party had seemed so anxious to cling at the time of the Clause Four debate. And wealth through growth was the essential formula for raising the standards of the less well-off without that radical redistribution of wealth and income which leading Labour politicians knew could not be forced on the country. What was more, Socialist technology came to the consumer with its own accept-no-imitations guarantee. In the first Industrial Revolution, technology, given its head, had created wealth and prosperity – but only for the few, and at the cost of misery and oppression for the masses. The guarantee that this would not occur in the new revolution was the presence at the political helm of Labour politicians, dedicated to the protection of ordinary people: 'the essential leavening which Socialism brings to the industrial revolution of our age', said Wilson at Birmingham in January 1964, 'is the leavening of humanity which was so clearly absent from Britain's first industrial revolution.'

That great burst of promised growth never came; and at the end of the decade, Britain had reached the curious position that while politicians and economists sought desperately for cures for our limping rate of growth, more and more voices (though louder, quite markedly, in the middle-class enclaves of Islington and Camberwell than in the back-streets of Consett and Ashton-under-Lyne) were heard declaring that we had already sacrificed too much to such growth as we had already got.

A series of symbolic events helped to broaden this kind of concern from the preoccupation of the few – which it had been in the early sixties, when word of Rachel Carson's *Silent Spring* was first beginning to get around – to a movement too big for politicians to ignore.

There was Aberfan, in October 1967, the pit heap sliding down, engulfing the school, killing 144 people, 116 of them children: that emblem of technology's unconsidered side effects, of no thought taken for tomorrow with a subsequent generation paying the price. There were the deaths of thousands of seabirds along the coast; the tragedy of thalidomide; the wreck of the oil tanker *Torrey Canyon*, spilling 100,000 tons of oil into the Channel. All these, having made their headlines, left a more lasting message behind. Pollution of sea and air claims a steady and mounting toll of natural life: seabirds may die from time to time in their hundreds, but they may die in smaller numbers every ordinary day. Even without a *Torrey Canyon* disaster, tankers will spill 50,000 tons of oil in our waters each year: as they grow larger and more numerous, the danger will increase.[6]

Technology had also presented us with that architect's dream of the sixties, the tower block, and the new industrialised systems to build it. The motive for building high flats and using industrialised systems was not just an architects' foible, though some were clearly more concerned to make their mark upon the skyscape than to give people agreeable lives within. The rage for system building was born of the same humane feelings which were later to move many people when they became aware, perhaps for the first time, of the tragedy of homelessness when the TV film *Cathy Come Home* was shown. Traditional methods, it was argued, could not house all the families who desperately need new homes now. Land was scarce, and deterringly dear; the countryside would be lost if the towns kept eating into it. To build high flats was the obvious rational course.

For a time, though there were grieved reports from Medical Officers of Health and angry condemnations from welfare workers, the social implications of this policy were less of a planning priority. In 1962, builders started work on 13,836 flats in blocks of ten storeys or more, of which 903 were in blocks of twenty storeys. By 1965, the total of flats in blocks over ten storeys had doubled, and the number in flats of twenty storeys or more was 6563.

In the summer of 1968, concern about high flats became a public rather than a private property when a block of flats in East London, Ronan Point, collapsed after an explosion. Already, by this time, the building of high blocks was declining: 14,393 flats in blocks of ten or more storeys were built in 1968, and 1969 saw a further decline. The proportion of new homes built by industrialised systems, which had risen from 19·9 per cent in 1964 to 41·2 per cent in 1968, also began to fall.

But the major target of the new environmental campaigners was the motor-car. In 1959, there were nearly nine million vehicles on the roads of Great Britain. By the end of 1970, the figure was around sixteen million, with the prospect of further rapid growth: there were forecasts that present numbers would double well before the end of the century. Polluting the atmosphere, killing something like 7000 people a year and maiming many more, puncturing more and more of the nation's peace with its inescapable racket, the car, though a source of pleasure, liberation and delight to many thousands of individual motorists was, in its mass impact on society, like a monstrous intruder which had invaded the nest and now, sated and swollen, was engaged in befouling it.[7]

In their report on *Traffic in Towns*, published in 1963, the group led by Colin Buchanan warned what damage the car would do to our cities if preparation was not made to accommodate and manage it. (There had been an even more graphic illustration of this the previous year when a tube strike in London brought thousands of additional cars into the streets and the centre of the capital was soon jammed solid.) Yet even Buchanan, the apostle of environmental values, proposed to sacrifice thousands of homes and spend millions of pounds to create cities fit for cars to be driven in. (Buchananism, wrote Mishan later, would 'take decades to implement, cost the earth, and would apparently remove us from contact with it.') The fate of people in Acklam Road, North Kensington, driven mad by a new motorway which roared past their bedroom windows, became widely celebrated. But anyone driving into London by motorway can pick out hundreds of homes with no one to speak for them, where the lives of families must have been demeaned and made miserable in order to speed motorists to their more enviable destinations.

The long battle over the Greater London plans for a multi-million pound motorway box, involving massive demolition, was a deeply significant one, not least because – as was now increasingly often the case – the opposition had mustered evidence and analysis which could match for thoroughness and expertise that of the official side. But the most powerful symbol of the conflict between technological progress and the defence of human values was the story of the third London airport.

Because Britain had never had an airport policy, but had proceeded by private initiative and official improvisation, the choice for a third London airport fell upon Stansted in Essex. A public local inquiry – set up on terms which carefully precluded any discussion of whether this site was right or whether another might conceivably be more appropriate – led the inspector to conclude that local objections were justified. It would be 'a calamity for the neighbourhood', only justifiable in terms of national necessity; and such necessity had not been demonstrated. This unfavourable judgement was subsequently treated to a 'searching inquiry' behind closed Whitehall doors by an official committee whose members were not named and whose report was never published. Only their conclusion appeared; which was, that Stansted was right.

This wretched piece of public decision-making (by a Party, moreover, which was supposed to be dedicated to rational planning) was defended in the Commons by the President of the Board of Trade, Douglas Jay (ironically to re-emerge later as a crusader against the London motorway box) in a speech which, one hopes, he may now find it embarrassing to read. Powerful and well co-ordinated local opposition eventually led Jay's successor, Anthony Crosland, to go back on the Stansted decision and submit the whole question of the third airport to a new kind of high-powered planning inquiry under Mr Justice Roskill. The Roskill team was equipped with one of the most lauded planning aids of the sixties, cost benefit analysis (described in their report as 'the best available aid to rational decision making'). This enabled it to put an economic valuation on each consideration put before it and draw up a budget for competing sites. The eventual report used the analysis rather more sparingly than had once been expected: there had been something of a storm when it was discovered that the team had costed the Norman church at Stewkley on its fire insurance valuation. This inquiry, which did not even rate Stansted as worth a place in its short list, came out in favour of an inland site at Cublington. But in a dissenting report, Colin Buchanan argued for a coastal site at Foulness.

In doing so, he broke away from the cost analysis approach and argued the crucial part of his case on boldly non-rational grounds. He recalled his feeling, his entirely unquantifiable feeling, as he stood on Ivinghoe Beacon and looked out over the Vale of Aylesbury, that to build an airport here would be simply 'unthinkable'. Against the findings of the researchers, he set his emotions as he looked at a Rex Whistler reproduction hanging in the hotel where the inquiry was held: 'as potent', he declared, 'as any of the evidence I heard'. He even included in his dissenting note a tribute to Sir Albert Richardson, a dedicated preserver of an earlier day and a traditionalist architect at whose name modern-minded and rational men had been known to break down and weep.

The approach of Roskill, and the Buchanan reservation, set a new, though hideously expensive, standard for issues of this kind. Assess all the evidence (not just a few accessible parts of it) as rationally as you can; balance the conflicting considerations; but (and this was Buchanan's moral) do not leave out considerations which you cannot quantify.

Much of the previous environmental campaign had been damaged by a hysterical note. Technology itself, rather than the uses of technology, had been identified as the threat. It was seen as a wrecking monster, set on eating us all, instead of as the sorcerer's apprentice, a fine servant but a dangerous master.

In a book of essays called *Conviction*, published in 1958, Raymond

Williams, a pillar of the New Left and no technological dreamer, wrote of those who condemned the gifts of technological power:

> I have seen all these things being used and I have seen the things they replaced. I will not listen with patience to any acid listing of them – you know the sneer you can get into plumbing, baby Austins, aspirin, contraceptives, canned food. But I say to these Pharisees: dirty water, an earth bucket, a four-mile walk each way to work, headaches and broken women, hunger and monotony of diet . . .'

In his Fabian pamphlet, *A Social Democratic Britain*, in 1970, Crosland said of the anti-growth men:

> Their approach is hostile to growth in principle and indifferent to the needs of ordinary people. It has a manifest class bias and reflects a set of middle-class and upper-class value judgments. Its champions are often kindly and dedicated people. But they are affluent and fundamentally, though not of course consciously, they want to kick the ladder down behind them . . .

Already, in fact, technology itself was cleaning up the environment. Technologists, faced with the problem (which they should have anticipated) of detergents polluting rivers, designed new ones which did not. Because of technology, the development of cleaner forms of fuel, the air of London was cleaner than for very many years. It had needed a disaster first – the London smog of 1952 – but cleaner air had come, saving not only the potential victims of occasional smog but also the potential victims who would have died, year in, year out, from breathing bad air – but less conspicuously. Lack of growth meant less money to spend on combating pollution, as when cuts in public spending caused local authorities to cut back on new sewerage schemes.

But the lesson which politicians had to consider, as the seventies began, and the rate of technological innovation increased, was this. Why did it take these tragedies, like smog, like *Torrey Canyon*, like thalidomide, like Ronan Point – to make us see the danger in what we were doing? Since the eventual and inevitable decisions as to how growth should be weighed against amenity would fall to politicians to decide, what could be done to educate them for the responsibilities which will come their way, and do to it in time for disasters to be averted?

This kind of question gave a new impetus in the second half of the sixties to the campaign for Parliamentary reform, and in particular to the creation of specialist committees on which ordinary members could see for themselves something of the problems and choices governments face, the advice they get, and the conflicting advice which they possibly do not.

The 1964–6 Labour intakes took up the cause of Parliamentary reform with an enthusiasm which caused some of their elders to mutter and grow redfaced.[8] In a debate on procedure in October 1965, the Leader of the House, Herbert Bowden, spoke rather tetchily of 'new Members, many of whom come here with the idea that they have the answer to all our problems . . .'. How, they repeatedly asked, and were not quieted by their seniors' scowls, can Government lecture industry about modernising and rationalising its procedures when it is content itself to muddle on in its present unstreamlined, irrational state? Twice, in August 1965 and May 1966, when Black Rod interrupted the Commons debate to summon them to the Lords, there to hear the traditional incantation of Acts given royal assent, some Members refused to go, continuing their discussion in the absence of the Speaker. The arrival of Richard Crossman as Leader of the House in August 1966, like the arrival of Roy Jenkins at the Home Office in the context of social reform, was the signal for activity to begin. Black Rod's maraudings were quickly curbed; but much more important, the demand for the establishment of specialist committees was met by the creation of two, on science and technology and on agriculture, with others, on education, immigration, Scotland, and the ombudsman, coming later.

All did not go smoothly. The Agriculture Committee infuriated the government by demanding to be allowed to visit Brussels to deal with what was unmistakeably a basic question in any discussion of British agriculture – the cost of entering the E.E.C. After a year, the committee was told it could not continue: it had never been intended, Ministers declared, that it should run longer than this. Supporters of specialist committees found this difficult to take. The committee, it was argued, had made a nuisance of itself, had offended some Ministers and some civil servants. So it had been dismissed. But was not making a nuisance of itself the proper function of such a committee?

The partial collapse of the experiment – though science and technology continues to be surveyed – did not destroy support at Westminster. In their book, *The Member of Parliament and his Information* (London, 1970), Anthony Barker and Michael Rush found that there remains a 'quite strikingly favourable' attitude to these committees among Conservative as well as Labour members. As with social reform, enthusiasm was greatest among those who had entered the House since 1959.

In the continued absence of any strengthening of research services available to Members, and the general reluctance to see the importation of research teams on the American model, the specialist committee seems the best hope of parading before Members the increasingly awkward political and moral choices which will have to be made in time.

Few Honourable Members come to Westminster with any great knowledge of biology. More, perhaps, though probably not enough, read science fiction. Yet in the next fifty years, not just in America but in Europe too, we can expect to see the development of remarkable new techniques of genetic engineering, with the possibility of determining the genetic make-up of unborn children and perhaps even altering the genetic pattern of existing individuals; the revival and spread of transplant surgery; the prolongation of life, which, with further cures for killing diseases, will lead to further increase in the population; the maintenance of sperm banks, for later distribution to suitable applicants; test-tube fertilisation of eggs which can then be implanted in a receptive uterus, enabling one woman to bear another's children; and a great many others, all of which may sound far-fetched but are, on any assessment, less far-fetched than a man on the moon used to sound not very long ago.

It may be said that these are not political matters. Party-political, they are not. But they are political all the same. As we have seen with the motor-car, there are some issues which do not lend themselves to resolution by Party politics and therefore tend to be left unresolved. Sooner or later, Members of Parliament will find themselves discussing, if not these questions, then others no less formidable. Technology will not wait for them. Unless the lessons of the sixties are learned, there may well be further disasters in store before the politicians can be brought to make their hard and inevitable choices.

NOTES

1. This irreverence was not confined to the Labour benches. Some Conservative M.P.s were worried by the behaviour of their younger colleagues. In a debate on hanging, one senior backwoodsman M.P., Brigadier Terence Clarke (Portsmouth W.), comparing them with his own generation of Conservatives, complained: 'Unfortunately, we have a few young people on this side who came in in about 1956 and who are of a rather different calibre. They are about as wet as the last three Home Secretaries, and the one I see laughing at the moment is the worst of the lot.'

2. The voting in vital divisions was:
   On leave to introduce the Sexual Offences Bill

		For	Against
	Labour	183	33
	Conservative	49	67
	Liberal	11	—
	Others	1	—
	Total	244	100

On the Third Reading

		For	Against
	Labour	83	2
	Conservative	12	12
	Liberal	4	—
	Total	99	14

On the Second Reading of the Abortion Bill

		For	Against
	Labour	161	13
	Conservative	51	15
	Liberal	10	1
	Others	1	—
	Total	223	29

On the Third Reading

		For	Against
	Labour	129	22
	Conservative	31	61
	Liberal	7	—
	Total	167	83

On the Second Reading of the Divorce Bill

		For	Against
	Labour	152	19
	Conservative	23	86
	Liberal	6	1
	Others	2	—
	Total	183	106

On the Third Reading

		For	Against
	Labour	89	13
	Conservative	16	42
	Liberal	4	—
	Total	109	55

Vote to make the abolition of hanging permanent

	For	Against
Labour	276	2
Conservative	53	180
Liberal	11	1
Others	3	2
Total	343	185

For a record of how individual M.P.s voted, see David McKie and Chris Cook, *Election '70* (London, 1970). For analysis of voting by Party, age, education etc., see Peter G. Richards, *Parliament and Conscience* (London, 1971). In the interests of brevity, I have referred in places to 'the reformers', as if they were one cohesive group subscribing to a single progressive package. In fact, some M.P.s fought hard for one reform and against another. Leo Abse (Lab., Pontypool), leading campaigner for divorce and homosexual law reform, strongly opposed the new Abortion Act. M.P.s not generally thought of as progressive were also to be found voting consistently for reform: Ronald Bell (Con., South Bucks) is perhaps the best example. But in general, as Richards concludes: 'Members favourable to reform on one issue are generally favourable to reform on others; equally, those who oppose change in one sphere generally oppose it in others.'

3. This point can be usefully illustrated by comparing the vote on Leo Abse's Bill to reform the law on homosexuality in 1965, which failed by 159 votes to 178, with the successful vote on the introduction of his later Bill, which got through by 244 to 100.

   Changes in membership of the House were important. Of those who had left the Commons between these divisions, 34 had been opponents of the earlier Bill, and only 14 had been in favour. Of new arrivals, 64 voted in favour, only two against. But, just as crucially, *69 Members* (46 Labour, 22 Conservative, one Liberal) *who abstained on the first Bill voted in favour of the second; and 74 Members* (48 Conservative, 25 Labour and one Liberal) *who opposed the first did not vote on the second.* (Two members changed sides: Mrs Alice Cullen (Lab., Gorbals), moved from support to opposition and Jack Tinn (Lab., Cleveland) from opposition to support.)

4. Harry Street, *Freedom, The Individual, and The Law*, 2nd edn. (London, 1967).

5. E. J. Mishan, *Growth: The Price We Pay* (London, 1970).

6. Pollution in time became such a popular talking point and source of political provocation that it was awarded its own Royal Commission –

a standing body chaired by Sir Eric Ashby and ordered to make regular reports. See *Royal Commission on Environmental Pollution: First Report* (H.M.S.O., Cmnd. 4585, February 1971) for a cool, some would say over-cool, tour of the territory.

7. For a remarkably knowledgeable and well argued history of the motor-car and the inability of the party-political system to cope with it, see William Plowden, *The Motor Car and Politics* (London, 1971).

8. A basic text for the reformers was Professor Bernard Crick's *The Reform of Parliament* (London, 1964) which, despite some undeserved aspersions on the architect Pugin, is very persuasive on the ways in which politicians could start setting Parliament to rights.

9 Politics outside the System

HUGO YOUNG

After Labour lost the 1959 election, the politics of protest secured through the Campaign for Nuclear Disarmament the greatest triumph over 'the system' since the war. But the victory, achieved when C.N.D. captured the Labour Party conference in 1960, lasted only a year. Pursuing orthodox democratic methods, the Campaign was swiftly defeated.

Before Labour lost the 1970 election, the politics of protest, transformed into the protest 'movement', appeared to be a good deal more durable than C.N.D. That one extraordinary incursion upon the consensus was now a puny and irrelevant memory. Protest encompassed not merely ragged idealists, backing worthy causes by constitutional means, but seemingly a whole generation with a comprehensive philosophy, a radical life-style and a contempt for the old methods of restrained persuasion. 'Protest' was inclusive and badly defined. But it could safely be said to operate outside the system, and to aim variously at political, social and cultural revolution, with an impact which quite overshadowed conventional pressure-groups working, like C.N.D., to influence and thereby strengthen the system of parliamentary democracy. During the Labour years, the movement seemed capable of making an indelible mark on British politics.

That is, superficially, the story of the sixties. Among the milestones pointing to it, the most significant are associated with Grosvenor Square and the London School of Economics, two arenas which witnessed the rebirth of radical politics in Britain. From these sites the basic revolutionary message, with many different modulations, was picked up at many other points.

Yet by the middle of 1970 this scenario, which from 1967 to 1969 had been adopted with great solemnity by New Left radicals and with fierce concern by their opponents, was already falling apart. Despite the luxuriant growth of anti-system politics in the later sixties their hour did not really seem any nearer at hand. The impact of protest was conspicuously less impressive than had at one time seemed possible. Where so recently there had been the promise of the barricades and the people's government (or at least the students' university) there was now the more familiar noise of apathetic muttering. What survived was the memory of radical methods, which were learned and exploited by liberal reformers. Of the substance of radicalism there was virtually nothing.

C.N.D.'s apotheosis in the autumn of 1960 was achieved within the rules of conventional politics. Resolving its early uncertainty about the proper relationship to adopt towards the system, the Campaign followed the advice of Kingsley Martin and other liberal elders to convert the Labour Party or face extinction. If Labour had won in 1959, C.N.D. would have had only a marginal existence. As it was, very soon after their third electoral defeat, Barbara Castle and other leaders of the Left began to join their rank-and-file and identify themselves with C.N.D.'s radical objectives: namely, the unilateral abandonment by Britain of her nuclear weaponry and the consequential (although this was less candidly admitted and less widely understood) assumption of neutral status in the world.

Backed by a growing number of trade unions, this fundamental departure acquired a political momentum which led first to an interim, then to a conclusive victory. In the summer of 1960 Hugh Gaitskell, the Labour Leader, was obliged to moderate his strongly-held attachment to the nuclear consensus. He conceded that Labour should abandon the independent nuclear deterrent and that Britain should henceforward rely on the United States to provide nuclear cover. Large though it was, this compromise was not enough for C.N.D. It excluded any move away from the NATO alliance and thus rejected the Campaign's central demand, which was that Britain should not merely renounce the manufacture and use of nuclear weapons but should explicitly disavow dependence on them from whatever source.

What Gaitskell passionately resisted the Party Conference overcame. By 3,339,000 votes to 3,042,000 it adopted the full neutralist package. For a year the movement had been taken over by the crusade.

In two particular respects, C.N.D. foreshadowed the initiatives of the protest movement. The first of these was its success in attracting young people into political action. This was the first major post-war cause seen by the educated middle-class young as having relevance for them. The young constituted an important element alongside the middle-aged liberals, pacifist trade unionists, proper intellectuals and committed clergymen who made up the voice of the Campaign. Later in the decade, the under-twenty-five age-group advanced from participation to control not only of anti-system politics but of several more conventional pressure groups.

C.N.D.'s second characteristic was the vestigial connection between its purpose and its effects. This too, in the eye of history, will surely give it an affinity with later growths. In 1961 it attracted 100,000 people to Trafalgar Square at the end of its Easter march from Aldermaston. A splinter group from it, Bertrand Russell's Committee of 100, subsequently persuaded 4000 people to sit down outside the Ministry of Defence. Later that year Russell's group attracted more than 1300 arrests and a fair amount of police brutality in Trafalgar Square, having adopted the tactic of civil disobedience which was to be repeated with infinite variations by successor groups.

How effective was all this? C.N.D. leaders have often claimed credit for the signing of the Test Ban Treaty between the main nuclear powers in 1963. This bold claim rests on the premise that, without the public feeling which C.N.D. undoubtedly focused on the issue, the statesmen of the world would have had no interest in pressing for some ban on nuclear testing. A fair amount of evidence and common-sense argues against such a conclusion. But unless one accepts it, it is hard to sustain the view that C.N.D. was other than a necessary outlet for moral indignation which had one swift and, as it turned out, deceptive moment of political promise.

The precise limits of C.N.D.'s influence are nowhere more pitilessly defined than by a main participant in these events, Harold Wilson. Wilson was an architect of the Gaitskellite compromise, to get rid of the Bomb but retain the nuclear umbrella. Moreover, it was through unilateralist support in the Parliamentary Party that Wilson got as many as eighty-one votes against Gaitskell in the leadership contest in November 1960. While not a root-and-branch unilateralist himself, Wilson had made enough sympathetic noises to be adopted as their candidate; and he endorsed a defence policy which promised the absolute surrender of the independent nuclear deterrent. For this, the central plank in Labour's defence platform throughout its opposition years, C.N.D. was mainly responsible. It is interesting, therefore, to see from Wilson's own account of his Administration how crisply the issue was despatched by Labour in power.

Recalling the Nassau Agreement, under which Britain acquired Polaris nuclear missiles to replace the cancelled Skybolt, Wilson writes:

In the debate which followed, and in my 20 months as leader of the Opposition, we had opposed the decision, and opposed still more the pretence that Britain had an 'independent' nuclear weapon,

In the first days of the new government in October 1964, I had discussed with Patrick Gordon Walker and Denis Healey the future of the Polaris project in the light of the information now available to us. It was clear that production of the submarines was now well past the point of no return; there could be no question of cancelling them, except at inordinate cost. We decided to go ahead with four of the projected five submarines and to ensure their deployment as a fully committed part of the NATO defence forces. There was to be no nuclear pretence or suggestion of a go-it-alone British nuclear war against the Soviet Union.

The brisk insouciance of this account does not conceal the fact that Labour maintained a policy whereby Britain kept ultimate control over a handful of nuclear weapons, which became a factor in the equations of the Cold War and in deterring (if not provoking) a 'go-it-alone' war with the Soviet Union. When C.N.D. was at its height, and Labour was adjusting its defence policies accordingly, the mere existence of the Polaris submarines would hardly have been enough to waft aside, 'in the light of information now available', the moral principles preached by the Campaign.

The futile history of C.N.D. in fact points to one further connection between it and the radical protest which exploded some years later. It illuminates and exemplifies the disillusion with the Labour Party which, perhaps more than anything else, provoked the intimations of revolution which were to be heard through 1967, 1968 and 1969. Even in the 1966 election the radical Left, including the students, tended to work for a Labour victory, in the hope that, released from the bondage of 1964's tiny majority, the Government would fulfil some radical hopes. When soon afterwards it became quite apparent that such optimism was to be betrayed in foreign and economic policy as decisively as it had been over defence, movement not merely outside 'the system' but away from it gathered speed.

This movement offered a challenge to the consensus which C.N.D. never attempted and which, indeed, had been the property of the outermost fringes of political activity throughout the post-war period. Marxist or quasi-Marxist critiques of society began to be advanced, which extended well beyond the specific origins of protest. These lay in a cause which was analogous to the moralities of C.N.D. – the occupation of a small country, Vietnam, by the army of a great power. But the rhetoric, although it fed on the escalation of the war, rapidly broadened, and the methods recommended by the American New Left for pressing it home became rapidly less restrained. It was not the American soldier or even the American war machine which was to blame for inhumanity in Vietnam, but the society which produced the machine which produced the soldier. Hence it was the society which must be destroyed. By late 1966 this call to action was being taken up in Britain by the Radical Student Alliance, a ginger group within the reformist National Union of Students, and the Vietnam Solidarity Campaign, which backed the cause of the Vietcong. British society came to be seen by radicals as indistinguishable from American in its corruption, its injustice, the deadness of its liberal nostrums and its ripeness for revolutionary change.

Anti-system politics were marked in Britain, as elsewhere, by an inter-linking, if not an alliance, between the street and the campus. Students made up the bulk of the protest movement – about three-quarters of those attending the most significant protest action, the march through London to Hyde Park in October 1968, had some connection with places of education. Similarly, radical ideals, however various and confused, underlay most of the disorder at universities.

The first 'sit-in' at a British university took place at the L.S.E. in March 1967. A shocking accident the previous month, when a porter died during a demonstration in the building, did not diminish the resentment felt by some against the prevailing disciplinary rules at the school, by others against its total management. The sit-in was a protest against the disciplin-ing of the president of the students' union and the president of the graduate students' association for trying to organise a meeting after the L.S.E.'s director, Sir Sydney Caine, had banned it. Behind this stood a deeper resentment, against the appointment as Caine's successor of Dr Walter Adams, then Principal of the University College of Rhodesia. Thus, within a year of the 1966 election, another aspect of the Wilson Govern-ment's policy struck lightning on the campus; first there was the un-qualified and repeated support for American policy in Vietnam, now the failure to make good Wilson's rash promise that Rhodesia's U.D.I. would be over 'in weeks rather than months'.

During the rest of 1967 the possibilities exposed by the action at the L.S.E. began to be understood elsewhere. In this process, two elements of opinion fed upon each other. On the one hand a righteous hostility was aroused against many college rules, which were characterised in the rhetoric as anything from 'paternalism' to 'institutional violence'. On the other hand stood the belief that the places should be pulled down and reconstructed as a model – the most vulnerable and most instructive model – for society as a whole. To the second, 'revolutionary' axis, the first set of grievances, which were often real and pressing, supplied the combustible material they needed.

In the spring and summer of 1968 the disruption of university life reached its peak. It became increasingly difficult for either British Ministers or American spokesmen to get a hearing on campus. Some speakers were threatened with duckings, others were drowned out, others had their cars blocked or spattered with paint. Without doubt it was, in every case, only a minority of students who saw themselves as participating in an embryo revolution. But equally they did not find it difficult to engage the sympathy of a much larger minority, and sometimes a majority, for action in protest against the running of the institution – whether in its disciplinary function (as, eventually, at almost all colleges and universities) or in its academic curricula (especially at art colleges).

By the middle of 1968 there were those bedded inside 'the system' who felt themselves to be seriously menaced by this chain of events. A leader in *The Times* at the end of the summer term spoke of 'a collapse of order in English universities'. In France a large body of students, led by Daniel Cohn-Bendit, had brought the country temporarily to its knees, by forging an alliance with the trade unions. They appeared to have come close to unhorsing President de Gaulle himself. Along with other foreign students, they influenced directly the conversion of the Radical Student Alliance into the Revolutionary Socialist Students Federation (R.S.S.F.) in Britain in June. The R.S.S.F.'s manifesto was an explicit summons to the barricades:

> R.S.S.F.'s aims cannot be achieved through parliamentary means and it therefore constitutes itself as an extra-parliamentary opposition. . . . It commits itself on principle to all anti-imperialist, anti-capitalist and anti-fascist struggles. . . . It commits itself to the revolutionary overthrow of capitalism and imperialism and its replacement by workers' power . . .

But it did not in the end happen here. For a time the students of the world looked as though they might forge themselves into a real International. But they did not. In Britain the advance to revolution never made very much progress, and the alliance between student and worker foundered on mutual class hostility. There were results, to be sure, but in a bitter, classical, British pattern they tended to strengthen the system rather than assist its destruction.

The anti-system radicals succeeded in bringing about some valuable liberal reforms. Disciplinary procedures were improved. Representation of students on governing bodies greatly increased. Consultation expanded. Committees were set up. Curricula were revised. The Committee of Vice-Chancellors and Principals met the National Union of Students in October 1968 and produced a *concordat* which attested to the capacity of the 'system' to yield gracefully and gobble up any threat to its own existence. The Commons Select Committee on Education and Science studied staff-student relations, thus conceding what earlier in the decade would have been inadmissible: the claim of students to be taken seriously. Structures were reformed: but structures still stood.

Another narrow, ominous but critical initiative contributed to this result. For adopting and encouraging a revolutionary perspective, two lecturers at the L.S.E. were dismissed and one student put in prison. The lecturers, Nicholas Bateson and Robin Blackburn, were felt by many to have been harshly treated. The student, an American post-doctoral researcher, Paul Hoch, who was jailed for persistently ignoring a court injunction, was less obviously martyr-material than Blackburn, in particular, whose punishment for supporting, after the event, an act of revolutionary destruction stimulated a wave of sympathy. It was notable, however, how frequently in the rest of 1969 and 1970 these sentences were remembered on campuses all over the country which had previously believed themselves to be beyond the law. They were a cause of the marked reduction in campus radicalism of all kinds during 1970.

By the end of the decade, anti-war protest itself, as an agent of radical change, had become a congealed memory. Its rise and fall ran almost exactly parallel with that of the university reformation, but there was not even a liberal reform to show for it.

From 1967 the Vietnam Solidarity Campaign, whose most voluble leader was a former President of the Oxford Union, Tariq Ali, was synonymous with the protest movement. The multitude of groups, institutes, campaigns, committees, parties, splinters and zealots nominally federated within it constituted an almanac of the more or less New Left. Ali's magazine, *Black Dwarf*, foresaw the Campaign's largest enterprise, the October March through London, 'as the beginning of a new movement'. It urged that all left-wing groups should get together and form the Extra-Parliamentary Opposition: 'Such a party cannot be built in isolation from the mass of those who are active on the streets against the Vietnam War because they are a politicised vanguard and will of necessity form the cadres of a new party.'

Some weeks before the march the 'system', through *The Times*, gave some credibility to this dream. The newspaper published a report warning, without any qualification, that 'a small army of militant extremists plans to seize control of certain highly sensitive installations and buildings in central London', while police were diverted to the demonstration. This report became something of a landmark for connoisseurs of false prophecy. But it effectively illustrates the panic-stricken state into which the authorities were driven at the time.

As a demonstration of opinion against the Vietnam war and the Labour Government's total endorsement of it, the march impressed by its size and, for the most part, its orderliness. But as the beginning of a united extra-parliamentary Opposition it was less convincing. Solidarity was not its middle name. Like the May Day Manifesto, published in 1967, the V.S.C. united hardly anyone on the Ad Hoc Committee for the March, beyond the war. International Socialism disagreed with the Young Communist League, the International Marxist Group with the Young Liberals, the R.S.S.F. with the Movement for Colonial Freedom, and the British Vietnam Solidarity Front with the Vietnam Solidarity Campaign itself. Ali, who for the 'system' became the very emblem of destructive radicalism, was denounced by some fellow-marchers as 'that international adventurer and playboy of the pseudo-Left'.

A survey of the marchers, conducted by the magazine *New Society*, revealed a wide range of motives subsidiary to the attack on the war. A fair number evidently thought they were there as a protest against capitalism in general, or as a gesture towards the destruction of British society by violent revolution. To this kind of sentiment the police's conduct of the march was not very helpful. There were no water-cannon, no teargas, no troops, no anti-riot shields, even in Grosvenor Square where the most radical splinter insisted on attacking the American Embassy. To revolutionaries the most jarring symbol of 27 October was the spectacle of police and demonstrators congratulating each other on the general decency of each other's behaviour.

In retrospect it is possible to see that date as the high point of British anti-system politics in the sixties. But images of the revolution continued to be perceived even though revolutionary political action tended from then on to diminish.

One such image was the pop concert, especially when it was given free. In the *Guardian*, Richard Gott reported that a Rolling Stones concert in Hyde Park in the summer of 1969, before an estimated half-a-million spectators, 'seemed to be taking place in a socialist society in the distant future . . .'.

To an old-timer, it would seem like the climax of an Aldermaston march, though without the politics. For one surrealist moment it was like being transferred to the Plaza de la Revolucion in Havana, with Fidel Jagger haranguing the assembled workers lately in from the cane-fields. ... The participants had a classless air, less disciplined, less puritanical than the middle-class protesters of earlier days. Today there is no protest, but merely a feeling – perhaps a false one – that a kind of freedom has been achieved in spite of, rather than because of, Wilson, Heath and Co.

Anyone who wants to understand the present political malaise in Britain, or who wants to have an inkling of what Britain will be like in ten years' time, should have been in Hyde Park on Saturday.

Nor was it only on the Left that protest flourished. Others too felt that only outside the system of parliamentary debate could they adequately express their grief with the Labour Government. At the same time as universities were facing the radical challenge, the country was obliged to confront a much more bizarre phenomenon.

It all began with five patriotic typists, Valerie and Brenda and Joan and Carolann and Christine. Over Christmas 1967, when Britain was in the pit of post-devaluation gloom, they asked what they could do for their country and decided that it was half an hour's extra work a day, without pay. From this modest beginning at the Colt Heating and Ventilation Co., Surbiton, the 'I'm Backing Britain' movement grew to encapsulate a national mood. In the first week of the New Year, collective self-denial became, ever so briefly, the vogue. One day twelve Ipswich mothers agreed to give up free milk vouchers, another day the municipality of Bootle officially Backed Britain, another the Governor of Tasmania telegraphed that all Tasmanians were 'thrilled at the finest action since the Battle of Britain'.

Such idealism could not survive untarnished for long. A rival campaign was launched by Robert Maxwell, the Labour M.P. and publishing millionaire, with the slogan 'Help Britain, Help Yourself'. Clive Jenkins, leader of the Association of Technical and Managerial Staffs, spoke for most trade unionists in deriding these inspirational self-sacrifices as 'economic illiteracy'. Enoch Powell called them 'silly and dangerous hysteria'. And even though these times themselves were both dangerous and hysterical, Backing Britain was dead within four months.

It had, nevertheless, drawn upon a feeling of despair which was visible across the political spectrum. When the five typists, after visiting the

House of Commons, complained about 'all those M.P.s lying around with their legs up', they showed they had something in common with *Black Dwarf*: 'We do not want any more petitions to Parliament. The House of Commons is as irrelevant as those who sit inside it.' People who sent in sixpence for Concorde or left a fiver to defray the National Debt seemed to believe that conventional methods of managing the economy and the national spirit alike were failing. So, palpably, did the advocates of Great Britain Ltd, who thought that government should be turned over to businessmen. For a time in 1968 this too had its day, as men like Cecil King, in his last days as chairman of the International Publishing Corporation, and Lord Robens, chairman of the Coal Board, climbed on the bandwagon. Nothing would have horrified these men more than to be reminded that they were arguing for a destruction of the 'system' as radical as that envisaged by anyone on *Black Dwarf*.

A new fundamentalism, then, was the distinguishing mark of extra-parliamentary politics as the sixties advanced. It tended to overshadow the more orthodox efforts to mount political campaigns in the style the British parliamentary system knows very well. Yet these were as numerous as ever, probably more so. Whether the cause was Biafra or child poverty or disablement or betrayal of British passport-holders, the law which decrees that all governments arouse sectional anger applied to the Wilson Administration with particular rigour. Not only the radical fringe profited from the collapse of confidence in Labour's idealism.

The pressure groups were small and large. Some, like the Campaign against Racial Discrimination (CARD) and the Disablement Income Group (DIG) saw their efforts issue in legislation. Others were much more futile. Three are particularly worth noticing.

The group most relentlessly in evidence was Shelter, which was founded in 1966 for the purpose of raising funds for housing associations. This modest and potentially obscure activity was quickly transformed into something more political. Under its director and publicist, Des Wilson, Shelter harnessed the talents of a large number of young people into the business of compelling the nation and its politicians to pay attention to the housing problem. Shelter was simultaneously an action group and a pressure group, seeking political support for its own purposes. By August 1970 it had raised £2·5 m. and rehoused over 4000 families. But more than that, Wilson himself had become a skilled exponent of the value of public relations as applied to social problems. Criticised for taking inadequate interest in the complexities of housing policy, and for over-colouring some of his evidence, Des Wilson left little doubt which of

Shelter's two functions he regarded as the most important. He was proud to claim that no other campaign had had as much television coverage as his. To those who felt that too often the message was merely the message, he answered that 'the P.R. activities of Shelter were aimed at public opinion itself – in other words not towards an administrative reflection of the best in society, but a more compassionate society itself'.

The Child Poverty Action Group worked by precisely opposite methods. Its objective was to persuade the country and the politicians to take poverty more seriously, a course which it pursued by rigorously intellectual methods. It did not lack publicity, and indeed by being a copious source of accurate information on complicated matters it was regularly heard from. But it was not interested in ballyhoo, merely in the constant refinement and repetition of unalterable facts about life at the bottom, together with recommended policies for changing their condition. Unlike Shelter, it observed all the Fabian canons of rationality.

By 1970 it was hard to be certain which of these two approaches to political influence had been the more unsuccessful. Leaving aside Shelter's own valuable efforts at providing dwellings, its impact on government was minimal: housing remained what it had always been, an unsolved problem. As for the C.P.A.G., it published its own confession of failure. During the 1970 election it reported, to the fury of Labour Ministers, that under six years of Labour, poverty had actually got worse.

A third group was wholly successful, and it is instructive to examine why. The Stop-the-Seventy-Tour campaign (S.T.S.T.) was put together to prevent a scheduled tour of Britain by the South African cricket team from taking place. It hoped to persuade the English cricket authorities to call off the tour voluntarily under the influence of sweet reason. But if persuasion failed, S.T.S.T. made it perfectly clear that it would seek to make it impossible for any games against the South Africans to take place. Through the winter and spring of 1970, S.T.S.T. united liberal opinion behind its objectives, which were strongly opposed by most of the cricket world, most of the Tory party and most of the country.

In the end, after first curtailing the tour to a few matches on a few well-guarded grounds, the cricket authorities called it off after a formal request from the Government to do so. In making this request the Government was clearly influenced only a little by the fact that most of its members abhorred apartheid; it had been careful throughout the debate to take the position that the tour was a private function. What the Government responded to was a crude threat to the peace, which was likely to take place at the very time when its custodianship was being tested in an election. As the *Guardian*, an opponent of the tour, wrote: 'The threat of violence . . . has influenced partially a decision by the Government. Mr Callaghan [Home Secretary] had no choice. But the precedent is still an unhappy one.'

But S.T.S.T. was an isolated event. By the time of the election the apocalyptic optimism which fuelled the protest movement in 1968 had drained away. Even in March 1969, a mere 2000 people assembled to march down Whitehall in protest against the refusal of visas to a North Vietnamese delegation. Outbursts against the Vietnam war occurred with steadily diminishing volume until, in April 1970, the march was taken over by Black Power and its route forcibly diverted from the United States Embassy to the Embassy of Trinidad and Tobago. The following month it was not Tariq Ali but Fenner Brockway, the veteran of C.N.D. days, who led the platform. The press spoke of ideological exhaustion and 'an anticlimactic failure'.

Similarly at the reformed universities, little stirred. As the new academic year opened, most newspapers carried warnings of continuous explosion on the campus. *The Times* insisted that 'the revolution is already occurring'. But all that it could cite in defence of this inexact analysis was, revealingly, the growing support for such system-oriented bodies as the Consumers' Association, the Advisory Centre for Education and 'the lobby for the environment'. At the London School of Economics a new president of the Union was elected on a manifesto he described as 'just a few jokes'. According to the retiring incumbent the new man owed his victory to 'the frivolous attitude here at the moment. The atmosphere has always been intensely political, until now'.

For all the radical excitements of the sixties, therefore, a question remained about their capacity to endure into the seventies. This was true before the election, and emphatically true after it.

Some people, far from being chastened by the failure of the radical style to radicalise British politics, believed that it would define the future. Inside the system, the chief exponent of this view was Anthony Wedgwood Benn, the former Labour Cabinet Minister. In a Fabian pamphlet published soon after Labour's defeat, Benn foresaw direct action as a key to 'the new politics' which must revitalise the enfeebled parliamentary system. Workers' control, civil disobedience and referenda on important issues were among his prescriptions. 'The case for a strategy of confrontations with bureaucracy is very strong', he wrote, 'and indeed without it it is hard to see how we can ever liberate ourselves.'

Maybe Benn was a little late. Even as he wrote, an uncomfortable fact was becoming clear; under the influence of a Government with strong anti-consensus inclinations, the parliamentary system was showing signs of revival. For the first time in two decades the differences between the democratic parties appeared to be basic. No longer was it plausible to opt out of the system merely on the grounds that both Parties sounded the same. On the Left the battles to be won were real ones. There was not only the reforming work left undone by the Labour Government, there was also a new and calculated assault on existing remedies which had to be met where it originated, inside the system.

This will not necessarily extinguish the radical fires. On the New Left the reply would be that restoring substance to the parliamentary debate will merely emphasise its fundamental absurdity, and its inability to be more than a wasteful distraction from the coming transformation of society on an epic scale. Moreover, if the Labour Party itself fails to regain credibility among the Left and centre-Left, that might provide an opening for the kind of politics outlined by Wedgwood Benn – but in a context where they would not be controlled by the party in the way he envisages.

There seems on the whole to be a better chance that in the age of Heath Toryism, politics outside the system will be conducted in a rather different spirit. The way was shown by the course of the debate on the siting of the third London airport. A commission appointed by Labour considered the question with all the most sophisticated apparatus of modern decision-making. They made a choice, in the middle of the Buckinghamshire countryside, which seemed to be dictated by all the criteria of an efficient society. But that choice was overturned by the incoming Government not because the members of that Government were any more country-conscious or any less efficiency-conscious than either Labour or the Roskill Commission, but because of public opinion. It had become politically impossible to choose an inland site rather than a coastal site.

Here perhaps was the beginning of a new protest movement: the protest not of a radical minority against society as a whole, but of the people as a whole against the evils worked upon them by a tiny handful of decision-makers. The methods available to them had been permanently coloured by the sixties' radicals; like S.T.S.T., the airport lobbyists were full of plans for direct action. And eventually, who knows, this concern for the environment might lead to the same objective as Tariq Ali's: a radical questioning of the bases of the capitalist, technocratic, profit-motivated society.

10 Northern Ireland

HAROLD JACKSON

It was late in the decade that any consciousness of the intractable problem of Ulster burst upon a reluctant English public. For fifty years the English had thankfully buried their awareness of Ireland in a deep tomb of indifference. Once the Home Rule issue had been settled, at least to the satisfaction of the mainland, there was only the occasional outrage by the Irish Republican Army – and they had become few and infrequent – to remind the shires and the suburbs that four hundred years of history was waiting to catch up with them.

The fact that the English had wished the whole nightmare away did not, of course, mean that the six northern counties of Ireland had ceased to progress towards the inevitable showdown between the one million Protestants and half-million Catholics who shared the meagre cake available to them. From the start of the moves towards independence there had been a fundamental contradiction between nationalist aspirations and economic reality.

The chance of Continental drift had ensured that Ireland would be a natural satellite of the English mainland. Its natural resources are sparse and its predictable fate as an offshore island was that it should be ruthlessly colonised by the larger island to the east, whose inhabitants felt obliged to secure their trading ties by conquest. The Angles had suffered this fate at the hands of the Scandinavians and Romans – both island tribes in temperament if not in geographical actuality – and visited a similar situation on their weaker neighbours. There has thus never been a point in history where relations between the Irish and the English have not carried a certain natural tension.

The political consequence was inevitable: a strongly-motivated wish to break the sequence and restore the identity of the conquered. But this emotional need must always come up against the insurmountable obstacle of economic dependence. Could this economic and political spiral ever be broken we would probably see the end of the Irish question. The unlikelihood of achieving such a break was the basic dilemma that faced Harold

Wilson and his Cabinet when the Ulster crisis burst upon them in October 1968.

On the face of it the points at issue in the rioting which disrupted Londonderry that Saturday evening were calculated to appeal to a Labour administration. A protest march had been planned by civil rights activists to draw attention to the unfair allocation of municipal housing after a particularly blatant piece of discrimination in Dungannon. But the movement had already broadened its appeal to take in the whole spectrum of political repression of the Catholics, particularly at local government level. 'One man, one vote' became the slogan that penetrated not only to London but across the continents. Catch-phrases are seldom capable of great political sophistication and this one probably brought more harm to the movement in the long run than benefit.

Since the partition of Ireland in 1921, the Unionist Party had held power in the North and had behaved like the besieged minority which Sir Edward Carson had mobilised to oppose Home Rule. Though the pattern of sectarian voting ensured that it would keep its hand firmly on the reins so long as the usual political divisions were short-circuited, each administration behaved as if it was about to be annihilated by the republican (and Catholic) hordes waiting at the border. This fantasy was projected internally too, and every Catholic was treated as subversive and a potential enemy of the state.

So the minority was held firmly in check and almost any means of pursuing this objective was regarded as legitimate. The establishment of a separate Parliament at Stormont – initially against the wishes of the Unionists – had given Westminster the perfect excuse to leave Ulster to stew. Originally its members had been elected by proportional representation but this was soon abandoned for the safer method of single-member constituencies, which made certainty doubly sure that the Unionists would sweep the board. Where there was any doubt the boundaries were drawn in a way that grossly under-enfranchised the Catholics: Londonderry, with a population two-thirds Catholic, always had a Protestant-dominated council.

In the sixties Terence O'Neill took up the premiership. A remote, patrician sort of figure with the squirearchical background regarded as essential for Ulster premiers, he none the less started the first cautious moves to a dialogue with the Republic and towards some sort of normality in a highly eccentric society. To outsiders, if any had bothered to look, it would have seemed the dimmest sort of gradualism at best; but for a hothouse society such as Northern Ireland it represented a galloping radicalism which it was ill-equipped to handle.

O'Neill had some perception of what he was undertaking, but it is doubtful if he ever realised just what he was unleashing. Apart from the occasional outbursts of activity from the I.R.A. across the border the Catholics had remained astoundingly docile, largely because of the English Governments at Westminster. Though Stormont was nominally entirely responsible for the internal affairs of the province, the convention had developed that social legislation in England was repeated in Ulster. The preposterous situation thus developed where the measures brought in by the Attlee government after the Second World War to establish the welfare state were bitterly opposed by the Unionist M.P.s at Westminster only to be docilely pushed through Stormont by the Unionist Government there. But at least they served to temper the more extreme aspects of Unionist rule and to hold at bay the discontent stirring in the minority. In essence it was little more than giving them cake, but it helped as a stopgap.

But the tentative steps forward taken by O'Neill took on a significance out of all proportion to reality. Ireland is a natural arena for extremes – though disentangling history or temperament as the cause is a barren exercise – and so the reactions were heightened accordingly. Wilson initially saw the anti-Unionist battle as a convenient stick against the Tories at home and his early opportunist pronouncements stressed this aspect. Later he woke up to the fact that his administration was once more being sucked into the bogs of Irish politics, a graveyard for Englishmen for three hundred years, and he backed off sharply. The onus of running the crisis fell on James Callaghan who, against all the odds, forged a considerable reputation for himself.

The introverted quality of Ulster politics does not mean that the province is insulated from outside influence. There can be endless argument about why the whole mess blew up when it did but, to adopt Marxist terminology for a moment, there was a certain historical inevitability about it all. It must be remembered that the whole area of politics in Ireland, North and South, is way to the right of the English norm. Thus what can be absorbed with only a small gulp on the mainland causes violent dyspepsia across the Irish Sea. The upsurge of the New Left in Europe and America, culminating in the Paris student riots of May 1968, looked like Red Revolution in Belfast.

The civil rights movement attracted students; it would have been astounding if it had not. To a man like William Craig, then Minister of Home Affairs, the increasing militancy of the campaign looked ominously like the wrath to come. In an odd way the issue of the Papal encyclical

Humanae Vitae, with its continued proscription of birth control, also played its part. It appeared in July 1968 and once more set off the deep-set fears of the Ulster Protestants that the minority would outbreed them. In the Ulster context, therefore, it seemed an absolutely natural decision to ban the Derry March and to enforce that ban with the baton charges and water-cannon that the Royal Ulster Constabulary regarded as its normal method of law enforcement. It was hard luck, so far as they were concerned, that a Westminster M.P. happened to be at the receiving end.

Though the subsequent riots served to draw international attention to Ulster – and certainly to increase the pressure on O'Neill from both extremes – Westminster played the situation coolly and saw no reason to intervene. There had been periodic crises before and they had always gone away: with a bit of luck this one would behave like the others. In fact it did not, if only because the vastly increased technology of communications kept public attention aware of what was happening. O'Neill thought he could outflank the hardliners in his own party and called a snap General Election in which he put up Unionist candidates to oppose the backs-woodsmen. It was a disastrous miscalculation in which he only held his own constituency by a whisker against the extremist Protestantism of Ian Paisley. Two months later O'Neill resigned. That was the end of gradual-ism. Extremism now took over and found its first expression with the election of Bernadette Devlin to Westminster.

The situation went steadily downhill from then on. O'Neill's successor, James Chichester-Clark, was a compromise choice whose main appeal to both sides was that he was regarded as malleable. It was about the worst conceivable reason for selecting a Prime Minister in the circumstances and Chichester-Clark's early weeks were spent with his finger in a fast-crumbling dyke. Events in Ulster have moved so far since then that it is hard to imagine the political atmosphere then prevailing. Even moderate Unionists at the time believed that they were faced with a little local difficulty that would be resolved with judicious firmness towards the minority. Their lack of grasp of the underlying realities was pinpointed by the decision to allow the traditional Protestant parade to march through the centre of Londonderry on 12 August and to bring in massive numbers of police to safeguard its passage past the city's Catholic stronghold, the Bogside.

To those of us from outside the Province it seemed totally suicidal, as it turned out to be. The city erupted in mid-afternoon and was in a state of near-anarchy within hours. The R.U.C. could barely contain the situation, let alone control it, and when the rioting hit Belfast two days later its hard-pressed forces were virtually overwhelmed. The Special Constabulary had been mobilised earlier (this was part of a wider contingency plan in which the army was also on the alert, though this was kept highly secret at the time) and just ran amok. The B Specials had earned a fearsome place in Catholic mythology and were seen as licensed Protestant thugs recruited to oppress the minority. In the desperate situation of the adjacent Protestant and Catholic ghettos of Belfast that August their reputation seemed well-deserved. The combination of lack of training, fear, trigger-happiness, and official status could have had even more disastrous consequences had Westminster not brought the army in to take over the security operation.

There was no choice in the matter by this stage, but London started to reap the whirlwind of its own indecision in the earlier stages of the crisis. There had been minor political concessions to the Catholics in the preceding months, but they had done nothing to ease the discontent. Catholic leaders had called for intervention from London but this had been resisted not only by the Unionists but by Wilson. Now he had been obliged to intervene without being able to choose his moment. Ulster probably provides the clearest case against pragmatism: it was never a situation which should have been allowed to develop under its own steam. There were never any options opened by allowing that to happen; they were just closing down all the time.

The great mistake had been to assume that the Catholics had a clear political programme. Certainly that was the way it looked to the casual observer, and this was the great disservice that the 'one man, one vote' slogan did to all the participants. No one actually stopped to ask what the effect of local government franchise reform would be. Given the one-third, two-thirds division of the community and the continued pattern of sectarian voting (which had been made all too evident both in the O'Neill general election and in the Westminster by-election which brought Bernadette Devlin's victory) reform could never bring the Catholics any more than a paper victory. It was not going to change the realities of power in the province.

But the civil rights campaign seemed to have mesmerised everyone into believing that it contained a solution. Obviously it had a firm foundation in its demand that United Kingdom standards should apply to all citizens and, from that point of view, was wholly laudable. But this perfectly legitimate struggle masked the fact that it did not really touch on the heart of the crisis, which had a far more mystic basis. What the Catholics were really looking for, though they did not admit this even to themselves (and have still not done so) was the best of both worlds – the freedom of spirit and action implicit in nationalism allied to the economic benefit of the £100 m. a year with which the English taxpayer bolstered the province's chronically ailing economy.

Clearly, this is not the sort of demand capable of rational expression, because it has no rational basis. Any attempt to translate it into political terms could thus only falsify. The position of the Protestants was equally unreal in that they proclaimed their allegiance to the Crown but were wholly unwilling to meet the social and political obligations this entailed. If Ireland had had something tangible to offer the English – such as a strategic naval base, as Malta has – there might have been some basis for a negotiated settlement. But it has not and the tangle that faced James Callaghan when he came to try for a solution was that he could only act in a general spirit of goodwill, since the logic of the crisis was that the English should wash their hands of it as soon as possible; that the Catholics were demanding concessions which were not going to meet their real wishes; and that the Unionist protestations of loyalty to the U.K. always carried the undertone that it was contingent on their being allowed to do as they liked without interference from the central government.

What followed was a remarkable piece of sleight of hand by Callaghan. In many ways he was the ideal man for the moment. His generally benign manner, allied to an iron will, served both to placate the Catholics and bulldoze the Stormont administration into a more evident reform programme. In an astonishingly short time Chichester-Clark was committed to reform of local government voting (which had already been promised) and revision of electoral boundaries, to disarming the police and disbanding the B Specials, to centralising housing allocation and thus circumventing local bigotry, and to establishing machinery to deal with allegations of discrimination at administrative level.

The Catholics were delighted and the Protestants dismayed. It appeared that violence was reaping its rewards, a point rather ineptly conceded by Chichester-Clark in one of his occasional and disastrous public excursions into philosophy. The inexorable logic of Callaghan's intervention – though there was no alternative to the course he took – was that the Protestants would see what they could achieve by counter-violence. The reform programme might look eminently reasonable to Westminster and the outside world, but to the Shankill Road, befogged by generations of Unionist propaganda, it came across simply as aid and comfort to the enemy. In a state of great emotion and considerable confusion the Protestants started their own riots. In a bizarre reaction to the recommendations of Lord Hunt's committee that the police should be disarmed, a mob in the Crumlin Road shot an R.U.C. man dead.

So, within three months of its intervention, the army found itself up against the contradictions of its own presence. From the start, the General Officer Commanding Northern Ireland, Sir Ian Freeland, had stressed that only the politicians could sort things out. It was true enough, except that the politicians had lost the ability to control the situation. The only real control, and that was pretty notional at times, was exerted by the British troops. So, though they continued to deny the fact, the troops were fulfilling a political role and every action became fraught with overtones. Arms searches, for example, were accompanied by howls of rage and allegations that they were only directed at one side's weaponry. Every dead rioter became an innocent martyr, though no one ever bothered to explain how it happened that he was present in the middle of a rioting mob. The fantasy element in the situation grew steadily.

It brought increasing bafflement to the English whose simple logic suggested that the easy way of not getting shot by the troops was not to riot. For the Irish there was an equally evident logic which dictated that the only way to demonstrate that they were being subjected to intolerable provocation was to be provoked. Any attempt by the authorities to maintain order was seen by both sides as a brutal repression of their legitimate grievances and therefore, by implication, support for the opposite faction. The idea of a reasoned dialogue, which underlay Callaghan's political strategy, was unattainable since no two parties were speaking the same language. But the Home Secretary acted with great astuteness. One point in his favour was that the Catholics were more sympathetic towards a Labour government, which was not tainted as the Conservatives were with formal links with the Unionists. He also managed to achieve a bi-partisan approach at Westminster which served to disarm the Unionists to some degree. He remained calm and judicious, showed understanding of both points of view, was constructive in his ideas and primed the Belfast pump with well-judged economic aid. His reputation grew measurably and his initiative could well have done the trick if he had one more element to count on – that the Irish were Englishmen.

But they are not; and the truth about the Callaghan programme, though this was certainly not deliberate on his part, is that it was well-calculated to appeal to the English as a solution but was almost irrelevant to the Irish. This may sound harsh but the blame cannot be laid at Callaghan's door. He was dealing with an irrational situation and could only rely on rational suggestions to meet it. His finest achievement in some ways was to ride out the storm with his reputation enhanced where it most mattered, in his own country. Considering what has usually happened to English politicians suddenly faced with Irish politics, that in itself is a glowing tribute to his political touch.

Looked at in the coldest light, his greatest long-term service to the English taxpayer was to lay a solid foundation for an eventual withdrawal from Ireland by doing all that could be legitimately demanded. He may not have convinced the Irish, but he has certainly offered the English the essential self-justification they need before selling anyone down the river.

But the results of his policy in Ireland were equally predictable. Bit by bit he closed down the options for both sides. For the Protestants it was made clear that there could be no backtracking on the reforms or on the pace of them. In the background hovered the threat of direct rule from London and the suspension of the Stormont Parliament. And the Catholics in turn had to accept the fulfilment of their demands and a cessation of their pressure. Since the demands had only been intended as a form of pressure and had been pitched at what had been regarded as an unattainable level, the minority was suddenly left in a vacuum. It had never articulated what it really wanted and here it was with its main weapon suddenly thrown from its hand.

There was a joint move away from established politics, which now seemed unable to offer any outlet. Ian Paisley and one of his extreme Protestant followers were elected to Stormont in by-elections and recruitment blossomed in the two factions into which the I.R.A. had now split. The battle-lines were being drawn more clearly and it became plain that the moderate element often referred to by Ulster Cabinet ministers and at Westminster was largely fictional. Not every Ulsterman was out throwing petrol bombs and loosing off Thompson sub-machine guns at the military, but there was a tacit acquiescence in extremism which spoke just as loudly. Riots ebbed and flowed and the number of troops went up and down proportionately. But the underlying momentum of the crisis increased: neither faction was looking for peace, each was out for victory.

Callaghan held the line until the Labour Government was defeated in June 1970 and it must have been with some thankfulness that he handed over the burden to Reginald Maudling. It was not a happy transition. Maudling's apparent lack of interest and heavy-handed touch got on everyone's nerves. The whole issue had become a matter of style rather than content and the High Table manner jarred all round. Basically both factions in Ulster were looking for a reason to reject Westminster's policy and Maudling offered a better one than had come to light so far. Not that the rejection was made evident. It took the form of endless nitpicking about the details of each proposal or of allegations that the reforms were not being operated in the spirit in which they were conceived. It may well be that no one could have resolved the difficulty, simply because there was no will for a solution on the part of Northern Ireland, but the tone of the Heath administration and the particular qualities of its Home Secretary could not have been more unfortunate.

If ever there was a lame duck it was Ulster and the Conservatives' declared willingness to let the creatures swim or sink through their own efforts increased the general feeling of insecurity in the province. In the event, the policy was not actually applied to the six counties – the Stormont Government, for example, took on a massive financial responsibility for the Harland and Wolff shipyard, still lurching wildly under the impact of expensive fixed-price contracts – but words count for more than deeds in the emotional climate of Belfast. The Conservatives' economic policy, bringing a dramatic rise in the numbers of unemployed, hit Ulster hard and again served to exacerbate the communal tensions which are largely rooted in the struggle for a reasonable living in an area of limited opportunity.

Nine months after Heath's unexpected accession to Downing Street Chichester-Clark threw in the towel. He had lasted far longer than most people expected but his administration had really been kept in office by the army. Military juntas are regarded as the product of banana republics and African tribalism, but a Martian might have been hard put to find any essential difference in the situation in Northern Ireland. The Government had, admittedly, been elected but it had lost the support of the popular will. Had an election been held when Chichester-Clark handed in his seals it is doubtful if any of his Ministers would have survived. The right-wing Unionists, led by William Craig, made a strong push for power but were again held back by the fear of Westminster intervention.

Brian Faulkner, who had spent a large part of his career waiting in the wings for just this opportunity, took office and immediately shot his credibility apart by appointing one of the hardest-line right-wingers to the Cabinet. He balanced this by going outside Parliament for his Minister of Community Relations, appointing a former Stormont Labour M.P., David Bleakley. But it was the appointment to his administration of Harry West which made the impact, convincing the Catholics once again that no Unionist Government could escape the clutches of the Orange Order and Protestant extremism. To outsiders, Faulkner was the obvious choice.

A gifted administrator and possessed of a far greater political skill than any other Stormont politician, he was seen as the possible saviour of the province.

But his ambivalent past and his supposed trickiness were anathema to the Opposition, which was coming under increased pressure from its own grass roots. For the bulk of the Catholics there had been an unreal assumption that the passage of the reforms would bring Utopia instantly. When they found that the effect on their lives was minimal, and with the general economic climate operating very heavily against Northern Ireland in any case, their call for positive action from their own representatives became more insistent. No Catholic M.P. could afford to be seen co-operating with the Faulkner Government.

The violence continued to expand. Explosions of gelignite became a regular feature of the Ulster evening and the choice of target became increasingly random. More British soldiers were picked off by snipers, who were showing greater skill and using better weapons. Within three months of Faulkner's taking office there was speculation about how much longer he could last: the pace of crisis was getting madder and madder. In an attempt to break the spiral he brought forward the first genuine home-grown political initiative. The core of the problem at Stormont had always been the impossibility of the minority ever taking part in the process of government by normal methods. Faulkner suggested the formation of parliamentary committees with the chairmanship equally divided between Unionists and Opposition and with members from both sides. The committees would be able to examine legislation before it was put to the House and make amending suggestions. The way the membership was proposed would ensure that every member of the Opposition could take some part. It was not perfect but it was certainly a better system than any that had existed previously.

It put the Catholics in a dilemma. There was really no ground on which they could reject the proposition formally, but equally they would lose all backing from their own people if they took part. Their initial reaction was cautiously welcoming but this barely survived its utterance. A riot in Londonderry led to the death of a young man, allegedly about to throw a bomb. There was the usual outcry and some objective evidence that, though he had been among the rioters, he had not in fact been armed in any way. The Stormont Opposition immediately demanded an independent inquiry, a request brusquely rejected by the Westminster Government. This was enough. All but one member of the Opposition withdrew from Stormont and the main group declared its intention of setting up an independent assembly. The Faulkner initiative was dead and the formal adherence to the electoral system was now foresworn by the Catholics. Even the dialogue of the deaf had broken down.

And so Ireland moved steadily towards its second civil war within two generations. The possibility of direct rule remained but no one in Westminster could contemplate it without a shudder. The moves towards the Common Market made Ulster seem small beer but there was the knowledge that it could absorb endless time and energy to no fruitful end. Both Labour and Conservative administrations had made formal pledges that there would be no constitutional change without the consent of Stormont and the Prime Minister of the Irish Republic was rapped sharply over the knuckles for suggesting that it was time this undertaking was forgotten. But the truth was that he was doing little more than articulating the unspoken wish of the English, who had by now had their fill of the Irish problem and its ramifications. Few people on the mainland cared who won any more: they just wanted them all to go away.

Notes on the Contributors

JOHN BARNES Born April 1937. Educated at Plymouth College and Gonville and Caius College, Cambridge. Elected Drosier Research Fellow at Gonville and Caius College, 1961. Appointed Lecturer in Political Science, 1964, London School of Economics. Co-author of *Baldwin*; currently working on lives of Beatty and Macmillan. Was historical adviser for *The Day Before Yesterday*.

CHRIS COOK Born June 1945. Educated at Wyggeston Grammar School, Leicester; St Catharine's College, Cambridge; and Oriel and Nuffield Colleges, Oxford. College Lecturer in Politics, Magdalen College, Oxford, 1969-70. Currently Senior Research Officer at the London School of Economics. At present working on *European Political Facts, 1918-1972* (with John Paxton), to be published by Macmillan in spring 1973. Has written for the *Guardian* and *Socialist Commentary*.

ROY HATTERSLEY Born December 1932. Educated at Sheffield City Grammar School and Hull University. Member of Sheffield City Council 1957-65 (Chairman of Housing Committee). Elected Labour M.P. for Birmingham (Sparkbrook) in 1964. Parliamentary Secretary, Ministry of Labour, 1967-8; Under-Secretary, Department of Employment and Productivity, 1968-9; Minister of Defence Administration 1969-70. Front-bench spokesman, foreign affairs, from 1970; Shadow Minister of Defence 1972.

HAROLD JACKSON Born October 1932. Left school at 15; joined the *Guardian* at 17. Frequently reported the Northern Ireland situation from October 1968. Publications: *The Two Irelands: A Dual Study of Inter-Group Tension* (1971).

VICTOR KEEGAN Born April 1940. Educated at Wimbledon College and Brasenose College, Oxford. Joined the *Guardian* direct from Oxford; became Industrial Correspondent in 1967, with special interest in nationalised industries and relations between government and industry.

ANNE LAPPING Born June 1941. Educated at the City of London School and the London School of Economics. Has contributed regularly for *New Society* and has also broadcast and written widely on the social services. At present working on *Weekend World*.

BRIAN MACARTHUR Born Febuary 1940. Educated at Helsby Grammar School, Cheshire, and Leeds University. Student President 1961–2. Has worked for the *Yorkshire Post*, *Daily Mail* and *Guardian* before becoming Education Correspondent of *The Times*. Since mid-1971, editor of *The Times Higher Education Supplement*.

DAVID MCKIE Born February 1935. Educated at Christ's Hospital and Oriel College, Oxford. Journalist: *Keighley News*, *Oxford Mail*, and (since 1965) the *Guardian*. Publications: *The TV File* (1967) and (with Chris Cook) *Election '70* (1970).

PETER SINCLAIR Born September 1946. Educated at Corpus Christi College, Oxford. Elected Student of Nuffield College, Oxford, 1967. Appointed Fellow and Tutor in Economics, Brasenose College, Oxford, 1970.

LESLIE STONE Born May 1934. Educated at Christ's Hospital, Oriel College, Oxford, and Harvard. Journalist and broadcaster; covered the Foreign Office as a Diplomatic Correspondent from 1960 to 1968.

HUGO YOUNG Born October 1938. Educated at Ampleforth College and Balliol College, Oxford. Joined *Yorkshire Post* from Oxford; then two years as Harkness Fellow, one at Princeton, one at U.S. Congress. Joined *Sunday Times* 1965; now (1972) chief leader-writer and assistant editor. Co-author of *The Zinoviev Letter* (1967) and of *Journey to Tranquillity* (1969).

Index